COLLEGE TEACHING BY TELEVISION

AMERICAN COUNCIL ON EDUCATION
COMMITTEE ON TELEVISION

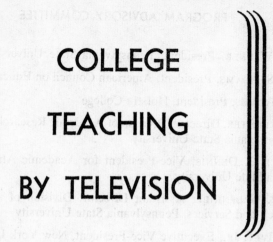

COLLEGE
TEACHING
BY TELEVISION

Report of a Conference Sponsored Jointly by the
Committee on Television of the American Council on
Education and the Pennsylvania State University at
University Park, Pennsylvania, October 20–23, 1957

Edited by
John C. Adams, C. R. Carpenter, Dorothy R. Smith

AMERICAN COUNCIL ON EDUCATION
Washington, D.C.

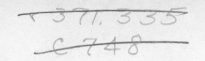

PROGRAM ADVISORY COMMITTEE

Foreword

AS A PIONEER in utilizing and appraising instructional television, Pennsylvania State University recognized more than a year ago a need, as expressed in the words of President Eric A. Walker, for "a conference on the improvement of televised instruction, designed to focus the attention of a number of selected key individuals from across the nation on the needs and the possibilities of improving teaching over closed-circuit or broadcast television." To meet this need, President Walker, on behalf of Pennsylvania State University, invited the American Council on Education to join in the sponsorship of such a conference, and the Council accepted the invitation with enthusiasm. It seemed especially significant to the Council to return to the Pennsylvania State campus in the fifth anniversary year of the Television Programs Institute which had been held there under its sponsorship in 1952. At the time of that institute, the aspirations for educational television were many and varied; yet they were but aspirations. It was well known that, during the intervening years, experience had disclosed much precise information concerning the use of television for instructional purposes. This information, however, had been gained largely by individual institutions and, hence, it seemed that there would be genuine value in providing an opportunity for bringing it together in such a conference as was proposed.

From the initial state of planning with Penn State for this conference, it was recognized that the participants should be teachers who had experience in offering one or more credit courses by either open- or closed-circuit television. The broadly representative roster, which appears at the end of this volume, resulted largely from nominations made in response to the Council's invitation to the presidents of colleges and universities to identify those for whom such a conference would have special value.

It is hoped that the report of the conference will aid many who are considering the role of television in American education. It is believed that a thorough study of this report will be useful to teachers and administrators as well as to others interested in improving the quality of teaching, for it seems clear that the technical materials of research and

v

evaluation that it presents constitute a wealth of data for study and consideration.

It is a pleasure to acknowledge indebtedness to Pennsylvania State University, not only for the excellent arrangements for the conference, but for the major contributions in the planning of the program by its Division of Academic Research and Services. President Walker headed the planning group which also included Vice-President Lawrence E. Dennis, who is a member of the Council's Committee on Television, and Director C. R. Carpenter and Assistant Director Leslie P. Greenhill of the Division of Academic Research and Services. To the latter two, special tribute is due for their faithful and energetic service, both in program planning and execution. The facilities of the university's Conference Center, under the capable administration of Reed Ferguson, proved highly satisfactory.

To President John C. Adams of Hofstra College go expressions of high esteem for his brilliant leadership as chairman of the conference. It is appropriate to recognize here his effective service as chairman of the Council's Committee on Television from 1953 until the end of 1957.

A broad base of financial support was given to the conference from the Fund for the Advancement of Education, the Alfred P. Sloan Foundation, Inc., and the Payne Fund, and the personal interest of officials of these organizations was indeed heartening. In particular, the assistance and encouragement given to the program committee by John K. Weiss of the Fund for the Advancement of Education was invaluable. His tragic death in an airplane accident in April 1958 was a great loss to education and because of our close association with him it had special personal meaning to us.

ARTHUR S. ADAMS, *President,*
American Council on Education

July 31, 1958

Preface

THE Conference on Teaching by Television in Colleges and Universities had its origin in the recognition that education by television had reached a stage of development that warranted turning attention especially to those problems of using the medium at the level of higher education. Specifically, plans for the conference were based on the assumptions that (1) television as an instrument of education has earned an established role in American education; (2) television's place in education needs to be greatly expanded and its effectiveness improved; and (3) the most crucial and promising possibilities lie in improving the processes of teaching and learning by television.

In making its plans the Program Advisory Committee recognized that the real educational merits and values of using television as a means of instruction must be increased—and every effort exerted to achieve progress. It was convinced that a large body of research results, experience, judgments, and opinions exist which must be brought together and made available for application in order to increase the effectiveness of educational programs being presented over television and to provide bases for decisions about extending the employment of television in higher institutions. The committee concluded that the resources of facts and principles need to be stated and then applied to the tasks of teaching and learning by television. Finally, the committee observed that while research on instructional television is extensive, its quality can be improved by making available information on the elements of experimental design and planning and on academic measurements and assessments.

Earlier conferences on the subject had, properly, had administrators in predominant roles; now, the time was considered ripe to provide a public platform for teachers to express their judgments, opinions, and conclusions. The committee decided, with enthusiasm, to invite to the conference distinguished teachers who had actually experienced the realities of teaching by television. From here, it was an easy step to decide that the central theme of the conference should be teaching by television, that the meeting should deal with sound and substantive information, and that the discussions should persistently emphasize the learning behavior of students.

To give substance to the aims, the committee invited outstanding authorities to prepare basic papers to be given at the conference. These papers were planned for several major areas: perspectives on televised instruction and education; theories and principles of learning related to televised instruction; research results on televised instruction; effects of college cultural patterns on students' learning by television; experimental design; assessment of academic achievement and of teachers; and evaluation of televised recordings. In addition there were to be several major addresses dealing with broad areas of educational concern.

The committee also invited each prospective participant to prepare a statement of significant concepts, ideas, or problems. In this manner the conference itself would benefit from a wide and liberal sampling of thought by responsible and experienced teachers, and the benefit would pass on to a wider audience through their publication in the proceedings.

In the publication here presented a Selected Bibliography has been added to the materials of the conference in order to round out information on research on educational television. While it is far from complete, it will be of assistance to those interested in the subjects discussed at the conference.

In order to add realism and a very practical aspect to the program, the committee arranged for the preparation and presentation of examples of teaching by television. Some of these were recorded; others were presented "live" by teachers. An effort was made to have a wide range of examples covering different kinds of content and varying in quality and methods of presentation. The soundness of this plan was proved when, at the conference, the demonstrations received critiques that were objective and analytical.

Finally, discussion panels and informal discussions were scheduled. Among these activities was an informal dinner at which members of the Penn State faculty who were interested in televised instruction acted as hosts to visiting teachers in their respective subject-matter fields.

These were the plans of the Program Advisory Committee. The extent to which these plans were fulfilled is evidenced by this publication which reports in detail the work and the thought of the conference. The results will be fruitful and validated to the degree that teaching and learning by television or by other means is improved and advanced in American colleges and universities and in American communities.

C. R. CARPENTER
Director, Academic Research and Services,
Pennsylvania State University

Contents

FOREWORD, *Arthur S. Adams* v

PREFACE, *C. R. Carpenter* vii

APPRAISING THE GAINS OF TELEVISED INSTRUCTION

Introductory Remarks, *John C. Adams* 1

The Penn State TV Project, *Lawrence E. Dennis* 2

Greetings from the American Council on Education,
Arthur S. Adams 6

A Perspective of Televised Instruction, *C. R. Carpenter* 9
EVALUATION OF TELEVISED INSTRUCTION; ADVANTAGES OF
TELEVISION; LIMITATIONS OF TELEVISION; EFFECTS ON
ACHIEVEMENT OF DIRECT VERSUS TELEVISED INSTRUCTION;
NECESSITY FOR IMPROVED INSTRUCTION; FUTURE ROLE OF
TELEVISED INSTRUCTION

Panel Discussion: A Perspective of Televised Instruction
John W. Taylor 19
F. Glenn Macomber 21
Harvey Zorbaugh 23

LEARNING VIA TELEVISED INSTRUCTION

Principles of Learning by Televised Instruction, *Neal E. Miller* 28
DRIVE OR MOTIVATION; CUE OR STIMULUS SITUATION; RE-
SPONSE OR PARTICIPATION; REWARD OR REINFORCEMENT;
FORGETTING AND REVIEW; LOGICAL LEARNING, GENERALITY,
AND CREATIVITY; SPEEDING ADJUSTMENT TO NEW NEEDS
AND OPPORTUNITIES

Conditions of Learning in a Closed-Circuit Television System,
Joseph H. Grosslight 42
ROLE OF TEACHER; MOTIVATION; OBSERVATION ADVAN-
TAGES; WE LEARN BY DOING—RESPONSE; KINESCOPE RECORD-
INGS

Panel Discussion: Significant Concepts of Televised Instruction
Discussion Method, *Keith McKean* 50
Students' Attitudes, *Richard I. Evans* 52
Training for the Television Teacher, *David W. Bergstrom* .. 54

Design of the Chicago TV Junior College,
Clifford G. Erickson   55

Re-evaluation of the Teaching-Learning Process,
Shepard A. Insel   59

TEACHING BY TV: DEMONSTRATIONS AND A CRITIQUE

Critique of Teaching by TV Demonstrations, *Richard J. Goggin*   64

IN SEARCH OF FACTUAL DATA

The Need for Evidence, *Eric A. Walker*   71

Research on Televised Instruction at the Pennsylvania State University, *Leslie P. Greenhill*   74
COMPARATIVE EFFECTIVENESS; APPROPRIATENESS; ACCEPTA-
BILITY; FEASIBILITY; GENERAL CONCLUSIONS

Further Facts on a National Scale, *Hideya Kumata*   83

COLLEGE CULTURAL PATTERNS AND THEIR EFFECTS ON LEARNING BY TELEVISION

Toward a Student-Oriented University, *John E. Ivey, Jr.*   87

I Think TV Teaching Is a Good Idea, But—, *Robert R. Blake*   92
INSTRUCTIONAL TELEVISION AND TRADITION; DIAGNOSIS OF
RESISTANCE WILL SUGGEST CURE

Point of View—Television, an Ultimate in Communication,
Arthur Henry Moehlman   98
TELEVISION AND TEACHER-STUDENT VALUES

PRACTICAL PROBLEMS OF IMPROVING TELEVISED INSTRUCTION

Elements of Experimental Design, *William S. Ray*   110
CONTROL FACTORS IN MEASUREMENT; THE PROBLEMS OF
BIAS; EVALUATION AND INTERPRETATION

Assessment of Academic Achievement, *Henry S. Dyer*   115

Assessment of Teachers, *H. H. Remmers*   122

Evaluation of Televised Recordings, *Harry K. Newburn*   127

Panel Discussion: Significant Concepts of Televised Instruction

Problems of Long-Range Outcome of TV Education
Dale B. Harris   131

What Will Encourage Faculty Acceptance?, *James C. Olson* 132

Adult Education, *J. W. Ashton* 134

Teacher Preparation, *David S. Brody* 136

Criterion Improvement, *Warren F. Seibert* 138

EDUCATIONAL PHILOSOPHY AND TELEVISION,
                                        Clarence H. Faust 142

Reservation of TV Channels for Education, *Ralph Steetle* 154

Cooperation of Educational Broadcasters, *Burton Paulu* 155

DEMONSTRATIONS OF TEACHING BY TELEVISION .. 156

REVIEW AND PREVIEW: A SUMMARY OF THE
CONFERENCE

Breaking the Barriers, *John E. Ivey, Jr.* 160
    INSTITUTIONAL BARRIERS; LEARNING BARRIERS; TELEVISION
    AND THE RESPONSIBILITIES OF AMERICAN EDUCATION

Review from the Fifth Milestone, and a Glimpse into the
Future, *Arthur S. Adams* 169

APPENDIXES

A. PAPERS SUPPLEMENTING SUBJECTS DISCUSSED
   AT THE CONFERENCE

Hope Lunin Klapper, NEW YORK UNIVERSITY, 175; *H. Burr
Roney,* UNIVERSITY OF HOUSTON, 177; *Martin H. Rogers,*
STATE UNIVERSITY TEACHERS COLLEGE, BROCKPORT, NEW
YORK, 179; *Edwin P. Adkins,* STATE UNIVERSITY COLLEGE FOR
TEACHERS, ALBANY, NEW YORK, 180; *David G. Monroe,* UNI-
VERSITY OF NORTH CAROLINA, 182; *Barclay Leathem,* WEST-
ERN RESERVE UNIVERSITY, 184; *Rev. Herman J. Muller,*
UNIVERSITY OF DETROIT, 186; *Vernon Davies,* STATE COLLEGE
OF WASHINGTON, 188; *Fred McKinney,* UNIVERSITY OF MIS-
SOURI, 190; *Harold P. Skamser,* MICHIGAN STATE UNIVERSITY,
191; *W. C. McNally,* MIAMI UNIVERSITY, 192; *Frank S. True-
blood,* LOS ANGELES CITY COLLEGE, 193; *Oliver M. Stone,* CASE
INSTITUTE OF TECHNOLOGY, 196; *Robert D. Brown,* UNIVER-
SITY OF ALABAMA, 197; *W. Bernard King,* IOWA STATE COL-
LEGE, 199; *C. N. McCarty,* MICHIGAN STATE UNIVERSITY, 201;
L. O. Morgan, UNIVERSITY OF TEXAS, 202; *Kurt C. Schreiber,*
DUQUESNE UNIVERSITY, 202; *Harris W. Wilson,* UNIVERSITY
OF ILLINOIS, 204; *Erna Gunther,* UNIVERSITY OF WASHINGTON,

206; *Ralph C. Leyden,* STEPHENS COLLEGE, 207; *Harold White-hall,* INDIANA UNIVERSITY, 209; *James F. Short, Jr.,* STATE COLLEGE OF WASHINGTON, 211; *Eugene F. Grewe,* UNIVERSITY OF DETROIT, 212; *Frederick J. Bogardus,* PURDUE UNIVERSITY, 215; *M. W. Fleck,* UNIVERSITY OF NEW MEXICO, 217; *Clark Griffith,* STATE UNIVERSITY OF IOWA, 218; *Ada D. Stephens,* UNIVERSITY OF TOLEDO, 219; *Harry E. Crull,* BUTLER UNIVERSITY, 219; *J. M. Sachs,* CHICAGO CITY JUNIOR COLLEGE, 220; *John R. Martin,* CASE INSTITUTE OF TECHNOLOGY, 221

B. SELECTED BIBLIOGRAPHY 224

C. PROGRAM OF THE CONFERENCE 227

D. CONFERENCE ROSTER 230

Appraising the Gains of Televised Instruction

MONDAY MORNING, OCTOBER 21, 1957

Presiding: PRESIDENT JOHN C. ADAMS, Hofstra College; Chairman, Committee on Television, American Council on Education

CHAIRMAN ADAMS: It is my pleasure, on behalf of the American Council on Education, to welcome you to this meeting; and, as your representative, to express our gratitude to Pennsylvania State University for cosponsoring this conference and for supplying us with every facility and comfort.

Several of us were here in April 1952, when the impact of television upon the educational system of the United States was first recognized in conference. At that time we decided to take a constructive look at this magical opportunity for strengthening the schools across the country, convinced that we should face up to the challenges and advantages of this new mass medium, which one member said might prove as significant "as the introduction of movable type."

So much progress has been made in these intervening years that it is certainly appropriate that we meet again during this fifth anniversary, appraising the gains we have made in such ways as may make our future work in educational television more meaningful.

It is also appropriate that we meet here because the Pennsylvania State University has been a pioneer in the use of television in education. It has attacked the problem in major ways, with major scope, and with major minds. Our host institution has even attempted that most complex of matters, to evaluate at each stage what it has been doing with television.

As the various colleges and universities experimented and explored in this new medium, there have been disappointments and setbacks from time to time; even so, the progress in educational television has been fantastic.

Remembering our first conference five years ago, some of us marveled

1

at the little National Guard house on this campus, that was lent to us for our television studio, a newly built creation into which important commercial interests had put brand new equipment. But the real marvel was that young students in a very short time had learned the mechanics of television apparatus and were using it with skill and taste. Out of that meeting came the bench mark for our work—a television policy for education.[1]

Each one of the conferences concerning TV that has been sponsored by the American Council has encouraged faculty participation. Again I say we are making fantastic progress, because at this meeting we have nothing but faculty participation. There isn't a person here who isn't actively a teacher or a lapsed teacher. That is as it should be, inasmuch as we intend to ask those who have been teaching by television how we can do the job even better. The focus of this meeting will be teaching—teaching students, how to use this medium in teaching, how to develop its potentialities, and how to cope with its limitations, if it has limitations. We want to peer through the medium to newly discovered areas of teaching strength.

Those who have deserted the green fields and become mere administrators are asked to speak cautiously, if at all. At this conference we are not interested in costs as such, in electronics, gadgets, and all those subjects peripheral to teaching which we have discussed at previous meetings. This conference is concerned with teaching by television.

We want to review theories and research findings relevant to this process. We want to observe and analyze selected programs of high order. I think we will all be happy if we allot ourselves time for hearing the important papers that have been written and for the discussion that will make them meaningful.

I know that you will be happy to hear from a representative of this great university, which is ensuring and enhancing our comfort, Vice-President Dennis.

The Penn State TV Project

LAWRENCE E. DENNIS (Pennsylvania State University): Thank you, President Adams. I should like to welcome the members of this confer-

---

[1] The proceedings of the institute were published under the title *A Television Policy for Education* (Washington: American Council on Education, 1952).

ence on behalf of the trustees, administrative officers, faculty, and students of the university, and particularly on behalf of President Walker, who is out of town today and will speak to you tomorrow. All of us hope that your visit will be enjoyable as well as profitable.

Now, permit me to speak with pride about the development of television on this campus. Between 1950 and 1953 we joined with our sister institutions in Pennsylvania to secure state support for a state television network. Those efforts failed in Pennsylvania, as they did in a number of other states. So in 1954 we re-evaluated everything that had been done, submitting a proposal to the Fund for the Advancement of Education in which we suggested that this university would be willing to undertake a program of instruction and research in the field of closed-circuit television. A grant was made, and in the spring of 1955 the first three courses—two in psychology and one in chemistry—were taught via a closed-circuit system. Under the terms of the grant, no changes were to be made in the teaching procedures used in the televised classes. TV was simply being introduced into a normal classroom situation.

In launching that project we received effective cooperation from companies such as Westinghouse and Dage Television, which provided vidicon equipment at low cost, and we received expert guidance from Ralph Steetle and his associates on the Joint Council on Educational Television.

Many of you have probably read our report on that project, which was published in 1955.[2] Since then our use of closed-circuit TV has grown. We now have fifteen different classes in our closed-circuit system, with an enrollment of 4,200 students. The project is in its sixth semester. The Fund for the Advancement of Education has been renewing the grant from year to year, and under our agreement the university is gradually absorbing the cost of the project.

Currently courses in sociology, psychology, economics, air science, accounting, music appreciation, and meteorology are included in the TV project. Early next year we will publish a second penetrating report detailing our scope and findings during the second through the sixth semester.[3] As President Adams has said, we have tried at every stage

[2] C. R. Carpenter, L. P. Greenhill, and others, *An Investigation of Closed-Circuit Television for Teaching University Courses,* Report No. 1 (University Park, Pa.: Pennsylvania State University, 1955).

[3] *Ibid.,* Report No. 2: *The Academic Years 1955–1956 and 1956–1957* (University Park, Pa.: Pennsylvania State University, 1958). Copies available on request to authors, Division of Academic Research and Services, 405 Old Main, University Park, Pa.

of our project to know where we are, how we got there, and where we seem to be going.

Paralleling the development of closed-circuit television at the university has been the growth of broadcast television on our campus. Originally we were assigned an ultra-high frequency channel, Channel 48, but because of the geography in central Pennsylvania, the UHF channel seemed impractical. So we sought other means for broadcast of television to our general and agricultural extension services. Fortunately, we have one of the truly enlightened commercial television stations in the country located some thirty-five miles from here, WFBG-TV in Altoona. We have entered into a five-year contract with WFBG, under which the university is being allocated specific times each week for the presentation of educational television programs from our campus. We have a minimum of three hours per week, during which we offer at present an agricultural extension course and two programs in music appreciation.

Under this contract we also are to provide WFBG-TV with certain public service programs from time to time. The university retains the right, however, to enter into similar agreements with other commercial agencies. Triangle Publications, the new owners of WFBG-TV, have purchased certain kinescope equipment for the university and will give financial assistance to our broadcast television project annually.

They have installed and are maintaining a microwave link that ties our campus in with the Altoona transmitter. They will enable us to tie in the University Park campus with the campus of our Altoona center by means of closed-circuit television (as soon as a permit is obtained from the FCC), and they are giving us access to certain educational films produced by the Columbia Broadcasting System, with which they are affiliated. This is a truly mutual contract and one that we believe is a landmark in the development of educational television.

The campus tie-in with our Altoona center will permit us to carry programs, by means of our closed-circuit microwave system, from the actual classes being taught here. Who knows? A year or two from now the Penn State centers may be tied in with a state network after all, either by means of closed-circuit or our broadcast television. We hope to effect a continuing and constructive relationship with our sister educational television projects, with WQED in Pittsburgh, and with the new educational television station in Philadelphia.

As you may know from visiting with some of our faculty members last evening, we are using the multiple system approach to our television installation. We already have one closed-circuit installation in the Sparks Building and another one in the Boucke Building, which is the classroom building that was opened in September. Our broadcast originating rooms are modest, as is the entire operation. We are gradually wiring the entire campus for television, however, so that we will have closed-circuit systems in all our major classroom buildings.

Credit for our progress in television at the Pennsylvania State University is due to many leaders and visionaries: Dr. Milton S. Eisenhower, who was president at the time of the 1952 conference and who helped get our closed-circuit project under way; President Eric A. Walker, who has been supporting it all along the line; and the trustees, who this year helped us effect the contractual arrangement with Triangle Publications. Much is also owed to the skills and efforts of Dr. C. R. Carpenter, Mr. Leslie P. Greenhill, and their associates in the Division of Academic Research and Services.

Certainly our progress is due in large measure to the cooperation of the faculty; for when all is said and done, it is the teaching that goes into closed-circuit television that is our main concern. I think it is extremely significant that this conference, as President Adams has indicated, is to be instruction-centered, its focus on teaching. In the last analysis it is the teachers who will make or break educational television, whether it is closed or open circuit.

At Pennsylvania State it happened that the development of our TV project coincided with a heightened interest in the improvement of instruction. This interest is traceable to the long-range planning which the university has been doing and to our reaccreditation by the Middle States Association of Colleges and Secondary Schools two years ago.

Members of our faculty who are involved in the television programs nominate their own courses. Those who have taught by this medium believe that participation has improved their teaching. Many of them have written articles for their professional journals about the challenges and opportunities in educational television.

I am happy to announce this morning, for the first time publicly, that, in recognition of the distinguished service that certain members of our television faculty have given to the university, we are sending letters of commendation to them and awarding them financial stipends made possible by the president and the board of trustees. In the future this special stipend policy will be a permanent feature of our closed- and open-circuit television projects.

Educational television still has a long way to go on the Pennsylvania State University campus in order to win complete student and faculty acceptance. Students are very sensitive to changes in educational philosophy. When the television screens first appeared in the classrooms, some of the students joked about how they would return to the campus years hence to see how their old 24-inch screen was doing. Since then, student acceptance and understanding of the project has been paralleling the grand acceptance demonstrated by most members of the faculty. We are proud of the television work we have been doing here, not only because of the contribution it has made to educational TV nationally, but because of its help in the improvement of instruction generally.

You will recall that a few years ago people used to say that television was an *addition* to the spectrum of devices such as the radio, films, books, and the like, that could be used in teaching. I think the word *addition* is less apt than *multiplication*. Television multiplies the impact of audio and visual teaching. The progress that we have made here at Pennsylvania State during the past five years will serve to make television a permanent and constructive part of education in America.

CHAIRMAN: What a heartening and remarkable record of pioneering and leadership. Mr. Dennis, I noticed that you brought a gleam of special audience response when you mentioned that a professor could get rich by teaching on television.

As you know, all of our conferences on educational television have been cosponsored by the American Council on Education, whose president, Dr. Arthur S. Adams, has always urged that this new medium be explored fully, its potentialities uncovered, and its challenges fully accepted to the end that it might become an effective tool in instruction generally. I think we would like to have Dr. Adams speak to us, if he will.

Greetings from the American Council on Education

ARTHUR S. ADAMS (American Council on Education): Ladies and gentlemen, it is a great delight to welcome you on behalf of the Council and to express our deep appreciation to the Pennsylvania State University for its spendid cooperation and for the hard work that has been put into making this conference successful. Our first conference, in

1952, was supported financially by the Fund for Adult Education, the Alfred P. Sloan Foundation, and the Payne Fund. This conference is being supported by the Fund for the Advancement of Education, the Sloan Foundation, the Payne Fund, and I am glad to say that the American Council also has money in this enterprise.

The work which was done here five years ago established a basis for thinking about educational television. At that conference we were all inspired by hopes for the future. I believe that some of those hopes have been realized. New directions have been found, new possibilities have been uncovered, and new problems have been encountered. Then, we were concerned with getting stations on the air, and I remember that, as Ralph Steetle and I rode from Washington to this campus five years ago, we observed that, if in five years there could be at least four good educational stations strategically located in the country, it would be quite an accomplishment. We have twenty-seven educational stations today, and by next week we shall have twenty-eight. So I think I am correct in saying that those hopes of five years ago have been fully realized.

In 1952 we talked a great deal about money and production technique. First, we were interested in getting stations on the air, and we wanted to know how much it would cost to do so. My, I remember some lively sessions on this subject! And, second, we wanted to know how to put a program together and how to put it on the air in an effective way.

During these past five years we have been fortunate that teachers everywhere have identified the potentialities in television, expressed an interest in them, and explored ways in which they might be realized. The Council has had a conference on credit courses by television and another on closed-circuit television,[4] both of them invitational as this one is. In each instance we have had far more inquiries from those who wished to attend than we have had funds to support such invitations. The vitality of the interest is apparent.

Today we shall concentrate our attention on the most important question of all: "What for?" When I was starting out in administration, I had a wise boss who said to me: "There is one thing that I want you to keep constantly in mind. When any idea comes to you—and I will send you a number of them—your first question must be, 'what for?' " I think

---

[4] The proceedings of these conferences were published by the American Council on Education under the titles, respectively, *Credit Courses by Television* (1955) and *Teaching by Closed-Circuit Television* (1956).

the question "what for?" is germane to our interest in educational television. It covers a multitude of queries that might be stated more elaborately: Why are we bringing the medium of television into the field of education? What are we trying to do with television? Where do we want television to take us? How are we going to use the peculiar advantages of television to achieve significant results we have not been able to achieve by other means?

Years ago, when I was studying a course in history, we were told that the times always produce the man to cope with them. Is television perhaps the timely advantage of our era that will help us to adapt to new needs, to newly emerging concepts of what we should be doing, and to educational problems that will be peculiar to the decade before us?

All of those questions and many others known to administration, faculty, and students are included in that query "what for?" When we look at the significant record of the past five years, we know that we no longer are questioning whether or not we shall use television in education. We are using it. We shall use it far more extensively. But let us go on asking "what for?" to the end that we remain on the broad thoroughfare of education, never deviating along tangents, always shaping the uses of this promising medium to our primary purpose—that of teaching more successfully the youth of this nation.

I am confident that by the time we leave here, we shall have improved answers to that question. I am confident that we shall go away from here on Wednesday with a renewed feeling of gratitude to the Pennsylvania State University for having given us the opportunity to meet here, to see the work that is going on, and to enjoy the fellowship that I already sense at this conference.

CHAIRMAN: May I take this occasion to say what I suspect is apparent to all of you. Special staff work, special arrangements, a great deal of effort have gone into the job of bringing this conference together. Dorothy Smith, who is secretary to the American Council's Committee on Television, is in large measure responsible for the preparation of material we will be using, for getting out the letters and invitations, and joining with others in selecting distinguished guests. I would also like to introduce John E. Ivey, executive vice-president of New York University, who will be giving us a summary paper at the close of these sessions. Ray Carpenter and Leslie Greenhill, who direct the Division of

Academic Research and Services on this campus, have helped all of us in preparing for this conference, and we are grateful to them.

We will now turn to one of the most forward-looking and experienced men in educational television, Dr. C. R. Carpenter, director of the Division of Academic Research and Services, on this campus. We know him. We want to hear about his recent experiments against the backdrop of his long-range experiences.

A Perspective of Televised Instruction

C. R. CARPENTER (Pennsylvania State University): This will be a panel effort. Panel participants have exchanged several drafts of our various manuscripts, and we are determined to be as inconsistent with each other as possible!

The development of "A Perspective of Televised Instruction" is one of the principal purposes of this conference. We are addressing ourselves to the task of proposing, analyzing, assessing, and comparing ways of improving teaching by television in colleges and universities.

At present there are many different perspectives. Each of us has his own, determined by personal information, experiences, and professional responsibilities. We are making a variety of judgments and are arriving at different conclusions about the characteristics, justifiable uses, and the over-all place of television in schools. It is certain that during these sessions our different perspectives will continue to change and broaden. Participants in this panel will merely begin to sketch the emerging perspectives.

It is not our intention to reduce the variations in our views, but to foster them. These different perspectives may well be our most valuable asset and principal coinage of these sessions. Therefore, let us speak freely on the real issues as we see them. Let us capitalize on the possibility that this free exchange of ideas may yield new understandings and even provoke imaginative and creative insights into the complex problems of teaching first and television second.

In this pioneering era of tele-education it is premature to attempt to arrive at a final consensus or to formulate doctrine. Our unity is derived from other facts: namely, that we all have common problems, interests, and purposes. First, we have been selected to attend this conference because of our responsibilities, achievements, and interests in teaching. We are all committed to the never-ending, perennial task of improving the effectiveness of instruction. Second, we have been selected because of our interest in televised instruction.

Evaluation of Televised Instruction

The basic question which must be raised in presenting a perspective of televised instruction is: What is good teaching? Teaching implies learning by others, and learning implies observable, detectable, and measurable changes in behavior, including especially the intellectual achievements of students. Good teaching means that skills are acquired by students, information is gained and assimilated, understanding is broadened and deepened, appreciations are extended and enriched, and character is built and strengthened.

Our assessments and judgments of televised instruction, therefore, must be made relative to the broad educational responsibilities of colleges and universities. We should not evaluate television merely as a means of presenting information or of teaching objective facts, however important these functions may be. We must decide for what particular uses, within the full range of academic work and institutional responsibilities, television is effective, appropriate, acceptable, and feasible.

When viewed functionally, then, what is television as it relates to the complex processes of teaching and learning? Essentially television is a composite of two integrated communication systems of visual and auditory stimuli, corresponding to the two great human sensory capacities of sight and hearing. These stimuli, which are instructional in character, are projected over cable or through the atmosphere and are then reconstituted on the faces of receivers, where the information is perceived by students.

A few observations on the cues and information which are transmitted to students would seem pertinent. The stimulus fields are planned and prepared in advance. They are selected, composed, and have limits or boundaries. The picture of what was before the camera is presented on a tube face, but with varying degrees of fidelity and effectiveness. Both the visual and auditory systems of television are used to strengthen and improve the quality of some kinds of information or instruction. They may also be used in such a way as to change, destroy, or reduce the fidelity and effectiveness of the instruction.

Advantages of Television

The most important advantage of television for instruction is the capacity of systems for receiving, transmitting, and presenting very large amounts of information. In this respect TV's capacity to handle information, both visual and aural, in a great variety of forms and patterns, is analogous to the capacities of high-speed digital computers. Moreover, the capacity of television is so enormous that it is a mammoth task to provide enough information of different kinds to utilize fully the possibilities of the combined audio and video channels. The instruction-handling capacity of television greatly exceeds the learning abilities and rates of students. Competent observers believe that the presentation on the audio channel often receives a disproportionately larger amount of attention and emphasis from teachers than does the presentation over the video channel.

To determine what are the optimum levels and rates of use for the audio and video channels for different subjects and different students is a research problem of great magnitude. Such research will show in all probability that the machine capacities of television greatly exceed the human capacities of both teachers and students to utilize them fully.

A second important characteristic of television instruction is its capacity to extend and distribute information to viewers; it is possible to present instruction to any desirable or necessary number of students, given the resources for the task. The only limitations facing the teachers are functions of cost, availability of motivated students, and administrative procedures and patterns of course management. The television systems do not limit the number of students participating in any course. In fact, great wastage occurs as a result of the relatively restricted use of televised instruction in terms of the numbers of people served.

A development now on the horizon has to do with the use of film and tape recordings; here, there are possibilities for increasing the capacities of television to extend instruction in both space and time to vastly increased numbers of students. Film and tape recordings are increasing the flexibility and the variations which can be introduced into instructional management procedures. For example, through film and tape recordings we have been able to prepare the core materials for courses in psychology, chemistry, languages, and mathematics, which soon will be made available to about twenty Air Force bases overseas.

The physics course given by Harvey White and recorded on film will soon be available to hundreds of thousands of high school students and perhaps to freshman students in colleges. The course materials presented by broadcast television in St. Louis, Chicago, and elsewhere are recorded and used repeatedly.

By linking the distribution capacities of television with the information storage capacities of film, the instructional input resources can be greatly increased and broadened. We can reach out to sources of instructional materials throughout the nation and the world and make them available to the students in classrooms, in dormitories, or in homes, and thereby produce significant changes in the substantive curriculum. This is already being done in Houston. Furthermore, educational material produced at great cost for other purposes can, through these means, be made available for classroom instruction.

It is a fortunate coincidence that we educators now have available in television a communication system with almost unlimited capacities for handling large amounts of information and extending its availability to millions of students, at a time when the demands for broader and better teaching exceed our present conventional resources. The capacities and potentialities of television are available just as we are being compelled to improve and expand teaching in colleges and universities. The *Second Report* of the President's Committee on Education Beyond the High School tells us:

This Nation has been propelled into a challenging new educational era since World War II by the convergence of powerful forces—an explosion of knowledge and population, a burst of technological and economic advance, the outbreak of ideological conflict and the uprooting of old political and cultural patterns on a worldwide scale, and an unparalleled demand by Americans for more and better education.

These forces have created enormously increased educational challenges of which we have not yet taken full stock and which our educational institutions as a whole are ill-prepared to meet. The gap between this Nation's educational needs and its educational effort is widening ominously.[5]

In view of our present limited teaching capacities and the necessity for a tremendous expansion in the immediate future, the evident inertia, resistance, and lack of financial support relative to televised instruction appear shortsighted to say the least. We have been deprived of the general momentum given by broad social and industrial support and we have often found actual opposition. Furthermore, educational

[5] President's Committee on Education Beyond the High School, *Second Report to the President* (Washington: Government Printing Office, July 1957), p. 1.

institutions themselves have not yet realistically aligned their procedures and budgets to provide for definite and planned use of televised instruction in their programs.

There are other characteristics of television that may be used advantageously in teaching. Demonstration materials can be shown more effectively and extensively. A piece of equipment, a specimen, or an apparatus can be presented as well or better by TV to multiple classes than by direct presentation to single classes. The intimate, analytical, and magnifying powers of camera lenses can be used to advantage. Situations can be presented by television that could not otherwise be observed by students without disturbing the procedures. Televising children in various test, social, and classroom situations is an example.

Limitations of Television

Now let us consider some of the characteristics of television that impose limitations on instructional possibilities. This medium usually provides only an unidirectional flow of instruction. Both images and sound in standard systems flow outward from the teachers through the systems to the students. This is different from the normal processes of human communications, which are cyclical and include reciprocal exchanges, and to some degree regulate what is said, how it is said, and at what rate it is said.

It is this particular limiting characteristic that provokes the most intense criticism of teaching by television. The same criticism can actually be made of books or of lectures delivered to large classes, where students rarely have a chance to question their instructor. In these situations, however, the instructor does receive visual cues from the students which help him formulate or regulate his performance. Nevertheless, the problem of "one-way flow" information, typical of televised instruction, must be defined and solved.

We must discover what kinds of reciprocal cues, either simultaneous or delayed, are essential and actually contribute to the effectiveness of teaching by television and thus to achievement by students. We must find the effects of questions and answers, of auditory and visual "feedback," and of the intense discussion of issues. We must assess how much effect overt student reactions have on learning. We must also assess the effects of covert responses.

In supporting educational television, we need not be apologetic because it imposes some limitations on ideal teacher-student interactions.

This ideal is rarely achieved by conventional teaching methods. What we need to do and what we can do is to define the problems and solve them where educational values justify the effort. The limitations on the interacting processes in teaching and learning by television can be solved by making adaptations within the full potentials and limitations of this medium, or by utilizing supplementary and auxiliary instructional procedures for which models already exist.

Although television usually lacks stereophonic sound, this could be provided. In the area of vision, television is limited to essentially monocular perspective. Also, most TV systems are monochromatic. The systems having color introduce some distortion of the chromatic scales. Other important senses like kinesthesis are not stimulated directly. The complete context or surroundings of the originating situations cannot be presented on the receiving sets. Often students in a receiving room see only the face and figure of the instructor. The physical limitations of cameras, lenses, and especially receivers restrict the quality of large fields of vision.

Generally, however, the quality of both picture and sound are above the thresholds of perception, cognition, and understanding of students. Given instruction which is meaningful and relevant to the viewers, the quality of picture and sound, unless it distracts attention, has little effect on learning.

Some students have said that televised instruction is cold, impersonal, remote; others that it is intimate, personal, and close. We have been told that it is monotonous, that too many things are taking place visually and aurally, that information is being presented too fast. In all these reactions, the students are assigning qualities to television which rightly should be assigned to the instruction itself. The medium of television has been confused with the message it delivers, and our use of linked terms like "educational television" and "instructional television" are responsible for part of the confusion.

Television is neutral; it is neither educational nor instructive; it is a means and not an end. It is simply an instrument that can be used to do certain kinds of educational jobs, and the quality and dimensions of these jobs are the primary consideration of educators who are interested in using TV. It cannot of itself perform important educational functions, and it cannot be expected to do so.

Today's television is not tomorrow's television. Electronic communications are not standing still. Adaptations will be made; there will be new inventions. Two-way vision and sound may be developed, if there is both a need and a demand for it. Electronic systems for measuring rapidly and simultaneously both the instruction and the reactions of students to it have been developed and demonstrated.

Television was not developed for educational uses. The enormous amounts of money that have gone into its development have been for its entertainment potential. We educators are in the process of adapting it to educational functions. In our area it has both advantages and limitations. As educational functions demand it, we must be prepared to work around these limiting characteristics of TV by providing supplementary, complementary, or auxiliary methods of instruction. This medium offers an opportunity to use a variety of techniques and methods for our purposes. Certainly television can be used, with the same or even wider effects than most conventional instruction, to produce variations. The variation in the quality of the instruction, other factors being equal, will have the same wide variation in effect as that already found in our colleges and universities unless there are certain controls imposed. We must attack the problem of how to provide an optimum amount of variety in instruction, both by TV and by other supplementary means, to allow for the great variability among students and to offset "mass media" or leveling effects.

Effects on Achievement of Direct versus Televised Instruction

The most challenging information that has been uncovered by our controlled experiments in educational television is that "no significant differences" in student achievement have been revealed in our comparisons between TV instruction and conventional, direct teaching. Preliminary efforts to break through this quality barrier to reach new heights of teaching effectiveness with television have not succeeded. Nevertheless, the whole weight of reason suggests that this should be possible.

Why do we get these "no significant differences" over and over again? Is it because our conventional instruction is so good that there is no room for improvement? Unfortunately this isn't true. Is it because our instruction is so poor that whatever we do makes no difference? No. Is it because we are using inadequate measuring instruments? It may well be true that we need instruments that are not only sharper and more reliable, but also more comprehensive and more valid. Is it because we have not yet defined and gained control over these forces that will enable us to advance the real academic achievement of students? It seems to me that this is a real possibility.

The experimental evidence, which has shown "no significant statistical differences" between well-controlled direct and televised instruction, can best be interpreted as follows: In those courses that have been studied, the essential requirements for acceptable teaching are being met by the capabilities of well-operated television systems. In addition, it would seem that the known characteristics of TV do not significantly interfere with the instruction as it is conducted. Whether or not the instruction is ideally what is should be, and whether or not optimum uses have been made of television itself are questions that need further investigation. Certainly we must determine what methods and procedures are the most effective supplements to televised instruction as a means of providing students with maximum opportunities to learn.

When we pursue this thought about providing students with maximum opportunities to learn, we begin to wonder if teachers have usurped from students their responsibilities for learning. Perhaps, in our anxiety to teach well, we fail to make students aware of their prime responsibility in the learning process.

Inexorably, televised instruction separates the roles of teachers and students in the interacting process of education. It becomes clear that the role of the teacher should be auxiliary to the learning of the students and that the primary responsibility for academic achievement rests squarely with the students. The greatest unused resources for educational advancement in America are the brains of our students. In this connection it seems possible that television might be used as an instrument to help wean students away from immature dependency upon their instructors and to encourage their initiative, self-discipline, individual effort, and unique personal development.

Necessity for Improved Instruction

In educational television we are acutely aware of the need to have good or superior instruction. Little is gained and much may be lost when mediocre instruction is televised, regardless of the number of students reached by this means. We are primarily interested in the educational gains of students. We are concerned about instructional quality as well as instructional efficiency and economy. We can conceive of the possibility that poor instruction might result in regression of students' academic growth. If television is to be successful on the campus, it must be based on instruction of the highest order. The positive approach is to concentrate research and thought on methods of developing superior TV teachers and of improving instruction. Naturally, this will not be limited to televised instruction but be part of our over-all effect through improvement in instruction and development of more effective teachers, now that we have come face to face with the imperative need for greater educational achievement in this country.

The position, taken by some educators, that we already know enough about the basic growth and learning processes is far from justifiable. On the contrary, the educational tasks which confront our nation and the world are of such immense magnitude as to warrant undertaking a program of basic research and development in the behavioral sciences, with special emphasis on the problems of teaching, learning, and social change. In order to meet evident needs, such a program requires resources and brainpower commensurate with those now available to the Atomic Energy Commission. One of the greatest weaknesses in educational thought is an underestimation of the dimensions of the problems to be solved and hence an underestimation of the resources needed to solve them.

For example, the exceedingly difficult and complex issue of segregation versus integration shows the dreadful price we pay for our ignorance of the determinants and controls of human adaptive behavior and social change, and the price we pay for our unskilled method of achieving social advancement.

Furthermore, when we expect the sciences of human behavior to give us definitive principles for use in teaching and for guiding our efforts in the restructuring of students' motivation, attitudes, and value systems, we are likely to be disappointed. The inadequacies of professional education are due in no small part to the lack of basic, scientifically validated knowledge of human behavior and its management. We have not been fully aware of the necessity for investing an adequate proportion of our physical resources and brain power in the research and development of the sciences of human behavior and experience. We may be forced to admit that, at this stage in the development of the sciences and arts related to teaching and learning, we are not yet prepared to achieve new, important, and urgently needed advancements in education.

Future Role of Televised Instruction

What will be the future role of television in our colleges and universities? We are confident that it has an important place in helping teachers and other educators to meet some of the heavy demands about to be made on them. Already we have taken an important step by making this assumption and proceeding forthwith to build TV into the structure of a few of our colleges and universities and communities. The rough outline of future architectural blueprints can now be sketched and proportions estimated.

Throughout the United States, as clear and evident needs develop that cannot be met by our present methods, the use of television will increase, at first slowly and then at an accelerated rate. Equipment will be improved and simplified and made more dependable. With sufficient demand, new inventions and adaptations can be expected. In time, appropriate kinds of systems will be available for different types of instructional uses. The relative cost of television systems will be reduced as the volume of production increases.

The larger institutions will make use of several different kinds of systems, some of which will be linked by cable or microwave, while other smaller systems will be operated separately and for special purposes. Closed-circuit and broadcast television will merge and be used together, simultaneously and interchangeably.

The principal use of television will be to distribute and extend high-quality instruction to students in those courses where there are large numbers of students or by broadcast to large, widespread audiences. In the near future the different kinds or operants of teaching and learning may be accurately defined, and a determination made of what teaching functions television can best serve and what functions should be served by other means. When TV's characteristics interfere, auxiliary means of teaching will be developed. Many special uses will be found for television, such as the recording of instruction, the distribution and projection of films, the pacing and guidance of science laboratories, and the magnifying and "remoting" of information, as well as the movement of information rather than the movement of people.

Engineering students can be taught liberal arts courses in their own building. We are planning something along this line also for home economics students but are not sure whether the girls will appreciate staying in their own particular complex, where there are few men. It might even be possible to break down the dichotomy of dormitory and academic buildings, providing multiple-purpose buildings in which students will live and learn with all the resources that they need, including libraries and television, immediately available to them.

By broadcast, instruction can be sent directly into homes, thereby greatly increasing the viewing audience. University centers may be connected with a parent institution. Different colleges and universities in a community can be brought together by TV to cooperate in developing and using their instructional resources.

Finally, our acute awareness of television as a means of instruction will disappear. Ten years from now television will not be news. Its place in education will have been found and established. That place will be analogous to the telephone, the automobile, and the airplane in our society. We will be aware of its values but not particularly conscious of the instrument itself. We will take TV for granted, but we can never take for granted those who use television for teaching, the educational purposes it serves, or the effects it achieves both for individuals and for society.

We can fervently hope that even now there is emerging a large group of prospective teachers who will become masters of the science and art of teaching by television. We can also hope that television will become one of their principal instruments of instruction which they can use with superb skill for achieving valid educational goals.

CHAIRMAN: That was a very rewarding paper. We could profitably spend several hours discussing each paragraph; but rather than have catch-as-catch-can discussion, three other experienced authorities in this work have studied Mr. Carpenter's paper. How well they have done their homework and whether they have contrary ideas, we shall see as we call upon them. The first of these commentaries is to be presented by Dr. John W. Taylor.

A Perspective of Televised Instruction— Panel Discussion

JOHN W. TAYLOR (Chicago Educational Television Association): I find myself in virtually complete agreement with everything Mr. Carpenter has said. I believe strongly that our approach must not be one

of trying to make the medium do what it cannot do. To put this positively: the present stage of technical development of the medium limits
us to lecture and demonstration uses on an open circuit. Television's capacity for extending and distributing information to viewers should be exploited to permit us to work around its functional limitations. Television
should be the means of making it economically feasible to provide small
group or individual instruction where it has been demonstrated that such
is necessary.

As a professor of comparative education, I became skeptical of the
American "credit bank" system in higher education. Europeans have long
employed the system of presenting, in lecture form, the materials deemed
important to students working for professional licenses. The German
university, for example, was probably the father of the seminar and
practice system. The implications of the use of television for lecture and
demonstration, coupled with group discussion followed by examinations,
must be explored and made use of in our future planning.

At Chicago we have not yet reached the point in our junior college
open-circuit experiment of being able to pronounce finally on costs. However, I am willing to predict that there is a break-even point somewhere
in the neighborhood of nine hundred full-time student equivalents for
televised instruction as compared with the on-campus costs of conventional instruction. I am further moved to estimate that the per-student
cost above nine hundred will drop to one-tenth or one-ninth of the
on-campus costs.

The statement made by Devereux Josephs' Committee—"The gap
between this Nation's educational needs and its educational effort is
widening ominously"[6]—is the key to the successful utilization of television in education. I say this because our profession is probably the
slowest of all to change its curricula and methods. In other words, I
would not ask for a better time historically to get the medium into use in
education. We must, however, keep the order of our goals in mind:
instructional improvement, instructional productivity, and instructional
efficiency and economy.

CHAIRMAN: The next panelist is Dr. F. Glenn Macomber, director of
the Experimental Study of Instructional Procedures of Miami University.
He has been directly involved in these problems and we would like to

[6] *Second Report to the President*, p. 6.

hear him amplify what has been said or strike out on new paths of his own.

Panel Discussion (continued)

F. GLENN MACOMBER (Miami University, Ohio): I have read Ray Carpenter's manuscript quite carefully. His instructions to the panel are to "supplement, criticize, and argue" the points of view expressed in his perspective. I find myself so much in agreement with the position he has taken, however, that there is no argument, nor do I have adverse criticism. I shall confine myself to supplementing the remarks of the speaker.

For the past two years we have been operating an experimental study in large-group teaching procedures in which we have been trying to determine the effectiveness of certain types of large-group instruction, including the use of television. We have been particularly concerned with evaluating the results, and during the next two years we are going to be concerned with trying to improve the instructional process.

Not only have we been concerned with objective examination results in large-group courses and in equated control courses; but also we have been attempting to determine how effective large- and small-group teaching is in achieving some of the intangible objectives of higher education —critical thinking and the ability to integrate one's knowledge in the solution of problems. We have, furthermore, been concerned with making attitudinal studies of our students because we think it is important to know whether or not they like television, just as we think it is important to know how they feel about other types of instruction regardless of what the achievement is. Detailed discussions of our findings relative to televised instruction can be found in our second annual report, which will be available shortly.[7]

A study of the data on final examinations administered in four televised courses taught during the spring semester of 1956 and four taught for the full 1956–57 academic year disclosed that results on eight out of the twelve semester examinations showed no significant differences in achievement. In four of the twelve cases, however, we found some significant differences. The differences in three of these cases favored the control sections over the televised sections and in one instance the

[7] "Experimental Study in Instructional Procedures," Report No. 2, Miami University (Oxford, Ohio: The University, October 1957), 64 pp.

difference favored the televised section over the control section. Of the total twelve cases the mean score of five TV sections exceeded that of the control sections, and in seven instances the means of the control sections exceeded the TV sections, from a small to a significant amount. Keep in mind, however, that out of the twelve cases the differences established in only four were deemed to be statistically significant.

We attempted a measurement of problem-solving ability and the ability of the student to synthesize his learnings in three of the televised courses. We did this through tests in which the students had to apply at least basic principles to problem situations. We found no statistically significant differences in two courses, but in the third course (in economics) there was a difference favoring the control section.

We were concerned whether or not students of high ability achieved more or less in televised and control sections than students of lower ability. We could uncover no statistically significant difference in the achievement of higher-ability students between the television and the control sections. The same held true for students of lesser ability.

We were interested in the student's attitude toward televised instruction and its effect on his achievement in the TV classes. Again we found no material difference. Students with a negative attitude toward televised teaching did just as well as those of equal ability whose attitudes toward TV instruction were positive. The same seemed to be true in control groups and, incidentally, in large lecture sections.

We developed opinionnaire-type instruments in which we asked the students to rate both the course and the instructor on a number of factors. We found that students tend to rate instructors higher in control sections than in televised sections. Also they tend to rate the courses higher in control than in TV sections.

Again, however, this has no relationship to achievement. Nor could we detect any significant differences between the television and control sections in their effect on students' long-time interests in a particular subject area. As high a percentage of students in the TV sections as in other sections signified that they would continue to work in the particular subject area. In general, the majority of students preferred to take courses in conventional-type classes rather than in televised or other types of large-group instruction. We did find in one instance, however, that a great majority of the students preferred televised instruction to small-group instruction. We are convinced that—given the right combination of instructor and course organization—it is possible to teach in such a way that students will actually prefer televised teaching to small-group instruction. However, I think it takes a rather rare combination of factors to achieve this result.

Another significant finding is that a majority of students who have had a course by television indicated that they would enroll in a second television course if assured of an excellent instructor rather than take their chances on section assignment otherwise. We noted that students became progressively disenchanted with television, even in the courses in which the majority still favored TV instruction at the end of the year. In general, students liked television less as a medium for receiving instruction at the end of the year than they did at midyear.

I would like to present two major problems which seem to strike at the very heart of televised teaching. I am coming more and more to the conviction that conventional courses have to be specially organized in line with usual course procedure and that transferring these to television just won't work satisfactorily. The other problem which needs a great deal of study is that of receiving rooms. We have been using makeshift rooms.

I am concerned with problems of ventilation and of placement of the receiving set so that it will be free from reflection, but with adequate light for note-taking by students. Of greater importance, however, is the problem of room size and arrangement. I am convinced that the typical rectangular room planned for thirty to forty students is not satisfactory, nor is the large auditorium with multiple receiving sets. The new type of room we need for televised reception will grow out of research.

CHAIRMAN: Thank you Dr. Macomber. Our final panelist will be Professor Harvey Zorbaugh, who has been chairman of the Department of Sociology at New York University, and executive officer for their Communications Arts Group. I know his experiences will be of interest.

Panel Discussion (continued)

HARVEY ZORBAUGH (New York University): I shall confine my remarks to what we have learned from studying our closed-circuit instruction that bears directly on Mr. Carpenter's point. I liked the way Mr. Carpenter focused our problem on teachers and teaching, and his insistence that we examine television in this context—not as a substitute for the teacher, not as a method of teaching, but as an instrument teachers may find of use in extending effective teaching.

New York University has had considerable experience with television. Our interest in the medium is vital. Our Radio and Television Office has for six years been cooperating with New York television stations in interpreting to the citizens of the metropolitan area the nature and role of a university and the fruits of its scholarship. It has provided active leadership and support to the Metropolitan Educational Television Association. It has completed two years of on-campus closed-circuit instruction, involving its Schools of Arts and Sciences, Education, Commerce, and Dentistry. It is designing experiments to explore some of the questions, to test some of the hunches that have arisen out of its use of closed-circuit TV.

Its medical school is projecting a program of postgraduate work in cooperation with county medical societies. This fall NYU embarked on an experiment in broadcast instruction for credit in cooperation with the Columbia Broadcasting System. This is our Comparative Literature 10 course, better known as "Sunrise Semester." The university is seeking to acquire greatly expanded time or a station, whichever proves financially more practical, to step up its educational use of television.

Much of this experience is relevant to the problems we are discussing. However, we have studied systematically only our closed-circuit instruction. Hence I will confine my remarks to what this study has yielded.

Mr. Carpenter spoke of a disproportionate use of audio channels over video channels. At New York University we have asked this question: "What, if anything, will imaginative production, as contrasted with merely televising the teacher's lecturing, contribute to students' learning?" The course chosen for this study, Man's Cultural Heritage, is a synthesis of sociology, social anthropology, and history. It is part of the core required of all freshmen in the School of Education. It is offered in the first semester and repeated in the second semester.

The first semester was televised "bare bones," camera and microphones picking up only the lecturer, with desk, chair, a blackboard, and an occasional map or artifact. Two imaginative producers, Richard Goggin and Richard Heffner, experienced in teaching and in television, sat through these televised lectures and subsequent discussions. They met with the instructors and addressed themselves to the question, "When this lecture is repeated next semester, what visual materials should we have to support its oral presentation?"

A wide variety of visual materials were used during the second semester, ranging from definitions through charts, graphs, maps, models, artifacts, photographs, film clips, dramatizations, and dances from primitive cultures by Pearl Primus.

The visual production proved a great selling device for televised instruction. Students were overwhelmingly of the opinion that it added not only to the interest of the course, but also to the amount they learned. Interviews with instructors and discussion leaders showed that they tended to share these opinions.

But did the visual production increase learning? The instructional team, headed by Professor Hope Klapper, who is with us this morning, devised a test of the knowledge of the subject matter presented which they hoped students would have acquired upon completion of the course. Each semester's students were tested on this instrument at the beginning of the course and again upon its completion. The difference between pre-test and post-test scores was taken as the measure of learning. The average of these differences was used to compare learning from semester to semester.

Visual production did not increase learning. Indeed learning, as measured by the test used, was somewhat less, a difference significant on the 5 percent level. Why? We have considered many hypotheses.

Mr. Carpenter warns that "the instruction-handling capacity of television greatly exceeds the learning abilities and rates of students." Does the explanation lie here? We think not. The instructional and production teams were experienced, highly competent, and imaginative. The visual presentation was simple and clear and, in the opinion of the instructors, genuinely supported the oral presentation. It should be noted, however, that many students indicated that the visual materials did not remain long enough on the screen.

Were the students involved in the two semesters significantly different? They were not, so far as intelligence test scores, high school averages, and average grades in other university courses are concerned.

Were the students left too largely to themselves in connecting the visual and oral materials? This may be true. The visuals may have held interest and attention for themselves, even detracting from the points in the oral presentation which they were meant to support.

This we propose to explore this year. We may find upon questioning students some days later that there will be more recollection of the visuals than of the points they supported.

Is the nature of the course a major factor? Stressing, as it did, facts, concepts, principles, and attitudes, is its content perhaps most effectively communicated by language, particularly to students who are accustomed to learning through the spoken and written word? We did a rough study of the relation of attentiveness to learning, attention to the screen being the criterion. In neither semester was there any relationship between attention to the screen and learning. I believe that our findings confirm Mr. Carpenter's assertion that this is a research problem of great importance.

Raymond Franzen, a brilliant and ingenious research statistician, suggests that we stated our problem falsely to begin with. Rather than asking, "Will there be a difference in learning between the two groups?" Mr. Franzen says that, the experience of the two groups having been different, we should have assumed a difference in learning and devised instruments to delineate it.

Charles Siepmann, chairman of our Department of Communications in Education, has wryly suggested, with tongue in cheek, that our testing methods show that teaching is already so ineffective that nothing can make it less effective. We who teach would prefer to believe that they show we already teach so well that our teaching cannot be improved. Or do they merely confirm Mr. Carpenter's suspicion that we need more valid, more comprehensive measuring instruments?

In concluding, Mr. Carpenter pointed out that those of us who are active in educational television are also acutely aware of the need for superior instruction: "Little is gained and much may be lost, when mediocre or poor instruction is televised, regardless of the number of students reached."

Data gleaned from our course on English Composition strongly support this position. In the sections in which television was used a common televised lecture was followed by discussion, clarification, and application of the televised lecture to the students' themes. Another group of sections was taught in the traditional way. There was a marked variation in achievement among the sections of both types.

Five instructors taught both a television and a traditional section. Data on achievement of these ten sections yield an estimate of the relative influence of method of presentation and of the instructor—allowing us to hold first method, then instructor, constant. Neither the mean, nor even largest variations, where the instructor is constant, approach in magnitude those where the method is held constant.

This suggests that the instructor is a more important influence on learning than is the method of presentation. When we group sections by method of presentation and initial level of knowledge, we find marked variability in learning within each group. The only identifiable variable to which this difference can be attributed is the instructor.

The instructors varied, of course, in experience; obviously they must have varied in competence. Unfortunately we have no measure of competence. This is by no means the whole story of the part played by the instructors however. They varied in their attitudes toward the use of television in teaching. We explored this question and the attitudes of the instructors seemed to be related to the achievement of their sections to such an extent that Louis Heil, who directed our evaluation, concluded that the instructors make or break the course; and one of the television lecturers observed, "The discussion leader is the Achilles' heel" of televised teaching. The effectiveness of televised teaching will depend, during the immediate future and until such time as TV's place in education is assumed, upon the teacher's attitude toward TV as well as on his competence.

CHAIRMAN: Thank you, Professor Zorbaugh.

Learning via Televised Instruction

MONDAY AFTERNOON, OCTOBER 21, 1957

Presiding: JOHN C. ADAMS

CHAIRMAN: Our first speaker will be Professor Neal Miller of the Psychology Department, Yale University.

Principles of Learning by Televised Instruction

NEAL E. MILLER (Yale University): The same general principles of learning probably apply to all media, but certain media present special opportunities and special problems. I shall emphasize the part of the televised presentation which goes beyond the mere image of a man talking on the screen, because I believe that it is in the added audio-visual potentialities that television and motion pictures afford opportunities beyond those available in conventional instruction. I shall also emphasize some of the difficulties likely to be encountered in the instruction of large groups by television.

While I believe that we know quite a few principles that are highly relevant to televised teaching, we do not know all of the relevant principles of learning. I want to underline Ray Carpenter's point that we need a great deal more basic research aimed at discovering and clarifying fundamental principles of learning. We also need engineering research to tell us how better to apply generally verified principles to a particular medium such as television.

Even if we did know all of the principles, there would still be an important place for people with the precious art of knowing how to apply these principles to the special conditions of teaching a particular subject to a specific group of students. My field is the experimental study of learning; I do not pretend to be an expert on the teaching of classes via television. If this talk is to be of any value, you will have to take the principles that I describe and try to apply them to concrete teaching situations that you have experienced in teaching by television. It takes a great deal of experience and art to translate scientific principles into

28

practical results. Furthermore, various teachers may use the same set of principles to achieve similar goals in different ways.

I intend to group the problems involved in teaching-learning under certain fundamental factors. These are:

a) *Drive* or as it is often called, *motivation*. The student must want something.

b) *Cue,* or as it is often called, *stimulus*. The student must notice something.

c) *Response,* or as it is often called, *participation*. The student must do something.

d) *Reward*, or as it is sometimes called, *reinforcement*. The student must get something that he wants.

Finally, I shall discuss a number of research problems and practical principles which do not fit neatly under any single one of the foregoing four factors.

Each of the general principles that I shall discuss is quite well verified by experimental evidence. But whenever anyone applies general principles to any complex practical situation, he needs further confirmation, because there may be some additional principles which he has overlooked that operate in a different direction, or because the specific conditions may not be well enough known so that he can predict with complete confidence.

This problem is not unique to the social sciences. The principles of physics involved in making an automobile, for example, are well known. Nevertheless, whenever the manufacturer (who has had a great deal of practical experience) makes a relatively new model, he has to road-test it thoroughly, because the machine is so complex that he is apt to slip up on some small but significant detail which will cause trouble in practical operation. By this I do not mean that the scientific principles are not necessary. No one could build a successful car without a knowledge of the discoveries of physical sciences. Although Charlie Wilson may express contempt for pure-science research, without man's understanding of electricity, which started with the pure-science study of tiny pith balls suspended on silk threads, not a single General Motors car would run. Nevertheless, the scientific principles alone are not enough; the car must also be road-tested.

Similarly, in our area we should not be dismayed if the application of the principles of learning to the complex conditions of televised teaching must be "road-tested." Some relevant testing has been done in studies of the variables that affect learning from motion pictures. A smaller amount of testing has been done on the newer medium of television. But we could benefit by far more research on how to teach more effectively by both motion pictures and television.

Drive or Motivation

Learning must be motivated to be efficient. In dealing with motivation to learn by television, we have to discriminate between two situations: (a) the use of television in campus or extension courses where motivation tends to be similar to that on the campus, and (b) the use of open-circuit broadcasts to a free audience of adults or children who are not paying to take courses for credit.

I believe we can err in judging the motivation—the interest—of the television mass audience by our own interests and those of our students. I believe that our students are a much more highly selected and motivated sample than we realize. Since almost everyone tends to associate with those whose interests are similar to his own, we tend to underestimate the degree to which motivations and interests can vary in different segments of the population.

Age makes an enormous difference in many motivations and interests. Sex typing is important. The differences between the interests of men and women become greater as one goes down from the upper strata into the large middle and lower classes. Social class tends to determine the types of people who associate together in informal cliques; hence it determines many aspects of their social motivation in addition to interacting with the sex differences we have just mentioned. Differences are associated with intelligence, education, geographical, region, ethnic origin, and other cultural factors.

While some motivations are common to our entire culture, it is not true that all peoples' interests are similar. The differences are greater than most of us realize. Therefore, whenever an educational program is planned for general broadcast, one must ask: What is the nature of the audience? Do we hope to hit the general public or only a highly selected sample, and if a selected sample, exactly what one do we expect to reach? What is the potential audience interested in? It may be necessary to make audience surveys to answer that last question.

College students are much more highly selected and motivated. In the future when the great wave from the increased birth rate hits us, it will probably be harder to get into college and stay there. Thus, the students will be still more highly selected and motivated. Nevertheless, there is some danger that college students will generalize the entertainment set from commercial TV to the classroom. Once this is recognized, it can be handled by some of the techniques we shall be mentioning.

The teacher can help to create the right atmosphere of motivation to work rather than to be entertained. Research on training films shows that the teacher is important in the motivation of the students, even if he is not present when the film is projected. In another study Allison and Ash found that telling students that the material in a film is important and telling them that it is difficult can improve their learning.

Motivation should be relevant.—Relevant drives produce relevant responses and the desired type of learning. Irrelevant drives are likely to produce irrelevant responses, which interfere with the desired learning. Some of the dramatic and artistic devices that are carried over from entertainment television into educational television may actually distract the students from learning. Such devices may interest and entertain the students, but one must always ask whether or not they direct or distract the student's interest in essential points. The problem is analogous to that of using jokes in lectures. A good joke which makes a relevant point is excellent; a joke dragged in by the heels may waste time and distract from the main theme.

With the free audience of a general broadcast one may have to go further in the direction of bringing in educationally irrelevant motivations in order to keep the audience looking at their sets. But in the college situation, I would venture that one can dispense with many of these tricks of the entertainment profession, concentrating on relevant motivation.

One of the stronger motivations acquired in school is to get good grades by doing well on examinations. Thus it is not surprising that research on motion-picture instruction has shown that warning students in advance that they will be examined on the content of a film can have the effect of increasing their learning. This should be true of television; an examination early in the course ought to have a sobering effect on any student who is transferring the entertainment set to the classroom.

The use of examinations brings up an important problem. Ideally we would like the student to be motivated to understand the material rather than to pass an examination. The possible conflict between motivation to pass and motivation to understand is involved in all forms of instruction. However, when instruction—either lecture or TV—involves large groups, this conflict may be intensified because the give and take of direct contact with the individual student is reduced.

One of the ways of solving the problem is to create the kind of examination that tests true understanding rather than factual memory. But it takes considerable ingenuity to test for understanding rather than for facts, particularly when one is making out objective tests to be administered to large groups. I fear that sometimes what we measure in examinations is determined more by ease of testing it than by whether it is really the thing that we want to achieve.

On the other hand, I want to point out clearly that it is possible to make out objective examinations that get at the student's understanding and ability to think. It is possible to present students with novel problems which they must solve for themselves in order to be able to select the correct answer. It is also possible to have them check the principles that they use in solving these problems. One can even test for the ability to discover and formulate problems. With sufficient ingenuity it is possible to use reliable objective tests to get at types of learning and performance which one might not think off-hand could be measured in this way.

The Educational Testing Service at Princeton has done a great deal in developing objective and essay tests that reliably measure some of the subtler aspects of education. As the use of educational TV increases, it may be important to try to get some agency of this kind to develop improved achievement tests that will efficiently and reliably measure progress in learning the kinds of things we are most interested in teaching. The development of improved examinations is important because the power to examine is a significant part of the power to determine what the student is motivated to learn.

New potentialities of televised tests.—In many instances the greater ability of television to present the essential details of the actual situation in a realistic way may afford the possibility of creating new and more pertinent types of examinations. We have not really begun to use the full potentialities of television to give tests of this kind.

I think it is possible to use television to teach our students entirely new things which they need to learn but which we haven't hitherto thought of teaching, because we haven't had the opportunity to make such teaching practicable. Similarly, by using the whole spectrum of the audio-visual medium of presentation, I believe that it is possible to examine our students for entirely new things that previously were scarcely practicable for us to test.

For example, in a course in the psychology of adjustment I can imagine using television to present a kinescope recording of a social situation which is followed by a series of questions asking which of the characters is most anxious and how he shows his anxiety, which of the characters is overcompensating, and which is displacing his aggression. Such an examination would go beyond measuring the student's ability to regurgitate the textbook definitions of various psychological dynamisms; it would test his ability to detect them when they are operating in a real social situation. The test might then go on to ask the student to predict what would happen next or to suggest (or choose between) various methods for making the social group function more comfortably and efficiently.

In art and architecture, geography, geology, and ornithology, I think it is quite obvious how the audio-visual potentialities of television could be used to create more realistic tests. I don't have the background to give examples for the subject material in which all of you are experts. But I hope you will be thinking of the relevant types of learning that could better be tested by television than by conventional paper-and-pencil tests.

Finally, it is unfair to television, and to the new curriculum which should be built around it, if we test students who are trained by this new medium only with the kinds of tests that have been devised to measure the material that is learned from the textbook or lecture.

Fear as a motive.—Whenever fear is used as a motive, it is important to point out clearly the appropriate ways of avoiding the danger and escaping the fear. Any response which leads to escape from fear or punishment is reinforced. If the instructor does not provide desirable means of escape, the students will find undesirable ways—looking away from the set, paying attention to something else, belittling or forgetting the communication.

The same is true of fear of examinations. If the examination can be passed by cheating or by merely memorizing, fear is likely to motivate those responses. If the fear is too strong, and the habit of reducing it by studying is too weak, it may drive the student's attention away from the books or the TV screen, which remind him of the fear-evoking examination.

Fear itself is not necessarily always bad. It can motivate either maladaptive or adaptive responses. The important issue is whether the student responds to the fear with undesirable or desirable responses. When a response produces a prompt reduction in the strength of fear, it is rewarded and tends to be learned.

How television can influence motivation.—We have talked about the importance of arousing in the student a motivation to understand the subject material. However, since the motivation to understand is not yet itself well understood scientifically, the teacher will have to use his art to elicit such motivation. We are just beginning to bring motivations of this type into the laboratory. I believe we may be able to learn something about how to strengthen and channel intellectual curiosity.

It is obvious that television has a powerful capacity to catch and hold attention. It is obvious that my children have learned a great deal when their interest is aroused by programs such as Walt Disney's nature pictures, *Zoo Parade,* or *Mr. Wizard.* We need research to devise better measures of the types of motivations that can be aroused by television. We also need to discover the principles governing how the potentialities of television can be most effectively used to motivate learning.

The motivation of the teacher.—I believe that our nation will not get very far in solving its grave teacher shortages by scholarship programs and other means of trying to entice young people into the teaching profession unless the economic rewards of teaching can be increased to be more nearly commensurate with dentistry, medicine, law, and business. Perhaps the economies achieved by teaching certain school subjects by television can be used, along with additional funds, to help to increase the salary of an outstanding teacher to within nodding distance of those of the average junior executive in business. Perhaps these economies can also save more of the teacher's precious time and talents for increased emphasis on those aspects of instruction which can be carried on only personally in small groups.

In the meantime certain immediate small steps can be taken. An administration which already is saving thousands of dollars each year by televised teaching can plough a little bit of it back into air conditioning the studios, so that the television teachers do not have to suffer under summer temperatures greatly increased by the heat from the lights.

Cue or Stimulus Situation

In order to learn, the student must notice something. Television has the capacity for supplying a greater variety of more realistic cues, especially when it makes the full use of kinescopes and other recorded materials that would be difficult to reproduce in every classroom, every year, in every college. Stop-motion photography can show the growth of plants. Microscopic objects can be enlarged. The geology student can be taken on a flight over the great mountains of the world, so that he can see where the glaciers have dug out the cirques and how the headward erosion of the cirques has created the particular configuration of the peaks and ranges. Drama can be seen and heard rather than merely read. Historic scenes can be recreated. By bringing the world into every classroom, words can be given richer meanings. We can avoid the curse of empty verbalism and increase the transfer from the classroom to life.

One of the principles of learning is that responses transfer best to similar stimulus situations. This is called a gradient of stimulus generalization. The greater capacity of television to reproduce many situations realistically, as we have already suggested, should help to facilitate transfer of training from the classroom to life. Other things being equal, an attempt should be made to produce demonstrations that are as similar as possible to the situations which the student will encounter. For example, a study at Pennsylvania State University has shown that it is more effective to present demonstrations from the subjective angle of view. This is because, when the camera looks over the demonstrator's shoulder, it sees the scene in the same way that the student will see it when he is trying to perform the task; but, when the camera looks at the demonstration from the position which would ordinarily be occupied by an audience, it sees a different scene. You will probably be able to think of many other examples in which learning could be facilitated by greater realism, or in other words, by reducing the amount of stimulus generalization required.

Focusing attention on relevant cues.—In many learning situations the actual object may be complex and baffling; there are a large number of irrelevant cues. One of the problems of efficient teaching is to build up discriminations, so that the student will respond only to the relevant cues and not be misled or distracted by the irrelevant ones. We can expect television to be more effective if it is used to focus attention on relevant cues. For example, Lumsdaine has shown that pop-in labels and other devices which help to focus attention can improve learning from motion pictures. We would expect other techniques, such as deliberate exaggeration or diagrammatic simplification, to emphasize relevant cues. Color should be an advantage if it is one of the most relevant cues, or can be used to emphasize the relevant cues; it should be a disadvantage if it distracts or complicates. Similarly other special attention-gaining devices should help if they direct attention to the relevant cues and hinder if they fail to do this. But artiness, which is important in commercial television, may not always help. One may be able to save time and money by leaving out unnecessary artiness which does not improve the focusing of attention on relevant cues.

Often a sample of the real life situation may be too specific. We want to teach a response which will generalize a whole class of objects or situations. This generalization can be helped by using techniques, such as caricature and diagrammatic simplification, which emphasize the cues that are common to all of the members of the class and minimize those that are not general. The process of abstraction can also be helped by exposing the student to a variety of specific examples of the class and focusing his attention on the common elements.

Various means of abstraction, or directing attention toward relevant cues, will involve deviations from strict realism and thus conflict with the principles of stimulus generalization. The relative importance of these two opposing factors will depend on the particular conditions of learning. In one situation finding the relevant cue may be more important, so that a cartoon may be superior to live photography. But in another situation realism may be more important, so that live photography will be superior. Thus, studies aimed simply at comparing the two techniques, without taking into account the specific requirements of the task, are likely to produce misleading and inconsistent results.

In this dilemma of abstraction versus realism, it is obvious that the problem can sometimes be resolved by directing attention to the relevant cues in the early stages of training, and in the later stages of training adding step by step the confusing elements that will be encountered in different real life situations.

You can see the complexity of the research problems that face us. We are just beginning to get sophisticated enough to advance from the stage of grossly comparing televised instruction with ordinary instruction to the stage of finding out how this new medium can be used most effectively and what particular purposes it can best be used for.

Our analysis of this problem is based on learning theory, which I believe is in general sound, but the specific application to instruction by television should be checked by further research. I believe it would be extremely valuable to learn more about the interacting dynamics of these two opposing factors—abstraction and realism.

Finally, we have been talking about relevant and irrelevant cues. But it is not always obvious which are the relevant cues. Before we can decide which cues to emphasize, we must make a correct job analysis of the expert's performance and the learner's task.

Response or Participation

In order to learn, the student must do something; he must pay attention, perceive, rehearse, reason, and try to remember. It is obvious that I am not giving the narrowest Watsonian definition of response but a broad functional one which includes thoughts, images, emotions, and other possibly central processes. In short, responses can be covert as well as overt. Responses are elicited by cues. They are also related to motivation. Students who are motivated to learn are less likely to respond by day-dreaming and are more likely to be rehearsing and responding with new trains of relevant thought.

While information theory can be useful, analogies from physical transmission and communication can also be misleading. The degree to which we can transmit information to the student depends upon the response units he already has. To take an extreme example, a lecture in a foreign language may contain as much potential information as a similar lecture in the native tongue, but the student may learn almost nothing from the former and a great deal from the latter. It is important to know what response units your students possess and what cues can elicit these responses.

The professor is likely to be selected for his verbal skill and to have a lifetime of experience in his subject. For him a few words rapidly evoke whole contexts of integrated, meaningful responses. But the student has not yet learned these complex, integrated responses. Thus, the use of the more complete audio-visual potentialities of television, the need for which is not always obvious to the professor who is immersed in his subject, may be extremely helpful in eliciting the proper responses from the students so that the words become more meaningful. The ability to elicit more responses by a wider variety of cues is a possible educational advantage of television.

On the other hand, a disadvantage is that with television the teacher does not get the same feedback, that glassy-eyed look of bewilderment which tells him that the students don't comprehend. Consequently, the TV instructor has to take special pains to find out what responses he can count on in his students and to assemble these step by step into the larger novel combinations that are his goal. Frequent examinations, used more for diagnosis than for grading, help to keep track of students.

Some advantages of the small discussion group are that one can get immediate feedback from students, give them opportunity to respond, and correct responses. These advantages are reduced whenever teaching is done in large groups, be they TV courses or direct lectures to large classes. Once the group is beyond the size allowing appreciable individual participation, it might as well be made very large to achieve the economies of mass instruction. Intermediate-sized groups, taught by lecture or by television, are likely to be inefficient.

Many experiments on educational motion pictures show that building opportunities for participation into the films increases learning. An early experiment demonstrated better learning of the phonetic alphabet when the students were required to recite "Able, Baker, Charlie . . ." along with the film. Such experiments are not explorations of participation versus nonparticipation, but rather experiments in which requiring the response to be made overtly intensifies participation and ensures that it occurs. It has been found that covert participation, or instructing students to rehearse mentally, improves learning.

A technical challenge of instruction via television is that of finding out how to get maximum active participation out of students. Ingenuity should be used in solving this problem. Various ideas, such as test items and workbooks dovetailed right into the instructional period, will occur to you. In most cases it is desirable to have the first participation occur as soon as possible after the instruction that is supposed to elicit the correct responses, be they skilled acts or creative thoughts. Analytical studies are beginning to show how participation achieves its effect, and what kind of participation under what circumstances is best. We need more such analytical studies.

Reward or Reinforcement

The student must be rewarded; he must get something that he wants. The factor of reward is obviously related to drive because, if the student does not want what he gets, he is not rewarded by it. Rewards can also function as incentives to increase motivation. A student becomes more interested in the types of study for which he is rewarded.

Immediate rewards are more effective than delayed ones. With a small group it is easy for the instructor to shape his students' responses—to lead them to the correct response by raising questions about incorrect ones and immediately rewarding approximations to the correct ones. In instructing large groups, by either TV or direct lecture, it is much harder to use immediate rewards in this way.

Knowledge of results has been found to be an important factor in producing learning. It serves as a reward to those who want to learn or to solve a problem; it also serves as a guide toward a better approximation of the optimum response. It is more effective the more immediately it follows the response.

We need to exercise our ingenuity to devise new methods of introducing more immediate knowledge of results, and hence reward, into mass instruction. The anticipation method can frequently be adapted for this purpose. In its simplest form the subject is presented with a cue, required to make a response, and then given the correct response for comparison. If correct, he is rewarded by the satisfaction of knowing that he is succeeding; if incorrect, he is supposed to correct himself by rehearsing the right response. Later the item is repeated until the student learns to anticipate correctly every time.

With sufficient ingenuity it should be possible to apply the general principle of the anticipation method to certain phases of instruction by television. I can even imagine each student having a series of keys in front of him. The teacher presents a problem to him by television, listing or illustrating possible answers to the problem. After thinking, the student chooses the solution by pressing the appropriate key. If he is correct, a counter on his desk adds another point to his total score; and if he is incorrect, a red light by the appropriate key shows the answer he should have chosen. The total number of errors is flashed on another counter in front of the instructor. If many students have failed to get the correct answer, the instructor immediately explains why a certain answer is the correct one. This procedure gives maximum participation and immediate reward. Perhaps this sounds a little like Buck Rogers to you, but so did earth satellites a year or two ago.

Machine-scored answer sheets or workbooks might be substituted for the keys and counters. The resourceful teacher will be able to devise still other ways of introducing problem-solving with immediate knowledge of the results into televised instruction. Mechanizing certain aspects of instruction does not need to make the instruction merely rote and mechanical. With sufficient ingenuity general principles can be taught in this way, posing problems that can be solved only by reasoning from such principles.

Mass instruction poses special problems, because one cannot diagnose the individual student's difficulties and shape his responses as easily as in a small discussion group. Therefore, the instructor has to do much more planning beforehand in order to produce sequences that will lead all students by easy stages from the simple responses they originally had to the more complex ones desired as the outcome of teaching. With ideal planning of instruction the student should be able to perform correctly and be rewarded by success.

In adult education one of the rewards for the student may be to talk afterwards about what he has learned. Thus, it is important for the program planner to know what kinds of information are likely to produce social or other rewards. One of the difficulties with educating the adult public about science is that, although this is the age in which everyone's life is profoundly affected by the products of science, it is not the scientific age in terms of public interest in science. In social conversation a brilliant equation is no substitute for a literary *bon mot*. Similarly, the rewards in the school system are not likely to have maximum effect unless they are backed up in real life.

This part of the discussion may sound discouraging, but I believe that, if we know the kinds of problems we are up against, we are less likely to waste precious effort on impossible goals and more likely to be spurred to use maximum art and ingenuity to achieve what must and can be done. Finally, we need more research devoted to finding out how to channel, develop, and use the rewards people get from solving problems, satisfying curiosity, learning, and achieving.

Forgetting and Review

As time elapses, forgetting tends to neutralize some of the effects of learning. Since forgetting usually occurs more rapidly at first and then more slowly, it is desirable to give fairly prompt reviews first, followed by additional reviews at progressively increasing intervals. Reviews also afford opportunity for the material to be organized into larger, more meaningful units.

Logical Learning, Generality, and Creativity

As more knowledge is discovered at an ever-increasing rate, there is so much for students to learn that it becomes exceedingly important to teach them general principles with the widest applicability. In our discussion of abstraction we have pointed out the importance of directing attention to those cues, which may be complex patterns or relationships, that are common to a whole class of objects. Abstraction is one way of learning habits that have wider general applicability.

Just as some types of cues have greater general utility than others, so some types of verbal or mathematical statements have wider general applicability. It is important to teach in terms of those general principles and then to train the students to apply such principles to specific situations. Finally, it is extremely important to help the student to see clearly throughout the processes how each step is related to the goal. When a student is taught in this way, he has been given the wherewithal for reasoning and creative thinking.

For example, Wertheimer has shown that many geometry students are taught to prove the theorem concerning the area of a parallelogram by going through a rote process of dropping perpendicular lines and joining them together in certain ways. Students who have mastered the solution in this way are likely to be helpless when the parallelogram is turned on its side and are not able to transfer the method to new figures, such as triangles.

It is possible, however, to teach students in a more logical way which follows the course of creative thinking. They are first made aware of the goal—that of changing the parallelogram into a rectangle so that its area can be determined. Then the dotted lines are seen as a means of chopping off one end of the parallelogram to create right angles. Students taught by this logical method, in which each step is clearly related to the goal of changing the parallelogram into a rectangle, will readily transpose the solution to new positions of the parallelogram and even to finding the solution for new types of geometric figures.

Teaching in terms of general principles, logically and meaningfully related to the ultimate goals, is of course good practice with almost any type of subject material through any medium of instruction. But this precept is far too often neglected. Many of our science courses teach cook book techniques, facts, and formulae without giving the students any understanding of the problems that were encountered in their derivation and the process by which these problems were solved. Such teaching fails to convey the spirit of science and the scientific method.

While we are preparing materials for instruction via television, we should ask ourselves whether we are merely teaching facts by rote or are teaching the most general principles in a meaningful fashion so that the student is receiving the intellectual tools that will enable him to continue learning and to think creatively for himself.

Speeding Adjustment to New Needs and Opportunities

As a student of learning and social phenomena, I am impressed with the degree to which we build on the past with the consequent difficulty of adjusting to new demands and new opportunities. For example, think of the history of the automobile—how it gradually evolved from a horseless carriage into a modern motor car. Although a certain amount of maladaptive hang-over from past habits is inevitable, I believe that we can minimize such anachronistic bondage if we recognize the problem and devote concentrated attention to it. Perhaps we in television are still arguing about whether we should remove the whip socket from the horseless carriage when we should be trying to design an entirely new vehicle and the road system to make that vehicle maximally useful.

In various parts of this talk I have hinted at some of the potentialities of television for using kinescopes and other forms of recorded material to achieve easily types of instruction or testing that would be too difficult to achieve otherwise. There probably are new facets of old subjects and even entirely new types of skill and knowledge which our students would greatly benefit from learning in school, but which in the past we have not thought of including in the curriculum because we did not have any suitable way of presenting them. All of us tend to copy the example of our own professors and to borrow from the storehouse of previous lectures and textbooks. This is good. But let us also consciously try to alert ourselves to the fact that television is a new medium with new potentialities which cannot be realized maximally by merely copying the past.

Perhaps more of us should be devoting thought to the creation of radical changes throughout our educational system, keeping pace with the tremendous innovations in other areas of modern life. While these changes may take time to execute, they will be facilitated if we can achieve a clearer vision of the goal ahead.[1]

CHAIRMAN: Thank you, Professor Miller, for a learned and stimulating paper.

Professor Grosslight, formerly a student and colleague of Dr. Miller, will present our next paper.

Conditions of Learning in a Closed-Circuit Television System

JOSEPH H. GROSSLIGHT (Pennsylvania State University): Professor Miller has outlined some of the principles of learning and their operation as they may affect our concepts of learning. These principles interact

[1] For principles of learning applying to problems of audio-visual instruction and an outline of research needs, see Neal E. Miller, *et al., Graphic Communication and the Crisis in Education* (Washington: Department of Audio-Visual Instruction, National Education Association, 1957), Part II. This book also contains references to relevant research studies.

with a set of conditions—in this case, television. We find many variables in the nature of the stimulus conditions: the teacher, motivation, participation, meaningfulness, overlearning, mass and distributed conditions, part-whole presentations, and many others.

These conditions are involved in all learning situations. For televised instruction, however, three of them seem to be of prime importance. They are found in the nature of the stimulus situation as defined by the teacher, motivation, and participation.

Role of Teacher

The problem of the good teacher involves an awareness of a separation of roles in the learning situation of the teacher on one hand and the student on the other, and of the interaction of the two roles. We are faced immediately with the lack of an adequate definition and of modes of measurement for this concept of the good teacher. Yet I believe that adequacy of instruction is more closely associated with the teacher than with methods of teaching. Here I find myself at variance with some of my own colleagues who are stressing the importance of methods of teaching. Method is important, but the ability of the teacher is paramount.

Motivation

The teacher is a prime influence in the learning process, but we lack adequate studies and measures of the fundamental stimulus characteristics of the teacher which elicit the responses in students that we call learning. I believe television does one thing to a teacher: it makes the poor teacher even poorer. What conditions of learning, magnified by television, are involved? In my judgment, it is a problem of motivation— motivation in and by the student so that the stimuli presented by the teacher have an effect. Too often learning in the academic tradition is defined as the imparting or transposing of information. Ideally, however, we feel that the role of the teacher is not only to impart information, but to stimulate the student into thinking, evaluating, transferring, and asking relevant questions. To do this the student must be interested and motivated, and he must participate in the learning situation. Consequently, the problem of participation is particularly related to that of motivation.

Let us hypothesize briefly some of the reasons for the greater role of motivation in the television medium of instruction than in direct teaching. We are dealing with the image of the instructor at least once removed. We might postulate that physical distance is greater between the student and the instructor; I suspect that physical distance is not the essential variable, but rather that distance perceived by the student is the major component of this factor. This perceived distance can be called the psychological distance. The problem of psychological distance in televised instruction would seem an important area for investigation.

It is true that in televised instruction the student perceives a larger image of the instructor and that he has a restricted stimulus field, but the critical question is whether these factors lead to greater identification with the teacher; or does the student, because of the distance factor, use his old responses of a simple viewer? Does he then assume a passive role in the learning situation?

I would like to comment on the restricted stimulus field offered by television before pressing the psychological distance variable further. Some people believe that television can be used to increase the student's focus and attention and reduce the psychological distance because of its larger image and restricted stimulus field. However, we can raise a question as to whether the restricted stimulus field does not decrease attention due to repetition and the constancy of the same stimulus. Research indicates that repetition of the stimulus and response often leads to variability of behavior; consequently, it is equally possible that the larger image and the restricted field may actually increase attention to distractive cues rather than to the cues relevant to learning.

When we first began television research, we televised from a classroom, letting the students in other rooms look in on the class. There were reports of inattention, letter writing, and sleeping. The next step was to move to an originating room with a smaller number of students present. This gave the technical side of presentation greater freedom, but did it decrease the psychological distance? When I participated in this method, I found a dilemma. If I talked to the students in front of me, the television classes were put in the position of looking in as distant viewers. When I talked to the cameras, I felt like an actor in front of an audience. This conflict was resolved, in spite of my reluctance to give up the face-to-face audience, by changing to presentations without a face-to-face group present. In this situation what can be done to give the student the feeling of close identification with the instructor; that is, to reduce the psychological distance, to encourage participation, and to increase motivation?

In televised instruction we need to ask what it is about the instructor stimulus that will increase both the drive value and the cue value for the student. In order to encourage learning, the stimuli must produce a reaction; the student must be paying attention and otherwise responding. In effect we are raising the question of interest in the instructor as well as in the subject. Stimuli cues for learning are often more effective when they have some compelling characteristic.

The compelling characteristic is most apparent in a direct interaction between two individuals. Therefore, what can be done in televised instruction to give the impression of a direct, face-to-face interaction between teacher and student?

With his role redefined in this fashion, the teacher must consider himself as addressing four hundred separate individuals rather than a common mass, assuming that the class is composed of four hundred students. This approach alters camera techniques. If the camera is viewed as the student, the instructor maintains what we call eye contact with the camera at all times. From my own and student impressions, I suspect that this eye-contact effect is even greater in televised teaching than it is with a large face-to-face group. This is an area of research in technique or art whereby the cue value of the instructor may be enhanced.

I would like to suggest that slick professionalism in presentation may be in conflict with the authenticity requirement. Human errors, such as getting caught up in my mike cord, getting a slight electric shock from a piece of demonstration equipment, or having a visual fall, seem to lead to the students' perception that this is a real human being in front of them. Occasional errors in presentation, I feel, increase the students' identification with the instructor, increasing the authenticity of presentation, and decreasing psychological distance. Also, from our observations, we believe that the live demonstrations are more effective than the recorded ones.

Earlier in this paper I raised some questions about the larger image and restricted visual field of TV receivers, as these relate to attention and variability of student behavior. Attention to a stimulus is greatly dependent on change and variability. A constant stimulus leads quickly to adaptation, and both cue values and motivation value are lost. This raises the question of introducing change in the method of presentation of instruction. Graphic aids, demonstrations, and variations of verbal stimuli are possibilities.

Observation Advantages

Television allows for superior viewing of both graphic and demonstration material, but what should be their characteristics, and in what proportion and manner of presentation should they be used? The graphics and demonstrations have an effect on the instructor's motivation. I find that these techniques increase my interest in the material that I'm communicating to the students. When we evaluated a generous use of visual aids versus an absence of them, we found no consistent, significant differences in student learning as measured by four objective examinations.

Some instructors seem to be effective visuals in themselves; for others, the graphic-demonstration procedure is a necessary supplement. Perhaps the graphic-demonstration procedure is a crutch which supports the somewhat ineffective teacher. At any rate, we still lack the answers concerning the effect that graphic-demonstration materials have upon motivation and distance for the student.

We Learn by Doing—Response

One of the conditions of learning is participation or response. We often say, "We learn by doing." Clearly, in TV instruction the problem of participation is paramount. It is in this area that we meet the greatest criticism of educational television. It is said that the system detracts from student discussion; the student can't ask questions on the spot. He can't obtain the feedback. Too often we conceive of participation in terms of overt response.

We do not stress the processes of covert responses, such as thinking. We need to ask what learned responses we wish our students to acquire, and then determine what methods of participation reinforce these responses. In our General Psychology course we not only want our students to learn factual information, but we want to elicit responses that involve critical evaluations of data and conclusions, consideration of the appropriateness of evidence, and transfer of generalizations of principles to different situations. In all of these cases, covert participation is a critical component of learning behavior. What conditions, then, can be built into teaching methods or situations that will increase student participation and in turn advance the learning processes?

Feedback too often is considered an interaction between two persons, student and teacher. We should consider also the recurrent feedback systems within each of the participating students, the setting-up of certain covert activities which cause him to question, criticize, and investigate on his own.

In instructor feedback, the two-way process is most important; stu-

dents are important sources of cues for controlling the instructor's behavior. I find that a lack of student-response cues is a limitation on my
own teaching behavior. As an instructor I am often at a loss to state adequately the precise conditions of effective discussion. Too often we mean
simply the condition wherein the student may ask questions. Such a
system has been effected in our own televised instruction. We have installed a two-way communication system in which the student can push
a button, wait for a response from the instructor, and then ask his question. His question and the teacher's response can be heard by all students
involved in the television class sections.

We all know that many questions are pointless and represent wasted
effort for all concerned. The use of the talk-back system requires evaluation. For some of our instructors, it is rarely used; for others, as many as
twenty-four questions have been recorded in a fifty-minute period. The
number of questions may be an indication of participation, but does
failure to ask questions indicate a lack of student participation?

The use of the talk-back system increases with the interest in some
topics and in some methods of presentation. The open-ended presentation seems to stimulate student participation. By open-ended presentation, I mean raising some issue or a discussion of some event that
capitalizes on the student's interest, but not answering or closing the issue
in the same session in which it is raised.

For example, we often start our General Psychology class with the
question, "Is man a part of nature?" Then we proceed to outline some
of the considerations involved in this question, but we do not answer it
then or even in the next session. The questions generally are numerous
over the talk-back system, and students come into the originating room
to talk to the instructor. Perhaps this is the behavioral equivalent of "tune
in next week to see what happens to Stella Dallas."

Another procedure that seems to increase participation is to set up a
task that requires the student to do something for its solution or understanding. For example, in a ball-drawing demonstration to relate probability and scientific hypothesis testing, we told the students to gamble
with fictional money on each draw.

The selection of students from the class itself to participate in various
activities seems to increase student participation and motivation. What
methods of selection increase the students' feeling of participation? Is
this best done by volunteers or by representatives elected to a panel? It
is possible that none of these methods of increasing participation ap-

proaches what we mean by and expect from the discussion method. It may be necessary to modify our teaching procedures in our traditional lecture classes and change to a limited lecture followed by the formation of small discussion groups. But this comparison under carefully controlled conditions has yet to be made.

Kinescope Recordings

We have recently completed sixteen half-hour kinescopes of a semi-professional nature for General Psychology. Can we accomplish adequate motivation and information levels by presenting these over-view kinescopes of each topic and then reducing the class to small discussion groups? How will such a class differ from an all-kinescope presentation and from an all-live lecture-demonstration presentation?

As a teacher of televised instruction, I have been concerned with these problems for the last three years. Because of its being wide open to observation and criticism, television has forced me to concern myself with the application of the principles of learning to the conditions imposed by TV instruction. I am convinced that the variables of the teacher, motivation, and participation—although present in all teaching situations—are of paramount importance in this method of instruction. Investigation of these variables will lead to improvement in televised instruction. Investigation will expose further the sacrosanct area of teaching in general to appropriate and controlled research.

CHAIRMAN: Thank you, Dr. Grosslight.

If you are following your printed program, Ladies and gentlemen, you will notice that the meeting at this point turns to open discussion.

General Discussion

HOPE L. KLAPPER (New York University): Professor Miller, you were discussing cue and response; to what degree does specificity of teaching limit the response that the student makes? Is there any literature on this subject? While we learned that we could make extremely clear and specific to students things that used to be confusing without the visual aids, we also discovered that students learned more without the visual aids. This has led me to wonder if it might not be better sometimes to leave students sufficiently confused so that they are forced to a degree of covert participation.

MR. MILLER: You are quite right. I think that question could be answered through appropriate research. I wouldn't like to believe that clear presentation would always mean poor learning. I think that there must be some way out of this, such as giving specific examples and then giving other examples less specific, and requiring the student to try to answer the question himself. You start out by giving a clear example. Then you go to a more difficult situation and don't tell the student the answer, letting him do his own thinking, try to reason it out and maybe even come back the next day with the answer.

SHEPARD A. INSEL (San Francisco State College): It occurs to me that one of our occupational hazards is the heavy emphasis on words, and that with the introduction of televised instruction, we are involved with a transition from word images to visual images. We are really quite unskilled, in terms of experience, when it comes to portraying in the manner of the dramatists. This isn't meant as a question, merely a comment.

L. O. MORGAN (University of Texas): I question somewhat Professor Grosslight's statement that authenticity is heightened by a decrease in psychological distance. I find in my students a tendency to believe everything they read in spite of what I tell them face to face. I think this is the case when they are reading a book at a great psychological distance, and when they are face to face with me, certainly the psychological distance should be less. Also our students place more faith in what is told to them by an obviously competent person than in what is told to them by someone who is less competent. As to the polished versus the casual performance, our experience has been that the former gets across to the students a little better.

MR. GROSSLIGHT: We cannot in any of these situations consider the authenticity problem separately. When we have shown films, for example, we have found the students slipping back into a casual-viewing position. I didn't mean to say or imply that we must build in authenticity to the point where they know this is a human being instructing because he happens to be stumbling about and proclaiming in the extreme that he is a limited human being.

We have taken pictures of some of our demonstrations—one involving a rat, for instance, in a discrimination and demonstration development—and shown this on television. I can tell you we didn't achieve the same degree of student response as when we actually had the rat before them, jumping out of the box and fouling us up.

Of course we can become awfully skilled. I can give a 28-minute lecture and make it as slick as possible, but I would strongly suspect that occasionally, if not too often, humanistic responses keep the student with me a lot better.

MR. MORGAN: I think our disagreement is centered in the definition of that term *polished*.

MR. GROSSLIGHT: Probably because I didn't define it. In many cases students will take the book's word and discount yours. This happens in some of my classes. It is a problem, especially since the professor is trying to teach them to think for themselves and not follow anybody's lead blindly.

CHAIRMAN: We have about fifty minutes left, which will give us time for a series of interesting, brief papers by other specialists. But first a word from Ray Carpenter.

Panel Discussion of Significant Concepts of Televised Instruction

C. R. CARPENTER (Pennsylvania State University): The Program Committee decided on a different approach to this part of the conference in view of the limitations of time. The committee was convinced that every participant at this conference would have at least one important concept of televised instruction that should be reported. We believed that the productivity of this session would be increased if we could bring all of these concepts before the conference.

We are impressed with all of the papers we have received. We wish time would permit presenting all of them.[2] Since we are limited to fifty minutes, however, we have had to select five papers for presentation. Our processes of selection are not very reliable; we have chosen five that seemed to fit in with the line of thinking that has been introduced here today. Tomorrow we will be forced to follow suit with another group of papers. So with apologies to those of you who are not being asked to read your submissions, we will proceed to the first selection by Professor Keith McKean.

Discussion Method—Panel Discussion (continued)

KEITH MCKEAN (North Carolina State College): Television teaching in the colleges and universities has so far negelected one of our most

[2] Papers not presented orally at the conference appear in Appendix A, pp.175–223.

effective teaching methods, the class discussion. Most of the educational programs feature a solo performance by the professor. Seldom do we see real college students in actual class session discussing the subject. My own experience suggests that a televised class discussion provides positive educational advantages to the teacher. The course I presented on television was one that lent itself to the technique. Called "Science and Society," the year's study was designed to explore basic ideas in science and then the parallel concepts in other fields of activity.

We focus first on the ideas characteristic of medieval science and society, then on those typical of the age of the scientific revolution, and finally on the patterns of thought that underlie modern science and society. The facts one must muster in such a course are necessarily abstract ideas, and the students should learn to uncover implicit and explicit assumptions, and to discover similarities and differences in these basic concepts. Class discussion in such a course is an effective way to get students to probe into the ideas reflected in a document or to compare them with other points of view.

A televised discussion class is a stimulus to the teacher, giving him an important check on how well he is getting his information across. I have lectured on TV without a class before me, and I found it unnerving and stifling to stand in the glaring flood of light and try to talk to a camera. When there are studio students, the session is enough like a real class so that teaching seems familiar and appropriate. Student expressions cued me more effectively than any prompter. Studio students are apt to react much like the viewers, so that the sensitive teacher is able to do a better job when their presence and participation prompts him.

The advantage of televised discussion for the student is even greater. My class was one half-hour of informal lectures and one half-hour of student discussion. I would set forth the concepts we were to discuss, and the studio students, knowing that they were going to have to deal with the topic themselves, paid especially close attention. They knew that they had an audience. Relatives and friends could see what they were up to in college. Televising the class helped to solve the problem of student motivation. The quality of their work was far better than usual.

The students quickly saw that they actually shared the professor's responsibility for making the course a successful venture. The studio students got into the habit of disciplined discussion so that they could carry on in all of their class meetings, whether before the camera or not.

Finally, the televised discussion class may also be better for the viewer than a straight lecture. As I mentioned earlier, the studio students tend to react as the outside viewers react, cueing the teacher and improving communications. I learned early in the year that a convict class at a near-by state penitentiary had voluntarily formed to watch the class. I arranged to visit them. I guess they became our control group. This worked well because they were proctored by an armed guard!

I found that the student discussion dramatized and greatly enlivened the abstract issues for those viewers. The discussion also stimulated them into electing their own discussion leader, so that they might carry on after we went off the air. Some of the college students visited the prison class to help lead the discussion. The convict class hung on all year long, despite the fact that their average formal schooling was slim. Some were illiterate. One-third of them obtained syllabi and kept up with the assignments. I am sure I could not have held the convict class without the teaching aid of the students, differing with me and with each other.

CHAIRMAN: Thank you, Dr. McKean. Our next speaker is Dr. Richard I. Evans.

Students' Attitudes—Panel Discussion (continued)

RICHARD I. EVANS (University of Houston): We had the nation's first noncommercial, open-circuit educational television station at the University of Houston. Our findings over the years tend to verify, as well as disagree with, some of the things you heard today. In 1953 we dealt with the effectiveness of college course instruction by television. Our conclusions suggested that attempts to evaluate television as a teaching medium forcibly call attention to the over-all problems of evaluating teaching in any medium. Television as a medium merely adds another variable to consider in evaluating the entire teaching process.

We did a study in which we found that 97 percent of an open-circuit television audience felt that educational television should be entertaining.

We went into the problems of students' attitudes toward instruction by television. Upon completing a psychology course by television, 70 percent of the students stated that they would like to take another course by TV; over 16 percent were undecided; 13 percent would not.

Students who began a television course with a basically hostile attitude toward the medium tended to develop a significantly more favorable attitude toward television as a result of taking a psychology course by TV. The results also suggest that, if students have a basically negative attitude toward a subject-matter area or an instructor of a television course, they will apparently often displace this toward television. In other words, expressed negative feelings toward television as an instruction medium may often be based on factors not really related to whether or not the course is presented on television. This is important in considering the question of impact. I happen also to be a faculty member of the University of Texas Dental School. It has one of the most elaborate closed-circuit television systems in the United States. We found out, with great interest in support of our findings, that first-year dental students who have a rigorous curriculum may be disturbed over television instruction because they are disturbed with the rigorous curriculum to which they are being introduced for the first time in this professional school.

Dr. Neal Miller spoke of the impact of various television presentation techniques. We found in general that the personality impact of the lecturer continues to be very important. When students were given a choice among presentations that featured a lecturer who just used a blackboard or drawing board, one who used more elaborate structured visual aids, and one who permitted the students at home to participate (such as responding to an ink blot), the lecturer with only a blackboard was preferred by the students. Next in attractiveness to the student are more elaborate visual aids, with participative techniques least popular.

We actually use "cold openings," which Dr. Miller speculated about. These consist of role-playing sequences where interpersonal relation situations are acted out. However, in spite of all the gimmicks, students still prefer a lecture and judicious use of a blackboard over other presentation methods. Even so, they apparently learn from all of these methods. A cautious use of all of them has its place. So-called visual aids in themselves apparently are not perceived as an adequate substitute for the integrating and stimulating role of the lecturer.

Dealing with an open-circuit educational television station, we have been deeply concerned with the problem of controversial material on television. Let me say briefly that I feel that the teacher should not be frightened of presenting on television anything that he would ordinarily present in the usual classroom situation, if it is handled in the same framework of academic objectivity. If we lose this objective approach and engage in emotional baiting, we may encounter difficulties. We have talked about such matters as sexual problems and racial prejudice, which, although customarily dealt with in psychology courses, are not usually encountered in open discussion around Houston. We found absolutely no

negative feedback. On the contrary, we received encouraging correspondence from both telecourse students and viewers from the general
TV audience. In response to a tight time schedule, this brings me to an
end. Thank you.

CHAIRMAN: Thank you, Dick Evans. Dave Bergstrom will read his
paper next.

Training for the Television Teacher—Panel Discussion (continued)

DAVID W. BERGSTROM (Miami University, Ohio): I am concerned
with the teacher's problem in making the transition from the conventional
classroom, where he is his own boss, to the strange land of the television
studio. When this teacher, experienced and capable in conventional
teaching, finds himself in the TV studio, he is in a new environment. Like
an animal which, straying from its natural woodland biome into the open
grassland, for which it is not preadapted, finds certain environmental
factors unsatisfactorily impinging upon it, the teacher may feel that his
personal welfare is in jeopardy. The factors are strange. He must adapt
to them and this may not take place very quickly. It appears clear that
not every teacher can look upon this entry into the television studio as a
delightful and exciting adventure. He is surrounded by lights, heat, the
movement of the cameras, and new and different things to work with; and
there are people—other than students—who must be there to make the
television medium work. He has two new masters: (1) the medium itself;
and (2) the people who must operate the medium and direct his performance.

Our great hope is that television will be our servant and not our
master. The people operating it should be co-workers, not servants or
masters. But these ends are not achieved easily. Let us concede that we
are not going to expect professional competency as a performer from
the teacher. A high level of professional competency, a blasé, matter-of-
fact, completely-at-home demeanor is not even desirable. But the teacher,
if he is to do his job well, must be happy, at ease, and willing to cooperate. He must also possess some sense that causes him to see what
television can do for him and his subject matter.

What does the secret voice of the teacher say when his director tells
him to speak more slowly, systematize his presentation, or move away
from the chalkboard edge? It says, "Oh, go to hell, don't bother me
with such trivia. I'm not Perry Como. I have a subject to get across."

Many of us performing on television fail to sense the simple aesthetic qualities that would be pleasing to the viewer. Maybe it is because we are not used to thinking about these elements in the conventional classroom situation. Still, the student, whose reaction is all important, is conditioned to the qualities of commercial television, and he may be making the comparison to our detriment. When the teacher compares himself to the professional performer, he may become uneasy and insecure.

So he may fight the medium and become more and more uneasy and unhappy about what he is doing, or he may extend himself in an attempt at perfection, this at the sacrifice of many other things in his professional life. His pride and reputation seem to be more at stake in television than in conventional teaching.

What can be done to facilitate the transition to the educational television medium? Workshops, presessions of a few weeks, conferences—these are fine and in no sense to be questioned. But it seems to me that something else is required over a more extended period of time, something that slowly, subtly, and emphatically effects a change in the teacher. He has many new adjustments to make. He needs a fresh outlook on his abilities in interpersonal relations. These cannot come about in two or three weeks.

Perhaps an in-service training program of six months to a year would be more appropriate and effective. It would be aimed at these cardinal objectives: (1) understanding of the assets and limitations of television; (2) development of desire to make the best use of the medium; and (3) catching the spirit of cooperative effort. Achievement of these objectives would involve some exposure to the technical and mechanical aspects of the medium, to the development of instructional aids, to the theory of operation, and to the jobs of those who operate the medium. He should be exposed also to the successful and unsuccessful experiences of others plus have a substantial amount of guided practice.

CHAIRMAN: Thank you, Mr. Bergstrom. Our next speaker is Clifford G. Erickson, representing the American Association of Junior Colleges.

Design of the Chicago TV Junior College—
Panel Discussion (continued)

CLIFFORD G. ERICKSON (Chicago City Junior College): The Chicago City Junior College experiment in open-circuit television is an attempt to discover how television can broaden the service of a five-branch community college in a large and complex urban center.

Our experiment assumes that television need not divert an institution from its primary objectives. TV College is not a separate college or a branch of the Chicago City Junior College. Students are enrolled in one of the five branches of our school. They receive instruction at home, and they participate in discussions and examinations in the branch of their enrollment under the supervision of a professional section teacher. The section teacher grades assignments and examinations and awards the final grades. In the autumn of 1957 there were 7,239 persons enrolled in 11,239 course registrations. Shorthand 120 led in number of enrollees, with 238 persons registered for credit and 2,269 registered in the non-credit group. A total of 531 credit and noncredit students enrolled in Mathematics 101.

Analysis of credit television student body shows an average age about fifteen years beyond that of the day classroom student. Their work shows a high level of motivation. Their determination was shown by 61 percent course completion in the first term and 71 percent completion in the second term.

In preparing for the presentation of telecourses on open circuit, it was necessary to view educational objectives in a new teaching context, and at times to hold valiantly to them when they seemed to suggest procedures counter to prevailing practices in broadcasting. The development of a set of educationally sound principles to guide teachers in the Chicago experiment is still evolving as the experiment continues:

1. Judgment on the validity of "rules" of educational telecastings should be deferred until sufficient evidence is available. There shall be freedom to develop a body of experience without restraint or limited experience here or elsewhere.
2. The goal is teaching, not performing. Showmanship may be utilized when it enhances the learning experience.
3. The focus of attention should be educational objectives, not audience ratings. The needs of the larger, not-for-credit audience shall not be met at the expense of the quality of the learning experience of the credit viewers.
4. The purpose is to teach students, not professional colleagues. Content and vocabulary should be set at student level.
5. Though the teacher's personality is a powerful element in the teaching-learning process, the prime goal is the learning experience of the student.
6. Though the television electronic link affords unique opportunities for the teaching-learning relationship, it is no substitute for the teacher's own creative development of the lesson. The television link may add an inordinate measure of credibility and authority to the teacher's statements in some situations. Care is therefore necessary to distinguish between the teacher's opinion and verifiable facts.

7. The teleclass should be approached as a new experience which may require new imagination and techniques to capitalize on the great opportunities afforded by the medium.

8. The television teacher should strive for active student interaction with the learning materials rather than for passive acceptance of polished presentations.

9. Student questions should be anticipated and their answers worked into the lesson material. The teacher can draw on his experience in the classroom and build on day-by-day experience in using the producer and director as trial students.

10. Audio-visual aids should be used only when they clearly enhance the learning situation and can be related to the objectives of the lesson.

Our television courses serve two kinds of students, those who are seeking to earn an associate in arts degree primarily through TV College, and those credit and noncredit viewers who wish to participate in one or more courses to improve personal or vocational competence. Some of the courses are primarily content courses and others are skill courses. This is by deliberate choice to test the versatility of television. The emphasis is not "teaching as usual"; rather, the television teacher is given adequate time and competent assistance in the development of new approaches which adapt the teaching situation to the potential and limitations of the medium.

Teachers are chosen from among applicants on the permanent staff. They begin this work months before air time. They benefit by trial kinescopes and closed-circuit teaching experiences before proceeding with the outlining of the course and the preparation of study guides and lesson plans.

Achievement data of three groups were compared, the outside television students receiving 30-minute telecasts, the conventional classroom students receiving 50-minute lessons, and the classroom students receiving 30-minute telecasts plus 20-minute follow-up classroom discussion and instruction.

1. In all subjects except biology, the television experimental group showed higher, though not significantly higher, achievement than the two control groups. Biology was significant at the 5 percent level, favoring the TV student.

2. Mathematics and English, where the groups were equated by the covariance method, using mental ability and subject pretest as correction factors, produced no significant differences.

3. In social science, when the matched pairs method was applied, using the Critical Thinking pretest as a base for equating pairs, there was no significant difference.

4. In the depth study in social science, using the matched pairs method, statistically significant student development toward the goal of critical thinking was achieved, although it was less than that achieved in several experimental discussion classes during the period 1953–55.

5. The apparent superiority of the achievement of the experimental television group can be presumed to be related to factors of age, maturity, and motivation—factors worthy of tighter control in the second year of the experiment. The comparison of the home TV students as a group with the control classroom students as a group showed the TV group achieving better scores in every subject. The TV student is older, more mature, and more able.

Course objectives and materials are unchanged, though tremendous creative activity is needed to adapt these to the new medium of presentation. The teacher is aided by a producer who is experienced in the adaptation of the learning situation to the TV medium and by a director who is skilled in arranging the technical elements that permit effective transmission of the learning experience. Our findings of the first year suggest that the following factors contribute to the success of the teacher in the Chicago situation:

1. Thorough preparation in advance of telecast time ensures adequate time for discussion of objectives, materials, and techniques for presentation with producer and director. The tension level seems to be inversely related to preparation level.

2. Simplicity in outline and directness of presentation contribute to the teacher's ease. Teacher effectiveness seems to be enhanced by adherence to course objectives and the omission of diversions.

3. Visuals should be under the teacher's direct supervision. A desk easel of visuals on cards is considered superior to remotely projected slides.

4. Studio facilities for rehearsals of visuals before air time must be adequate to give the teacher the assurance that the technical crew understands his objectives, materials, and sequence. Any uneasiness on this score will affect the quality of the teaching.

TV College brings to the college program a new group of students who otherwise might not have begun higher education. This group is equivalent to a full-time enrollment of 549 college students. A conventional college would require a professional staff of twenty-five and a building of moderate size to render an equal service. Significant is the large number of women who are preparing for a career in teaching. Also significant, the drop-out rate was higher in the low-ability group of TV students; this tended to make the TV group more select as the semester progressed.

The experience in Chicago seems to imply that regular college classes can be taught by television without the presence of a teacher. Our data relate, of course, to televised instruction to more mature, highly motivated adults.

CHAIRMAN: Thank you, Mr. Erickson. We now turn to Mr. Shepard A. Insel.

Re-evaluation of the Teaching-Learning Process— Panel Discussion (continued)

SHEPARD A. INSEL (San Francisco State College): As with all innovations in established systems, instructional television's greatest value to education is that its utilization demands a careful re-evaluation of our conceptions of the teaching-learning process.

The approach to the use of educational television has been, with few exceptions, that of dealing with problems of administering educational programs. This has relegated to a secondary consideration the question whether televised instruction achieves the purposes of education, and if so, in what way, and at what cost?

The appropriate goal of instructors teaching under any conditions is that of facilitating learning. It is also generally accepted, both culturally and experimentally, that experience is the best, though by no means the perfect, teacher.

Our research and our own experience suggest further that optimum learning takes place when the learner is motivated to learn. However, the relationship is not at all clearly delineated, because it can be demonstrated that some learning can occur in the learner with a minimum of observable motivation.

Both experiencing and motivation imply involvement, and one who is learning is by definition in the process of change and therefore of growth, be that change of perception, language, conception, attitudes, or values. Finally, the process of learning or change in the individual requires a state of readiness and, at every step of the experience, some process of testing, confirmation, approximation, redirection, assimilation, reorganization, and so on.

Much of present educational television as I have experienced it is at the descriptive level, frequently verbal. The instructor reports, describes, and/or explains experience. This experience, or interaction with stimuli, may be represented in any field from arithmetic to zoology. The student takes in this description and tries to interpret it in the light of his auditory-visual comprehension and past experience. However, he cannot test the accuracy of his reception by asking for a restatement. Nor can he challenge a point of view which somehow conflicts with his own experience or orientation. The student may continue with his misinterpretation, accept a false assumption, or perceive experience and the tests of experience as descriptive phenomena, and continue on his uncritical way. Only at some distant examination does the student get an opportunity to confirm any perceptions. In short, it appears that current televised instruction provides for an active presentation by the instructor and a minimum opportunity to participate by the student, and emphasizes the receptive aspect of experience.

Thus, it would seem to me that the most significant problem confronting us in the current use of television as a medium for the teaching-learning process is that of finding ways to minimize the constriction that the medium imposes on the processes of teaching and learning. The consequence of this constriction is that with which we have been faced traditionally in education, namely a superficial, less-than-satisfying learning experience. A further threat is that, as instructors become more isolated from the students, teaching may even become tangential to the learning process.

A still more subtle hazard is that the student has less opportunity to test and learn to trust his own experiences as, by and large, his best guide to learning. In effect, increased dependency on authority and expertness becomes the lesson. The lessening of opportunities for the instructor to get feedback to his ideas also reduces and constricts his own learning potential, since he has fewer checking devices available to him in the TV setting.

Nevertheless, the consideration remains that television, as a medium of unidirectional communication, is eminently deserving of the broadest exploitation that our investigations can provide to expand the learner's framework of experience. For myself, the experimentation in instructional television reaffirms the concept that a more productive point of view in teaching is to assume that the instructor is really another medium of communication and testing of experience, as is the textbook, the small group, or the laboratory. This concept has freed me to become much more experimental with my role of fountainhead or source of learning.

This mediating concept leads me to suggest one approach to making instructional television less constrictive. If I begin with the premise that the learner gains most from his firsthand experience, then my task as an instructor is to develop a situation which approximates as closely as possible the experiential set of the learner. The laboratory approach toward science is superior to just talking about what goes on in the laboratory.

From this process of viewing realistic aspects of life which are subsumed under education, the learner is confronted with many more sides and issues than words allow, and this offers many more opportunities to question. To round out the process the learner shares his perceptions with other learners in small discussion groups. Consequently, not only is feedback available to the learner, but also he is given the opportunity to use the experience to initiate points of departure towards other insights.

When we undertake to provide realistic experiences for others, additional problems emerge. The very existence of individual differences will mean that some learners will not be ready to take from the experience that which the instructor sees as desirable. Furthermore, controversy becomes a necessary part of those experiences that have enough significance to be complex. In this regard, the individual may learn something other than what the instructor would have him learn. Finally, learning which goes beyond the superficial aspects of experience reduces our standard evaluation techniques to some degree of inappropriateness. The bare emergence of these problems indicates that our progress is rather marked in approaching our broadest objectives.

In summary, it seems that mere reproduction of the standard, unimaginative classroom procedure by television probably reduces its learning value even further. The task confronting those who value instructional television is to examine and identify its shortcomings in the long haul of the teacher-learning process and then to rectify them or compensate for the loss. This means perhaps a deliberate departure from the traditional approach to instruction and thereby the forcing of a fresh look at the problem of facilitating learning.

CHAIRMAN: Thank you, Dr. Insel. By dint of the warmhearted cooperation of the speakers, we are running well within our time. Would you like another five minutes of pertinent questions and comments directed to these papers or to other matters that came up today?

General Discussion

EUGENE F. GREWE (University of Detroit): In our evening program, where we offer courses by television for a half hour on Monday, Tuesday, and Thursday evenings, the TV students report to the campus on Wednesday evening for an hour's follow-up with the TV instructor or some other cooperative person.

MR. ERICKSON: At Chicago we tried television control classes, where 30-minute instruction periods over TV were followed by 20-minute discussions led by the section teacher. We dropped this because we felt it was an entire area of research by itself. We couldn't assume that one teacher has in his equipment the ability to cooperate with another teacher.

REV. HERMAN J. MULLER, S.J. (University of Detroit): That is the system we are following in our closed circuit. Our afternoon classes are routed over the open circuit, and we have one of our control classes with a 30-20 ratio of TV instruction to classroom discussion. The professor who leads the discussion in history always takes notes during the telecast, I notice, and he does well with quizzes and with the discussion generally. The students seem to like this arrangement.

MR. EVANS: Where we pressed instructors into service as discussion leaders following a telecast, we found that those who were hostile took advantage of the situation to make sarcastic remarks about the lecturer and undermine the program. We also found that relatively few didactic-type teachers could do much of a job as discussion leaders.

ERNA GUNTHER (University of Washington): In our Department of Mathematics, Dr. Allendorfer gave a course in college algebra with three lectures a week. He assigned problems, and he had teaching fellows meet the TV students. They corrected the problems and had discussions with the students.

J. R. MARTIN (Case Institute of Technology): Since this question of feedback between instructor and student keeps coming up, you might be interested in what we have been doing for about a year, part of the time not very well, and now very well. We have cameras in the remote classrooms with a monitor in front of the instructor so he can see the students' faces registering interest or disinterest and can direct specific questions to a student. The receiving rooms have open microphones, so that any student in any remote room can ask the instructor a question without a special signaling device. The instructor answers the question directly and the discussion is heard by all. It is also possible that the receivers can be set so that the classes can see each other and have interclass discussion, with the instructor observing how this goes on.

HARVEY ZORBAUGH (New York University): I am going to throw a sour note into this discussion. We have been talking a lot about ways to get more discussion. I am sympathetic with this. I would suggest, however, that experience indicates that there are brilliant lecturers from whom students have learned a great deal. There are also very able discussion leaders from whom students have learned much. I don't want to see us take the position that television must freeze the brilliant lecturer out of that medium.

MR. ERICKSON: We often speak of the need to keep the teacher effective as the course moves along. We are experimenting with the use of telephone inquiries. We have an open-circuit presentation with no students present. The teacher uses telephone inquiries at assigned office hours to find out how well he is doing in adapting his teaching.

H. BURR RONEY (University of Houston): At what point does the attempt to keep the instructor happy give you such diminishing results that you might as well not bother with teaching at all? If you devote all your attention to his state of mind, what happens to your students?

MR. ERICKSON: I wasn't implying inordinate concern for the teacher. We are concerned that the teacher have some reaction from his students. We feel that students should be given an opportunity to ask questions.

MR. RONEY: I agree with Professor Zorbaugh. He said that there may be diminishing returns from our efforts to promote discussion and solve the problem of feedback.

CHAIRMAN: Ladies and gentlemen, it is time for adjournment until this evening.

Teaching by TV: Demonstrations and a Critique

MONDAY EVENING, OCTOBER 21, 1957

Presiding: RICHARD J. GOGGIN, Chairman, Department
of Television, Motion Pictures, and Radio,
New York University

The conference participants reconvened in a classroom building, equipped with closed-circuit TV, for demonstrations of college teaching by television. Eight course excerpts, each covering a different subject, were from five to ten minutes in length and were presented either live from the studio or by means of film or kinescope recordings. The audience was in a large lecture hall, equipped with four hundred elevated seats and six 24-inch TV sets.

Conference participants who demonstrated their teaching in live productions were: William G. Mather, Pennsylvania State University (sociology); Ross R. Middlemiss, Washington University (mathematics); Rev. Herman J. Muller, S.J., University of Detroit (history); H. Burr Roney, University of Houston (biology); and Oliver M. Stone, Case Institute of Technology (engineering drawing).

Those seen on kinescope were: Fred McKinney, University of Missouri (psychology); and Harold E. Whitehall, Indiana University (linguistics). In addition, excerpts from the filmed physics course by Dr. Harvey E. White, University of California, were shown. Dr. White was unable to accept an invitation to the conference.

Critique of Teaching by TV Demonstrations

CHAIRMAN GOGGIN: I will confine my critique to production values, teaching methods, and the teachers themselves. The abbreviated excerpts make it difficult to judge what the individual teachers would have accomplished in fifty minutes. Would we have tired of these personalities over a longer period? Were those teachers who seemed less sparkling really so, or were they merely slow starters? How many were done a disservice by being removed from the normal condition of their own studios and from the source of their own production and technical aids and assistants?

Certain things do stand out. All courses were word-oriented lectures or lecture demonstrations. The visual component—presumably the more important and distinctive component of television—was subordinate. We saw no large-scale attempts, visually or aurally, to use creatively the medium of television and its tools and techniques. Some audio-visual devices and approaches were used from time to time, but generally only as peripheral supplements to the primacy of the word. It is because of this that one critic I know insists that what we are seeing in schools and colleges is not so much instructional television as televised instruction.

Such a remark could be challenged as being unduly harsh or merely a facetious play on words. It may be both, but there are more than a few scattered grains of truth in it. While putting "master teachers" in front of television cameras and photographing them for a full class period will undoubtedly be of benefit in helping to meet the interwoven problems of rising student enrollments and the relatively diminishing number of highly qualified teachers, this actually doesn't make any more use of television than its minimal electronic functions as a transmitter of sound and sight from point to point.

Those who, as theorists, consider the spoken word as fundamental and, in time and quantity, as the largest and continuing part of instruction, see no dilemma, no problem, in such minimal use of television. They are quite willing to settle for this. All research studies and evaluations up to this time conclude that there is "no significant difference" between student learning achieved through instructional television and that achieved through conventional face-to-face, classroom teaching. We are not, apparently, losing anything by minimal use; let it suffice. Further, and in all fairness to the television teachers and production specialists, it should be admitted that the lack of time and money generally prevent them from exploring the medium of television in more than a tentative way. Time is even more important than money. It takes time to work out reorganization of subject matter; it takes time to conceive, reject, or accept new approaches to teaching, new or distinctive recreations of ideas in visual and in dynamic terms; it takes time to transform or implement all of this in production materials, in techniques, and with tools. No wonder that many practitioners in the art, as well as the theorists, are willing to settle for the minimum.

Few of us would suggest that television is radio with pictures. Yet instructional television seems to give little universal and convincing evidence that there is much more to television than sight appended to sound. The "no significant difference" suggests that, in spite of this, nothing is lost. But may not this be merely a statistical illusion? Isn't there a likelihood that we may be losing a greater teaching and learning potential that might come out of a concerted attempt to explore and later use the medium creatively? A number of educators, psychologists, researchers, teachers, and television production men are concerned about that "no significant difference." Even in minimal use, television is different from the classroom; with maximal use, which clearly would give us instructional television and not just televised instruction, and with a searching and unbiased re-examination of evaluation materials and methodology, we might well discover that "n.s.d." is no longer applicable.

Let me state here without contradicting my plea for maximal use of television, that I believe firmly that the personality of the teacher is the crucial factor in any instructional television program. The outstanding teacher can be made more effective with maximal use. The average teacher can use this creative approach with notable increase in impact. The poor teacher, who finds his way into television as well as into classrooms, may be even poorer on the screen, but he needs this kind of support desperately.

In this evening's excerpts, several teachers, perhaps bearing in mind the familiar dictum of how to compose the opening of a short story, used various teaching devices and physical apparatus to attract audience attention, arouse curiosity, and create interest right at the start. Charts, maps, graphs, pictures, and small figurines were shown; materials were employed to make simple ideas more immediately understandable. Television used only reportorially or photographically has a more obvious and immediate affinity for those things that are tangible and perceivable to the senses of sight and hearing—things that are to a large extent self-evident. With subject matter beyond the realm of the physical, as in the humanities and some of the social sciences, symbols take over, and getting to the heart of the matter is of necessity less direct. It is more complex.

The occasional references made by several teachers to common experiences of the audience made applicable to the subject matter, as in the instance of the laws of probability and gaming, achieved a measure of identification with the content not otherwise apparent. Humor moderately injected, carefully controlled, and appropriate to the subject matter, the dignity of the teacher, and the level of sophistication of the class, can be used effectively. This was done in several of the excerpts to brighten what might otherwise have been tedious moments, to establish friendly but not familiar contact with the audience, to personalize and humanize the teachers, and by contrast and comparison to illuminate certain points.

This evening's teachers showed appreciable competency in their fields; they reflected great interest in their subjects; but there was a marked range of personalities. Some were warm, natural, outgoing; others were more distant, cool, and even more remote on television than they probably are in the classroom. The important element of contact, which only the teacher can establish, is an essential ingredient in teaching and learning. It perhaps was significant that the degree of audience acceptance achieved by the teachers in the various excerpts was in direct proportion to the amount and kind of contact. Spontaneity of applause and favorable comment went hand in hand to the extent that the teachers made their personalities felt. The element of the theatrical is not to be despised or disregarded.

Some visual and other production aids were poorly done for television. We saw inadequate freehand script rather than carefully lettered words. There was too much printed material on the screen at one time or too much written on one line. I saw improper contrast ratios from white to black in the monochromatic gray scale. There was some inconsistency and lack of harmony and unity in scenery and decoration. The lighting in some cases was substandard technically and artistically. One effective visual aid utilized was the superimposition of captions at the bottom of the television screen; these were new words that the teacher was using or words that were difficult to spell. It saved time at the conventional blackboard and was visually arresting.

In two of the film excerpts guests were present. In one instance it was primarily to provide visual and aural variety, but the production device as used did not sufficiently integrate the guests pictorially or content-wise into the body of the lecture. The audience was left with a hit-and-run feeling that was vaguely disturbing because it was less than satisfying. The other excerpt had a positive integration of guest and teacher, the guest being a specialist in a specific aspect of the course. Each reinforced the other; yet the teacher consciously subordinated himself.

Other flaws in this program were poorly written vignettes and insufficiently trained student actors. This diminished the effect of the dramatization by removing credibility. Deficient production devices may do more harm than good. Students are quick to spot them and unfortunately the enjoyment they get out of ridiculing them exceeds the knowledge they get out of the program as a whole. Nevertheless, the inclusion of guests, the writing of special vignettes, and the staging of them for dramatic and subject-matter purposes are positive steps toward wider and deeper creative use of television and are to be commended.

The Ideal Television Teacher

Remembering my statement about the overriding importance of the teacher in instructional television, I would like to set down five points that seem to sketch out a profile of the ideal television teacher. First, he must be proficient and enthusiastic; there is neither necessity nor excuse for putting a teacher without these primary qualifications on television. Next the television instructor should have a warm, outgoing personality. He should be an eager but not compulsive talker, with a touch of the theatrical about him.

Third, he should be capable of being adaptable and flexible. He should be adaptable to the problems of staging in television, to the handling and utilization of visuals, to the production and technical demands of the medium, to the unfamiliar and sometimes terrifying environment of the studio. He should be flexible in the reassessment of the content of his material and to the reorganization of it for the best television purposes.

Fourth, he should be creative, or at least resourceful, when it comes to the conception of ideas and methods as they relate to the new interpretation and television presentation of subject matter. Production people can be of help, but they can't be competent in all fields. The ideas and dynamic approaches must spring out of content; it is the teacher himself who in the final analysis is best suited to supply the inspiration.

The television teacher should be courageous and confident. He should not be afraid of the medium because of its differences. He should not be wary of trying something new, of getting away from traditional content and presentational approaches. He should not worry over what his tradition-bound colleagues may think of him for appearing on television. He must be willing to balance any possible personal loss of direct student stimulation with the hope that through television he may not only reach more people but may become a more effective teacher.

This may be a large order, but I believe it is part of the emerging profile of the ideal television teacher.

There are a few minutes left for discussion.

General Discussion

WARREN F. SEIBERT (Purdue University): I would like to ask Mr. Stone a question: At Case Institute, how many rooms are linked to the originating room for purposes of discussion?

OLIVER M. STONE (Case Institute of Technology): In the graphics course we have one section in the live room and two remote sections. Dr. Martin can tell you more about the equipment used.

JOHN R. MARTIN (Case Institute of Technology): We have two remotes two-way and one remote which is one-way visual, although all are joined together as far as sound is concerned; that is, any speaker in any room can be heard by any other speaker in any other room. The cost of our entire installation was less than $10,000; this includes building the equipment, two camera chains, eight or nine receivers, synch generators, and so on. I don't want to take the time of the group to elaborate on this equipment, but I have literature on it with me and would be happy to discuss it with any of you personally. The point is we do it by radio frequency distribution. Each camera is on a channel. We can presently use four channels. We can use up to six by adding two more new amplifiers.

EDWIN P. ADKINS (State University of New York, College for Teachers, Albany): This one camera picks up the class and brings the view to the instructor?

MR. MARTIN: That is right.

MR. ADKINS: How well can he see the faces of his students?

MR. MARTIN: We have a camera which is constantly scanning the class; it has a remotely controlled turret lens, lens selector, and focus pan and tilt, by which a person at the back of the room picks out a particular student if the instructor wants to talk to him close up. The instructor can call for this student and the person has a chart of the seating so that he swings to the student and brings him close. We also have a single, wide-angle lens, with a seating chart. If the instructor knows his students, he can recognize him pretty well.

There is another application of this equipment that I call a teaching aid. I teach a course in microwave on the third floor of a building and have only twenty-five boys in front of me. On the fifth floor is the microwave laboratory with its equipment, delicate and yet weighing tons. I cannot take this equipment down to the third floor, and it is difficult to take the class to the fifth floor every time we want to inspect a piece of equipment we happen to be discussing. When I am ready to show a piece of equipment, I merely say, "Al, let's have a close-up of this particular item." The equipment comes on the screen. A student asks a question; I answer it. The student, therefore, has an immediate front seat throughout, a better one than he would have even if the equipment were in the room. All this can be done with a large group.

CHAIRMAN: I realize that we haven't had very much time for open discussion this evening, but we are now about twenty minutes past cutoff time.

In Search of Factual Data

Presiding: JOHN C. ADAMS

CHAIRMAN: We cannot begin our day better than to meet and thank the president of this distinguished university. President Walker.

The Need for Evidence

ERIC A. WALKER (Pennsylvania State University): Dr. Adams, members of this conference, I want to add my greetings to those you have already received. It perhaps seems a little incongruous to welcome you after you have already spent a day and a half with us. Let me assure you that I think it is a high honor to be associated with the American Council on Education in this conference, designed to promote the use of television in educational institutions.

In 1952 I was busy trying to run the College of Engineering on this campus. That was the year this institution joined with the American Council on Education in cosponsoring the first national educational television conference. I am sure that in those days we knew almost nothing about television and its place in education. We had no estimate of student or faculty reaction to it, how we should use it, or what public response to it and acceptance of it might be. We had the courage, however, to plot a course, trying to find the answers to those questions.

Ever since the time of Socrates we have been trying to extend the influence of superior teaching to large groups of students. I understand that Socrates' followers developed manuscripts based on his lectures as they remembered them. Medieval universities were usually founded on the possession of a few manuscripts. About the time Gutenberg invented movable type, it was thought that you could take superior lectures from the superior teachers and print them into books, thereby solving this problem of extending the influence of the best teaching. Books, radio, and now television have this aim in common.

Here at Penn State we will not grant a graduate degree for graduate

71

work not taken on the campus. Why? Because we say that the students do not have the benefit of an academic atmosphere. Not until we can develop some sort of a communications mechanism that can transmit this academic atmosphere, whatever it is, will we ever completely replace the teacher. In some way—and you won't do it by a book or by radio or by television—the student has to feel the enthusiasm of the teacher; he has to become immersed in his spirit of inquiry and doubt and wish to know. This cannot be transmitted by any electronic device.

Nevertheless, I shouldn't want to discourage you. As an administrator, however, I want from you some hard, cold, quantitative facts about teaching by television. These are the facts that I can use when I am questioned by trustees, taxpayers, parents, and students. Ray Carpenter, director of our Division of Academic Research and Services, and his associates tell me we have already developed some of these facts. For example, we know that our television system, on the basis of a thousand hours of operation, costs us about $26 per hour. I understand that we have also developed the fact that the break-even point, at which our profits begin to exceed our losses, comes at about two hundred students; that it is impossible to teach a course by TV less expensively if there are fewer than two hundred students.

I am sure that you can get superior teaching on television just by picking out the superior teachers and putting them on the screen, but it is more difficult to measure whether the result is superior learning by the student. And how about the less-talented students? Are we going to lose more of these? And should we just abandon them anyway? How about the very bright students? Are they going to be challenged as much by television as they are by face-to-face contact with the professor?

How are we going to divide up our student body and decide upon class assignments so that these occasional and valuable professor hours can be used wisely where they will do the most good?

I am afraid of the attitude of students. I have been somewhat uncertain since the beginning of our experiment five years ago. Even a few students can wreck the whole experiment. Certainly the faculty can wreck our experimental program. I am sure that, when the inferior teacher begins to feel insecure in his job, he is inclined to deprecate the entire idea. I have had mothers and fathers tell me that we are becoming so impersonal the students see their professors only on a television screen.

I am afraid at times that we are confusing the exposition of a subject with education. I don't think the two are the same. The other day I was talking to a lady who is active in state government, and after she told me that her oldest son had graduated from Penn State, she said that she was certain her youngest son would never attend our university. I was curious about this and asked, "Why, didn't the older boy like Penn State?"

"Oh, he loved it," she said.

After that I was really puzzled and asked why she wouldn't want the younger son to attend the university where her older boy had been so happy.

"Oh, you've become a big factory," she answered.

"Did your older son tell you that we're a big factory?"

"No, he loved Penn State. But you see I was at his commencement and I saw all those thousands of degrees being given out. I just know you've become a big factory."

Yes, she was certain that we are a big factory. Never once had she wondered or asked how many students we have in a classroom. She didn't ask if our students have advisers, or "Do your students have contact with the professors and advisers in planning their curricula?"

It is this type of erroneous impression that frightens me. I hope that in studying the impact of television on education you people won't stop with just a classroom. I think you may have the key to a re-examination of our whole educational process.

I get tremendously disturbed when I think about the poor manner in which we manipulate the logistics of teaching. Step out of this building at ten o'clock in the morning and you will see what I mean. We have thousands and thousands of students trotting from one building to another to get their lectures, rather than move the much smaller number of professors. We do it this way only because we have always done it this way. I am not convinced that these traditional schedules that operate from eight to five on the basis of 50-minute periods are necessarily the best schedules. I am not convinced that we are designing our buildings properly, or that we must standardize on a two-semester, nine-month year and on 136 credits for graduation.

When I see professors turning their backs on students to put formulae on the board, pulling down charts and using equations and demonstrations in the way we do, I am not at all convinced that this is the way to do it. But the administrators aren't going to change any of these things. It is up to the faculty.

I wish that all of our faculties could sweep away the cobwebs, saying, "If we were redesigning a university to bring superior teaching to all the students, how would we do it?" and not, "How do we use the buildings that we now have?"

Unfortunately, we ask ourselves, "How do we fit it into the hours we now have and the credits we now have?" That is all I have to say other than to wish you every success in your search for factual data.

CHAIRMAN: We are grateful to you, President Walker, for speaking to us frankly and for touching upon themes that are essential to this meeting. Your cautions and reminders are directed to the heart of our general discussions, for the focus of this conference is the teacher, the art of teaching, and the student—with television as the serving medium. We are profoundly grateful for the hospitality and courtesy which you and your staff are extending to us.

This morning we will proceed to a review of the relevant research results on instruction by television. The first paper will be presented by Mr. Leslie P. Greenhill, associate director, Division of Academic Research and Services, on this campus.

Research on Televised Instruction at the Pennsylvania State University

LESLIE P. GREENHILL (Pennsylvania State University): In its use of television for instruction, the Pennsylvania State University has emphasized the application of research as a means of gathering dependable information on which to base decisions.

During the three years that television has been used in our instructional program, nearly half of the money spent has been invested in research and a little more than half in TV operations. About one hundred studies have been conducted. Approximately sixty of these have been experiments in which comparisons have been made under controlled conditions with respect to defined variables. Some have been evaluated in terms of effects on students' achievement; others have related to students' attitudes or preferences. The remaining forty studies have been of a descriptive type in which information has been gathered about student or faculty reactions to a variety of problems.

It is impossible to review all of these studies here. This is also unnecessary because some of them have been published in our first report, which was issued two years ago.[1] The majority of the others will be described in a second published report, which we hope to have in print in about three month's time.[2]

I would like to focus attention on the recent studies that are apt to be significant to those of you who are engaged in teaching university courses by TV. We have found it convenient to classify our research studies under four main categories, which are by now well known to most of you. They are: (1) comparative effectiveness; (2) appropriateness; (3) acceptability; and (4) feasibility.

Comparative effectiveness embraces those experiments in which comparisons have been made between televised and direct instruction with respect to effects on students' achievement and course-related attitudes. Under *appropriateness,* we shall consider the range of courses in which television has been used at Penn State, and the patterns of use that have been developed. Studies of *acceptability* deal with reactions of students and faculty to televised instruction. Under *feasibility,* we shall consider briefly equipment and personnel requirements for televised instruction.

Comparative Effectiveness

During the past five semesters we have made such comparisons in seven different courses. These run the gamut of the types we have televised, ranging from the natural sciences through the social sciences to the arts. In some it has been possible to repeat an experiment with two different sections of the course; in others comparison studies have been repeated with minor variations in successive semesters, and in all of them, two or three tests of achievement have been given during the course of an experiment. At least thirty different comparisons between televised and direct instruction have been made.

In all of these studies the same teachers have taught comparable groups by the two methods in each instance. In most courses the two methods have been taught at successive class periods, and students have been assigned at random across the two sequences. However, in some earlier studies the performance of students in the television class-

[1] C. R. Carpenter, L. P. Greenhill, and Others, *An Investigation of Closed-Circuit Television for Teaching University Courses,* Report No. 1 (University Park, Pa.: Pennsylvania State University, 1955).

[2] *Ibid.,* Report No. 2: *The Academic Years 1955–1956 and 1956–1957* (University Park, Pa.: Pennsylvania State University, 1958). Copies available on request to authors, Division of Academic Research and Services, 405 Old Main, University Park, Pa.

rooms was compared with that of students who were taught directly in the room where the instruction originated.

The results of these studies consistently show no significant differences in student achievement between televised and direct instruction. Similar absences of differences between televised and direct instruction have occurred when comparisons have been made in terms of relative effects on students' course-related attitudes.

We are becoming increasingly confident that the academic achievement of students at Penn State is not suffering as a result of the use of televised instruction. It should be mentioned that in many of the comparisons, much larger numbers of students were included in the television sections than in the directly taught groups. Thus, television is making it possible to extend the teaching of experienced professors to larger numbers of students than is possible under conditions of direct instruction. The question now is not whether to use television, but how to use it.

Appropriateness

During the five semesters that Penn State has been using closed-circuit television, some twenty-five different courses involving forty-six teachers have used it regularly in one form or another in the presentation of their instructional programs. Another five courses have used the TV systems for the professional training of students in television techniques.

Many different ways of using television have been explored, and several of these have been tested experimentally. The varied uses of television may be summarized briefly as follows:

1. For the presentation of entire courses, with the instruction originating in one room and televised to a number of receiving rooms. This may be considered the instructor-multiplier function of television. The largest single section in a television course included 810 students.

2. For the presentation of lecture-demonstration parts of courses to be supplemented by tutorial, recitation, or laboratory sessions. Under this procedure students receive supplementary instruction in small groups, led by graduate assistants. In some courses there are two televised lectures and one tutorial session per week; in others there is one televised lecture and two recitation sessions, the pattern depending on the nature of the course.

3. For magnifying demonstrations in a large lecture hall so that many students can be taught at one time, all of them obtaining a good view

of the demonstrations. Courses using this application include: Introduction to Engineering, Electrical Engineering, Introduction to Education, and General Chemistry.

4. For observation of remote events. Television appears to be particularly useful for teacher education courses, where student teachers are observing teaching demonstrations without intruding on the actual teaching situation. Remote viewing such as this also permits simultaneous analysis and discussion of the teaching process.

5. For professional training in TV techniques.

Within this range of patterns, a number of variations have been tried and some have been evaluated experimentally. We have studied and experimented with television originating-room conditions. We have looked into the question of the number of students that might be present in the originating room. Most instructors, when they first teach via TV, express a preference for a group of students in front of them. In some instances, 100 to 150 students have been present; in other instances, from four to 20. However, some teachers televise courses without students in the originating room. The trend seems to move from the former to the latter as a teacher gains experience. Now only in special circumstances do we have students in the originating room. This arrangement gives maximum flexibility of operation and avoids a conflict for the teacher between giving attention to the television viewers and giving it to the class in the originating room.

Our only study on the desirability of having students in the originating room was in a course on Principles of Economics. During the first part of the spring semester of 1956 the instructor taught this course on television with a class of twenty students in the originating room. For the second half of the semester he taught the course without the class in the originating room, addressing himself exclusively to the students in the receiving rooms. On a questionnaire, 70 percent of the 315 students reported that they had no particular preference for either procedure; 20 percent preferred to have some students in the originating room; and 10 percent thought it was better to have no students there.

Comparisons of student achievement in relation to the size of the groups in the television receiving rooms were made in five different courses. Class sizes ranged from fifteen to two hundred; and in all comparisons no differences in achievement relating to class size were found. In a student-preference study, however, we learned that students prefer the smaller receiving rooms seating from twenty-five to fifty.

We looked into the matter of opportunities for discussion, questions, and answers in televised instruction. A cluster of studies relates to the problems of personalizing instruction by providing opportunities for follow-up discussion.

1. *Rotation:* A system of rotating students through the television originating room was tested. No differences in course achievement were found among the groups that remained in the originating room through-out the experiment—those that remained in the receiving room and those that rotated every two weeks between the two.

2. *Thirty-five minute lecture plus fifteen-minute discussions:* In a General Psychology course, comparisons were made between several different methods of using a 15-minute discussion period following a 35-minute lecture-demonstration on television. Groups in some receiving rooms participated in discussions led by graduate assistants, others observed by means of television the discussion sessions which were conducted by the principal instructor with a small group of students in the originating room. A third category of groups were not given any discussion; they were permitted to review their notes, read the textbook, or leave. Actually quite a few of them stayed and did some review work.

This study was repeated in two different sections of the course, but the various types of discussion procedures produced no measurable effects on student performances in either section. The students who participated in the discussions led by graduate students were much more favorable, however, to the idea of the split class period than were the others.

3. *Two one-hour lecture-demonstrations a week followed by recitation period:* As I have already indicated, in courses where supervised problem-solving or laboratory work is deemed desirable, it is the practice to have televised lectures interspersed with recitation periods generally supervised by graduate students. This procedure was evaluated in two studies. In the first one, student preferences were obtained relative to two teaching situations: for the first part of the semester each class period was split into a 35-minute lecture on TV followed immediately by a 15-minute recitation; during the latter part of the semester two 50-minute lecture demonstrations via TV were followed by a 50-minute problem-solving session each week. Seventy percent of the students expressed a preference for the two-lecture-one-recitation pattern, and 29 percent preferred the split-period arrangement.

During the spring semester the value of the 50-minute problem-solving sessions was subjected to experimentation and evaluation in the economics course. The 120 students who scored in the upper 40 percent on the first examination in the course were randomly divided into two groups. One group was required to attend the weekly problem-solving sessions. The members of the other group were required to solve the same assigned problems independently in their own time. All students attended the two televised lectures per week. After four weeks they took a common examination. There were no differences between the groups on the items covering facts and principles, but there was a significant difference on the problem-solving items in favor of the group which had attended the supervised problem-solving sessions.

4. *Two-way communication:* We now have six of our television classrooms equipped with two-way microphones, enabling the student to signal the instructor and ask questions. In two different courses we compared the performance of students in microphone-equipped rooms with that of students in rooms not so equipped. The opportunity to ask questions had no significant effect on student performance. Student reaction to the availability of the two-way communication system is favorable. From 67 to 92 percent, depending on the course, believed that the microphones should be available, even though the majority rarely used the microphones.

Several other supplements to televised instruction have been studied: the use of lecture notes, tutoring by seniors, and workbooks. Neither the use of lecture outlines, nor the provision of individual or small-group tutorials by senior students has yet been evaluated experimentally, but student reactions to both procedures have been highly favorable.

The use of workbooks containing problems, exercises, and self-examining questions was evaluated in an experiment conducted in the General Psychology course. On an examination covering what had been taught in the course, there were no differences among the groups using and those not using the workbooks. On a special examination, which covered material specifically treated in the workbooks, the groups which had their workbooks corrected regularly by senior students performed better than those that did not use workbooks at all and those who were not required to hand their workbooks in for correction each week.

We have compared the use of television in an auditorium as a magnifier of charts and other demonstration materials, with the use of TV as an instructor multiplier, in which situation an instructor taught several groups of students simultaneously from a small television originating room. During part of the fall semester last year the instructor in an education course taught a group of 175 students in a large classroom. Television was used to magnify visual materials of various kinds. The students were free to ask questions in the usual way. About half way through the semester the students were moved into several small television classrooms, and the instructor taught from a small television originating room. The two-way communication system was used.

After about four weeks of this treatment the students were asked to vote on the procedure that they would prefer for the remainder of the semester. Sixty-one percent voted to remain in the small television rooms and 39 percent voted to return to the auditorium.

In the same course during the entire spring semester this year the same two methods of using television were compared in consecutive sections of the course, with students randomly assigned to each method. In the first hour, students were taught in the auditorium with television used as a demonstration magnifier. In the following hour, the other section was taught from the small originating room. This time the evaluation was made in terms of student performance. No significant differences in achievement were found.

The final subject I would like to consider under this general heading of appropriateness is the comparison between highly visualized instruction and traditional lecture-blackboard instruction, both presented over television by the same teacher. Proponents of educational television have claimed that its use facilitates and encourages the presentation of visuals, such as prepared diagrams, photographs, live demonstrations, motion pictures, panel discussions, and the like, and that through the use of these learning will be improved. Others assert that college students ought to be mature enough to deal with material presented to them largely in the form of verbal symbols.

In order to test these two opposing propositions, experiments were conducted in Air Science and General Psychology. In each course students were randomly assigned across two class sequences. On an examination in Air Science the group which received the intense visualized treatment made a mean score of 20.62, while the lecture-blackboard group scored 21.52.

In the psychology course the scores were almost identical on each of three successive tests for those receiving the visualized and the lecture-blackboard treatment. These findings will be checked in other studies.

They suggest several hypotheses for future research: students may need to be taught how to learn from highly visualized presentations, with which they are not so familiar as they are with the lecture-blackboard; the types of verbal tests generally used to assess achievement may not be measuring some of the kinds of learning that result from visual presentations. A third hypothesis is that, where the material is largely conceptual, college methods of instruction may be relatively unimportant. The important factors may be student intelligence and his motivation to learn. Finally, it is possible that much more radical changes in methods of presentation and students' study activities will have to be devised before differences in learning will emerge when comparisons are made with traditional teaching-learning practices.

Acceptability

We have made extensive use of opinion questionnaires to assess students' reactions to televised instruction, but we have become increasingly dissatisfied with them. First, the validity of verbal responses that entail no immediate personal consequences for students is open to question. Second, it is clear from many responses to questionnaires that attitudes toward television are intermixed with attitudes toward the course, the instructor, and his method of teaching.

Consequently, we devised the "behavioral choice" method. We believe it offers a breakthrough in methods of measuring attitudes toward television instruction. We expose students to a reasonable period of televised instruction, say five weeks, which is followed by a similar period of instruction by the same teacher in a direct-teaching situation. At the conclusion of these two experiences, the students are offered an actual choice between direct and televised instruction for the remainder of the course. Their relative preferences are easily observed in the choices they make. It is also possible to obtain a measure of verbal preference before the behavioral choice is offered and to compare the two. Also the choice is important to them because, once having made it, they have to stand by their decision for the remainder of the semester.

In the fall of 1955 in General Chemistry about 33 percent chose television and 67 percent direct instruction. In the spring of 1956 in Business Law about 47 percent chose television and 53 percent direct instruction. In the spring of 1956 in Political Science 70 percent chose television and 30 percent direct instruction. In the fall of 1956 in Introduction to Education 61 percent chose televised instruction in the small television receiving rooms, and 39 percent chose direct instruction in the auditorium where TV was also used to magnify visual materials.

Our most recent experiment using behavioral-choice methods was conducted in General Psychology last spring. The first section of the course received a highly visualized treatment on TV for the first nine weeks. The three hundred students were then moved to an auditorium and given conventional, direct instruction for about three weeks, after which they were invited to vote on the procedure to be followed for the remainder of the course.

The second section of students received a conventional lecture-blackboard treatment over television from the same teachers for nine weeks. They were then moved to the auditorium to receive three weeks of the same type of instruction, after which they too were invited to vote for the teaching procedure they preferred, television or direct, for the remainder of the semester.

It was hypothesized that more students among those originally in the highly visualized television sections would prefer television than among those whose original treatment on TV was the lecture-blackboard method. In the section with the visualized treatment, 61 percent chose to return to the televised instruction, whereas of the group that originally had the lecture-blackboard treatment for television only 53 percent voted to return to televised instruction. Accordingly, in both sections a return to televised instruction was made.

The reasons most commonly given by a student for preferring televised instruction are that they can see and hear better, and that there are less noise and confusion and fewer interruptions in the television receiving rooms than in large classes. Those preferring the large, directly taught classes believe that they have closer contact with the teacher, that they can concentrate better, and that they can ask questions more easily. It would appear that student acceptance, or rather lack of it, is not a serious barrier to the use of televised instruction at Penn State.

Feasibility

We have found that suitable vidicon television systems are adequate in picture quality and sufficiently reliable in operation for a wide variety of uses on the campus, ranging from broadcasting and the presentation of complete courses to the simple magnification of demonstrations.

During the current year we are putting much emphasis on studies of the cost of televised instruction in comparison with regular instruction.

Dr. Walker spoke of our preliminary findings. With less than two hundred students, televised instruction is more expensive than the traditional method.

General Conclusions

Our research findings at the Pennsylvania State University have been such as to give us confidence that students can be taught as effectively by means of television as by direct methods of instruction, that there are many ways of using television to achieve valid educational objectives, and that student acceptance is no serious barrier to the use of TV for regular courses where its use is justified. Finally, through its use large numbers of students can be taught by a single teacher, with the help of some senior students as assistants, at costs that are favorable to television if the enrollment in the average televised course exceeds two hundred. Thank you.

CHAIRMAN: Thank you, Mr. Greenhill, for that summary of a long period of distinguished and systematic research.

Mr. Hideya Kumata, to whom we are indebted for his excellent *Inventory of Instructional Television Research*,[3] will present his paper next.

Further Facts on a National Scale

HIDEYA KUMATA (Michigan State University): Although this brief review will be limited to direct instruction by television, this does not mean that we are not cognizant of other offerings on educational television, which after all make up the bulk of programming. It would be unfortunate for the educational-television movement if ETV became firmly identified with direct instruction or credit-course offerings only.

What is the scope of direct instruction? Taking figures from our survey at Illinois, from the survey by the Continuing Education Service at Michigan State, and from the survey by the TV Committee of the American Council on Education, there have been at least four hundred credit courses, on both closed and open circuit, offered in the last six years.

[3] Ann Arbor, Mich.: Educational Television and Radio Center, December 1956; out of print. Information concerning many of the studies cited by Mr. Kumata in his paper may be found in the *Inventory* or the *Supplement to the Inventory,* which is now in press.

At least seventy institutions have been involved. This count excludes in-school enrichment programs—something that hasn't been mentioned here—and non-credit courses.

As for subject matter, almost every college subject has been attempted by the various institutions. Numerous courses in the humanities have been offered by television, with history and Shakespeare predominating. Social science courses are next, with psychology leading in this category, followed by political science. Then education and natural science courses follow in frequency. In education there is no single subject which stands out, except for music education, namely, the teaching of piano at the University of Houston. And in the natural sciences biology is the most popular course.

Within this framework we can ask about the research that has been done. If you look at the literature, I think you will come quickly to the conclusion that we are not coordinating our efforts. Attempts have been sporadic. Excluding the Penn State studies, we have not attacked the problem of instructional television systematically. One of the main troubles is that there are very few publication outlets for the results of research, so that one has to know of research going on through personal contacts or he never hears of it.

The pattern of "no significant differences" emerges for information gained by students in face-to-face as compared with TV conditions. There have been at least sixty studies aimed at answering the general question whether the mode of communications makes a difference, and, with very few exceptions, the answers are that there are "no significant differences."

It would seem that we ought to turn our attention to other matters. In previous discussions on this subject, I have been critical of duplication; however, I have come to the conclusion that one has to fight the battle of acceptance for use of television over and over again. Policy-makers do not accept conclusions in this area based on research which has not been done on *their* students, *their* instructors, and *their* courses.

Some of the Purdue and Miami studies hint that conventional, or face-to-face, teaching is superior to television. Possibly this may be a function of the type of information test used, although on the other hand these may be chance results. In comparing studies one must be very careful to distinguish between open-broadcast and closed-circuit conditions.

Aside from the captive-audience aspect of closed circuit as contrasted with the free choice of open broadcast, several things are apparent from audience studies. First, there are more females in the open-broadcast audience for telecourses. The ratio of females to males ranges from five to three up to as high as eight to one. Female predominance is the rule even in evening broadcasts.

There is also an age difference; the typical open-broadcast student is in his forties. This has been true from the Frank Baxter course in Shakespeare to the recent Chicago Junior College courses.

Third, the level of motivation differs. Some hint of this may be gleaned from the extremely good grades that open-broadcast telestudents get and from a look at some of the answers to opinion questionnaires.

Fourth, open-broadcast telestudents are usually married and have children. You can see that it is not fair to compare a normal resident, daytime class with open-broadcast telecourse students. Open-broadcast courses offer a choice between televised instruction and no instruction at all, not, as in college, a choice between TV and an alternative form of presentation.

Let us turn to the area of attitudes. As in many attitude-change studies made previously, there seems to be little relation beween attitude toward television and the amount learned. This means, for example, that if you are interested only in information gain in a captive-audience situation— closed circuit—then attitudes toward television are of small concern.

Some studies have shown that there is a significant difference in favor of television after students are exposed to a TV course. Generally, however, studies have shown that for closed circuit there is a decrease in favorability toward the medium after exposure. Open-broadcast courses show a rather high acceptance and liking for televised teaching.

Attitudes toward television as a teaching medium may be summarized in the following way: Acceptance is high at the grade school or school enrichment level and at the adult level. Acceptance is mixed at the high school and college levels, but generally negative.

The instructor himself is a crucial variable. In a study done at Michigan State University the experimenters tested along a mode dimension; that is, television as compared with face-to-face situations. They included a prestige dimension also, with three degrees of expertness. There was an instructor dimension, with three different instructors being used. As for attitudes toward the subject matter, it was learned that the significant findings were interactions involving the instructor, that is, some instructors were more effective in changing attitudes toward the course when they were on television, and other instructors were more effective when they were face to face.

Let us turn to the problem of feedback or two-way flow. We find that students and teachers alike are critical of the lack of feedback in the closed-circuit situation. However, the State University of Iowa studies in teaching a discussion course show that even when such facilities are provided, receiving rooms are noticeably reluctant to use them. In one study at Purdue talk-back facilities were provided after numerous complaints. The only question asked was whether students would be tested on the material presented. Here again student learning is not related to attitude toward the feedback problem.

In instructor attitudes toward television teaching, the majority of the faculty is negative to the idea. It is interesing to note here, however, that the most avid supporters of teaching by television are usually those instructors who have actually taught over the medium.

The question of high and low ability and television instruction has been raised ever since the Army basic trainee studies were made. In the several studies available since then the conclusions of the Army study, in which students of low ability seemed to do better when instructed by television rather than face to face, have not been borne out.

In the time that has intervened since the *Inventory of Instructional Television Research*[4] was published, the conclusions have not changed substantially, although the amount of literature has grown tremendously. I have purposely cut this review short to save us our coffee break.

CHAIRMAN: Not only did Mr. Kumata give us an excellent review, but he left us five minutes for opinions and questions.

General Discussion

NEAL E. MILLER (Yale University): While it is good for purposes of scientific control to have the same teacher give televised and non-televised instruction, that is not your practical problem. Your problem is your best teacher on television versus your average teacher in the classroom. Has research been done on this question?

MR. GREENHILL: I think we are getting to the point now where we can do research on that question. We have two studies projected for

[4] *Ibid.*

this coming semester. Our plan is to compare graduate assistants with experienced instructors on television.

CLIFFORD G. ERICKSON (Chicago City Junior College): Since we give full time to television instruction and have five branches spread across the city, we have been driven to using other teachers in the comparison groups.

LLOYD MATHER (Pennsylvania State University): Perhaps immediate testing doesn't show very much in student achievement, but the long-range retention of a student may be quite different depending upon the method by which he was taught. Has there been any testing in which retention has been a factor?

MR. KUMATA: Yes, there have been several studies in which retention was of interest. Usually the testing has been done about six weeks after the end of the instruction. Here there are no significant differences between television and face-to-face students. There was one study in which eight months intervened before retesting. It indicated that television instruction was superior to begin with and still superior after the eight-month interval.

CHAIRMAN: Our coffee break is due.

[A short recess took place]

College Cultural Patterns and Their Effects on Learning by Television

CHAIRMAN JOHN C. ADAMS: Three distinguished panelists will discuss the effects of college cultural patterns on students' learning from televised instruction. Our first speaker is Dr. John Ivey, executive vice-president, New York University.

Toward a Student-Oriented University

JOHN E. IVEY, JR. (New York University): In all the discussions we have had, I get the feeling that we are trying to pry television into a well-frozen curriculum, into the highly structured system of living in a college or university community.

Practically all the research that has been done has taken place within the framework of a course presentation, within the concept of existing curricula. It has been curriculum-oriented and professor-oriented, rather than student-oriented. If these general impressions are true, I would like to take off from my major assumption, namely, that the future of higher education in the United States, if it is going to be significantly improved, is going to have to emphasize the creation of superior learners.

If we focus on development of superior learners, we are dealing with a problem of acquired behavior, just as learning to teach well is acquired behavior. If this premise is true, then much of our discussion about the cultural conditions under which televised instruction has been taking place becomes more and more important. We cannot study what goes on in the classroom as an abstraction from the remainder of the college culture.

We must assume that a university is a large cultural system. There are people who have values, attitudes, patterns of living, institutional relationships, personality, and security committed to doing things the way they have traditionally been done. The orientation of work, play, and creative activity is well structured.

This large cultural system of students, faculty, administrative officers, board of trustees, and the lay public that surrounds it, is a social machine. It is organized to attain certain very specific ends. The more clearly the educational purposes can be defined and the machinery set up to achieve those purposes, the better the university cultural system can be patterned to produce specified and definable outcomes. If the purposes of the university are unclear, the perceptions of purposes are greatly confused among the faculty, administrative officers, and board of trustees; the procedures for operating the university are not well geared to a set of clear purposes; and we have an anarchic situation.

Under such circumstances the university cultural system is an area of confusion, misunderstanding, and personal and group tension, which cannot but lower the productivity of students, faculty, and administration. Certainly the student and his welfare cannot be kept in clear focus by university educational officers. Nor can the student be expected to emerge from this confused situation with any clear perception of himself or the educational process.

Our problem here is to explore some of the elements of the university cultural system so as to examine their implications for directing the educational process toward the purpose of helping students become superior learners. Well, let's start by putting the student in the center. This is the person we are worried about.

The student exists, as far as the university is concerned, in a series of learning groups at the present time. These learning groups are primarily centered in course or subject-matter groups. Each of these groups has a sociological structure. It has a leadership pattern. It has interaction patterns. It has a value system toward the teacher, a value system toward the content of the course. It has attitudes brought in from outside the classroom. Every student has come in with certain acquired skills and attitudes about how to learn.

The second community that the student exists in we will call the student community in the university at large. This is the community that is concerned about student government, athletics, activities in dormitories, extracurricular social activities, informal relationships with professors, and so on. This group also has certain patterned attitudes toward studying, making higher grades, the behavior of the "smart fellows." It has much to do with setting the *educational tone* of the university cultural system.

The system of student-faculty interaction is the third community in which the student exists. Such interaction takes place pretty much within what we call *curriculum*. It takes place within a physical structure, which, to a certain extent, has frozen the curriculum and the sociological relationship of professors to one another and the students to professors. This can be analyzed with the present techniques we have in social anthropology, psychology, sociology, and psychiatry.

Some people contend that the present interaction of the student and the professor is a substitute for the family pattern. You have a matriarch, or patriarch, who sets the rules of conduct, and the students come in and react, bringing their aggressions and dependencies on their father or mother, perhaps transferring them to the professor. All these forces operate in a classroom just as surely as the reactions operate in relation to the curriculum and its contents.

We are all familiar with the expression that a university is a community of scholars. The university faculty community is the fourth community on the campus. Sociologically, in many universities, there exists a harmonious concept of a community of scholars. But in many other institutions there are tremendous blocks, aggressions, and tensions existing among the various members of this academic community. Sometimes it is divided on college lines and/or relation of faculty to control administration, sometimes on departmental lines, sometimes between the chairman and the members of the department, sometimes in the faculty senate, sometimes in the American Association of University Professors, sometimes in the clubs they belong to. But this whole university community conditions the manner in which the professor participates in the student interaction system, which at the present time primarily occurs in the curriculum area. But there is a regular organized, unorganized, or disorganized community system of faculty academic and social life in a university.

There is still another community, that of university government; and here we have some interesting problems that have a strong bearing on the way the institution operates. Who is going to make policy—administration or faculty? How are these power relationships going to be resolved? We have a regular community system bound up in the governmental structure, which can be very authoritarian, or very democratic, or it can be in the twilight zone between these two extremes.

The community of relationships between the university and the lay public that it serves has a great effect on how this system operates internally. This public may be parents, or it may be the legislature and the citizens of a state, depending on whether it is a public or a private institution. These are what we call subsystems of a university cultural system where the forces and organized patterns of community life are geared to a common set of educational objectives; then this entire cultural system becomes synchronized, organized, and moves in one direction.

The student is in the center of all this, feeling the effects. This entire association is organized in such a way as to permit or block growth. The student brings into the classroom certain inherited and acquired characteristics. He brings in certain attitudes and values, some of them held by the various community groups in the university, others peculiar to himself.

The professor is on the other side of the fence. He comes in with a certain concept of the course he is teaching, a certain concept of the subject matter and the substance he is going to put over, a certain concept of how what he is doing here is going to be viewed by the whole community.

My hunch is that one of the reasons why we found "no significant differences" in the testing of what goes on when the television tube is between the professor and the students, and when you take it away, is that the major variables in learning are in the total university com-

munity and not in the relationship among professor, student, and the
television tube.

If this is possible, we need to pursue research to determine what
factors in the university cultural system can produce individuals who are
superior learners. What is the peculiar role of television in accomplishing this purpose? What is the role of the professor in this kind of undertaking, as contrasted with the premises that have dominated most of our
television research to date? How may the social communities in the university cultural system be better shaped to create the superior learner
with the motivation and skill needed for such independent intellectual
operation?

To Learn How To Learn

The discussion thus far is based on the premise that the learning process involves acquired behavior, just as good teaching represents acquired
behavior of the teacher. If it is an acquired behavior, then the focus of
university teaching ought to be more in the direction of helping the
students learn how to learn. The student should be provided with the tools
to learn how to learn. The university cultural system should encourage
values which encourage independent and group learning, with the
teacher, more or less, being a wise counselor and guide in the learning
process.

For the most part the approaches to the problem of how colleges are
going to take care of the large numbers of students forecast for the
1960's have been hinged on the assumption that we will maintain our
curriculum and the time presently required of students for completing
our system of academic credit accounting. These assumptions are barriers to the development of students as independent, superior learners.
More emphasis is required on the possible ways of encouraging students
to grow and develop at whatever rate they are capable of, instead of
moving in lock step in course credit acquisition. Such a premise greatly
changes the concept of the educational capacity of a given number of
teachers in a given physical plant.

We can develop research into the problems of student growth as
superior learners and its effect on the student-professor relationship. We
can unhinge the relationship of the student and the professor to a system
of faculty interaction now largely course-oriented and curriculum-oriented. We can build into our student community a value system oriented
toward intellectual and educational objectives as much as, if not more

than, it is oriented toward football and extracurricular activities. This is a great uncharted area for administrators, professors, and trustees.

If we are interested in the superior learner, then we ought to work with students in a manner that will conscientiously teach them how to learn under different circumstances and from different media, and provide the physical environment in which this can take place.

The great value of television may be that it provides a means to help study and experiment with this situation. The long-range effectiveness of TV may be in helping to find how we can organize the variables of the university cultural system other than through direct interaction between professor and student. The importance of these variables to learning situations must be assessed. We can then move toward emancipation from present concepts of curriculum and educational organization, creating student-oriented instead of curriculum- or faculty-oriented universities.

CHAIRMAN: Thank you, Dr. Ivey. Our next panelist will be Dr. Blake.

I Think TV Teaching Is a Good Idea, But——

ROBERT R. BLAKE (University of Texas): Behind many remarks heard at this conference has been the question of tradition, "how we ordinarily do it," "what students ordinarily expect," "what instructors ordinarily want to do," and so on. Teaching by television involves change from conventional ways of doing things and change can be disturbing unless resistance to change is understood and worked with intelligently.

My remarks are addressed to an analytical way of thinking about tradition and cultural change. I shall give you three examples, assessing them analytically. Two of them—smoking and bathing suits—are unrelated to television and serve to provide a clearer basis for analysis. The third example is concerned with television in classrooms. My argument will be that all of these can be analyzed in the same way.

Although problems of change are apt to appear different in content, that does not mean that the structural way of thinking about them is different. Standard patterns of behavior, regardless of the specific content they represent, are subject to analysis in a single basic manner. If we understand a way of thinking about them, based on democratic practices, we have a means of controlling and shifting tradition to suit our present requirements, rather than being victims of tradition when we most need to bring about change.

Smoking: The Traditional Way of Thinking about It

"How much do you smoke?" I ask a student, and he answers, "Oh, a pack a day."

"Why?" I ask, and he tells me, "Got the habit."

I ask him how long he has been smoking this amount and he tells me three or four years. He goes on to say he can't stop smoking because he has acquired the habit. I want to know what he means when he says he has acquired the *habit*. I wonder if he ever smokes more or less than the established tradition of one pack a day. I learn that around examination time, he steps this up to two packs a day. I also discover, after additional questions, that he doesn't smoke while he is visiting his parents during holidays or vacation time because they don't approve of smoking. They would be shocked to learn that he had taken up this habit.

What is this student saying? I could show you his traditional level of a pack a day on a diagram and then show how driving forces—the pressure of examination, the bias or censure of his parents—shoot this level much higher or so low that it runs beneath the diagram.

We keep talking about why he smokes. He says cigarettes taste good, they help him to feel sophisticated; and here we have two more driving forces to support his tradition of a pack a day. "Why don't you smoke four packs a day?" I ask. That question produces a résumé of statistics, linking cigarettes to cancer and heart trouble—a restraining force that hews away at his tradition of a pack a day. The cost of a package of cigarettes, like the current linking of tobacco to illness, is a restraining force that keeps his tradition at one pack rather than two or four a day. At the end of our conversation, we learn that he veers from tradition on two occasions, at examination time and while he is visiting the folks at home. These are new forces that are momentarily added, driving his consumption up or restraining him from smoking. He shifts his personal traditions with changing forces in the field of experience. His behavior varies with his situation. Tradition changes in line with new facts.

Bathing Suits

A bathing suit is interesting to think about, and if you look back at the old Pathé News reels of World War I, you will see a very different situation than if you go to Atlantic City today. It used to be skirts down to the knees and sleeves down to the elbow. When we think about bathing suits and how they have changed through the years, we automatically link these changes to the force fields inherent in the passing years.

In 1915 there were driving forces operating to make for lesser amounts of coverage, freedom to swim, comfort, and so on. But there were stronger restraining forces to keep bathing suits from getting skimpier also, strong moral imperatives. Today we don't look at bathing suits with such stringent modesty; the skirts and sleeves can be discarded. Comfort, freedom to swim, and attractiveness of appearance have remained strong driving forces to eliminate even more of the traditional suit; but by the time fashion achieved the ultra-abbreviated Bikini, the moralistic factors were still strong enough to say, "That's going too far!" Fashion may operate as a force inducing change, but its operations have to be within the basic force field of pressures acting on the individuals who are to wear the suits.

Thus, any behavior that can be viewed as having a "level" or a "flow" or an "average amount over time," can be regarded as held in place by forces that are driving in an upward direction and by restraining forces preventing the behavior from moving higher.

Tradition is a "level," a characteristic way of doing things. It is subject to change by changing the forces in the field, either adding driving forces, removing restraining forces, or some of both. Take smoking again. How do manufacturers of tobacco deal with changing the level? They advertise, showing the sophistication of smoking; that is, they add a new driving force. Yet they also try to remove restraining forces, such as putting forth long cigarettes with filter tips which might possibly reduce fear of cancer. In other words, advertising sensibly takes the total force field into account.

Instructional Television and Tradition

Teaching by television is little different from starting any new, unfamiliar practice, against the background of old, traditional ways. Let's deal primarily with restraining forces that prevent change in the direction of educational TV. Resistance may arise toward any practice that requires shifting away from existing cultural habits toward new, unexplored patterns of behavior. Negative attitudes toward instructional television are no exception. Although socially condoned, a retort that reeks with resistance to change is, "Well, understand, I think it's a good idea basically, but . . ." Any of fifty reasons after that *but* say that the person really doesn't want to do the thing that he is protesting is a good idea.

Frequently reasons for being against something are subjective and personal, unrelated to an objective appraisal of the situation. When a professor says, "Well, understand, I think instruction by television is a good idea basically, but . . ." this may be his way of refusing to come to grips with real problems by avoiding the medium altogether. His pronouncement is a cover for a negative attitude rather than a valid argument against the proposal.

Popular ways of resisting change are challenged here, with suggestions as to how this "resistance to change" may be overcome:

"You can't teach talking into a camera, you've got to interact with people, too . . ." The verdict rendered by this remark is centered on the social aspects of communication, not on the technical limitations of television, which intrude to separate professor and student as a learning unit. What is responsible for this categorical denial that TV can be useful as a communication medium? Students partly are responsible. They feel that they learn only when they get direct reactions from the teacher. The teacher also is a culprit, feeling that the spontaneity in classroom interaction is an indispensable factor in teaching success.

How might this source of resistance be coped with? Well, is interaction necessary under all conditions? We can ask this question, even though we know that the classroom situation provides opportunities for interaction and that such interaction can be satisfying to professors and students.

Two lines of evidence suggest that interaction isn't necessary under all conditions. One is that examinations taken under both conditions indicate little or no superiority of learning for the traditional classroom situation. People seem to learn as much one way as the other. Resistance to change can be met by evaluating the equality of the products obtained under the two conditions. The evidence says that, other things equal, you don't have to interact with people for them to learn. In the light of objective data, the argument that you can't teach effectively by talking into a camera doesn't hold up.

Another way of combating this resistance to change is in the practice try-out. Invite the professor to try his hand at teaching in a closed-circuit situation with a few people in the audience. He may find that he can teach, talking into a camera. He may even find that the techniques that he devises for getting material across are more suitable than those he traditionally used in his face-to-face classes.

"You can't get the feedback you need because people can't ask questions when they're hot." Here is a recognition that teaching is more than merely disseminating information that it may involve communicating ideas through sharp interchanges, with conflict, disagreement, and resolution. Sometimes questions need to be examined when they pop into the mind, rather than being answered at a later time. Also a question can bring out new information which clarifies the issue, so that succeeding material makes more sense. No doubt about it, there is a lot of insight behind this particular *but*. Some courses and some professors simply may not lend themselves to the TV medium, and in these cases the reaction is realism, not resistance.

In other situations this protest is resistance. The need to ask questions in order to gain clarifying information suggests that the professor may not have thought his arguments through or may not have presented his ideas in a sequence that permits comprehension; the program pretesting that TV demands, which can lead to a more thoughtful and orderly progression of ideas, can decrease the need for hot questions.

From another point of view, asking questions may be more in the service of psychological needs than educational requirements; a teacher may provoke questions to exercise his authority by answering them, thereby meeting his own needs. This motivation is apt to be denied most vehemently by those who are most guilty.

The opportunity to ask questions can provide students who need to be accepted with an opportunity to be dependent on the professor rather than thinking for themselves. This situation appeals to students who want the professor's whole attention spotlighted on themselves. "Ask him a good question at the beginning of the course," some students say, "and you'll have the halo effect the rest of the term."

Then there is the student who doesn't ask questions; he interrogates. He appeals to the professor, who needs argument and division of opinion to feel that he is really teaching. So if television prevents questions while they are hot, it may be a mixed blessing. When resistance to TV shows up in the hot-question attitude, it needs to be examined from the above standpoints. Assessing the psychological factors in the situation of confrontation that makes it appealing to the professor and to the students may diminish resistance based on psychological needs. Challenge the assumption that you can't get questions when they're hot. Technical improvements are moving forward. It may suffice here to acknowledge that the TV medium does not necessarily prevent functional student-teacher interaction from taking place.

"It'll put us out of business." Some resistance arises from administrative aspects, a professor's belief that television has a way of decreasing the need for professors. Television can make a single professor available to a wider range of students. Lack of enthusiasm for the medium may be rooted in this emotional concern, which really is irrelevant from the effectiveness of television. Yet to speak of this objection is unattractive because it implies that a person is sensitive to exploitation, and that is something an individual isn't supposed to be.

If people won't admit their objections to the exploitation aspects of television, how can you deal with this source of resistance? It is difficult, but you can meet the unverbalized objections with factual evidence, distinguishing the real from the fictional. By doing so, you can reduce the personal anxiety surrounding exploitation so that a realistic examination of television is possible.

"The older professors in the department would be certain that they made a mistake when they hired me if I were to do that." Another set of reactions are based on the concern for self typified in this statement. A significant shift in teaching methods, such as that represented by instructional television, is difficult for a younger professor to spearhead.

The conclusion that the older members will take a rejecting attitude toward the younger member who shows initiative in the TV realm can be forestalled. The decision to use television can be taken by the department, rather than by any single teacher. In this way a department will be able to exercise control over the manner in which individuals make use of instructional television rather than allow it to develop as an offshoot, controlled by the initiative of those whose motivation is not necessarily in the interests of the department. If the decision to explore educational television is taken as a departmental action, with committees appointed to implement the plan, then fear of rejection from the older professors need no longer be a source of concern.

Diagnosis of Resistance Will Suggest Cure

Traditions function in subtle ways, but they are subject to analytical treatment and to conscious determination rather than slavish adherence to requirements of the past. Analytical methods are available for organizing one's thoughts, one's way of examining and treating a problem.

A full-scale type of analysis can identify many of the problems and suggest ways of meeting them. You can identify the forces operating in a field to prevent change. You can examine typical attitudes that reveal resistance to a new pattern of behavior, teaching by television. Some of these attitudes are not based on a realistic appraisal of a given situation but on personal emotional reactions. Included in the resistance toward TV are anxieties about inabilities to perform under television conditions, fear of exploitation, violation of the standards for good teaching as held by older professors, and anxieties that the loss of interaction through the use of this medium may decrease the quality of the instruction. As in dealing with resistance to change in any setting, the basic premise here is that accurate diagnosis will suggest the cure.

CHAIRMAN: Thank you, Professor Blake. Our next speaker is Professor Moehlman, who also will discuss the impacts of television in the college culture pattern.

Point of View—Television, an Ultimate in Communication

ARTHUR HENRY MOEHLMAN (University of Texas): Granted that television is an increasingly dynamic instrument in college and university teaching, the medium's unique strengths and weaknesses should be examined with regard to its inner logic or philosophy as a means of instruction and its operation within the cultural climate of universities. Television cameras are obedient, quickly rolling robots with multiple lenses, which can take a teacher in many guises to huge numbers of students. It may be that the television cameras have more power than the atom in affecting our lives through learning. Maybe the flexible field of view and power of the TV lenses will give students greater opportunities to learn. With television the student can experience factors of knowledge at first hand and with increased reality. If television is one of the ultimates in communication, then university education must explore and utilize its potential with insight and imagination.

The Texas TV project, *Adventures in Education,* provided an opportunity to study the impacts of instructional television in the college culture with regard to the *Aura* (teacher), *Genius Loci* (TV stage and network), and *Organic Unity* (colleges and universities in state context). The TV project was run by the Texas Education Agency during the academic year 1957–58. This project was supported financially by the Fund for Advancement of Education. The program series concentrated on teacher recruitment and education. Research, writing, and presentation of the script was done by one instructor (the present writer), working as a team with the producer, Lyle Hendricks, and the executive director, Dr. Lee Wilborn. The plan was set up with the dual objectives of (1) teacher recruitment and teacher education for enrolled students—arts college graduates and seniors; and (2) social interpretation of the significance in society of education to teachers in service and to the general audience. The series was telecast from WBAP–TV in Fort Worth over an eighteen-station network, including twelve live stations, every Saturday morning. Six other TV stations used kinescopes of the programs. All colleges and universities worked with the T.E.A.

Some program titles included in the series were: "Universal Education as the Guardian Genius of Democracy"; "The Teaching Profession Vital to Society"; "The Teacher, the Law, and the Structure of United States Education"; "Supervision and the Improvement of the Quality of Instruction"; "Parents and the Community as Teachers"; and "Teachers Teach Themselves and Participate in Humanity's Vast Future."

The achievements and findings which came into focus as the series developed have provided illuminating data on *Aura, Genius Loci,* and *Organic Unity* relative to TV education in colleges and universities. The *Aura,* or projection of personality, is defined as the college teacher, involving problems of design in maintaining the unique characteristics of the instructor, and both projection and communication of ideas by personality and other instruments on the stage. The *Genius Loci,* or spirit of the place, is defined as the producer-director working with the TV sound and light stage. *Organic Unity* is the culture pattern of the college and the university; it is also the context, environment, and climate of thought forming the cosmos of television education.

The problem is one of a genius for synthesis between television, education, and the three great areas of knowledge—humanities, social sciences, and natural sciences—which form a tripod, and without any one of which our TV instrument as a new medium of education would not operate effectively. The experience we gained in *Adventures in Education* has already been invaluable in aiding our exploration of the philosophical and operational bases of TV education in the culture pattern of the college.

Why does education play such a powerful role in human society?

Man is unique in his capacity for conceptual thought and is the only form of life able to change self and universe through education in symbols. Symbols are signs for reality, or lines enclosing a concept or idea expressing reality. Man alone can manipulate symbols to visualize what he knows or desires. Therefore, humankind alone can use conceptual thought to transcend time and space and create new dimensions for living. As James Branch Cabell put it, "Man alone among animals plays the ape to his dreams." As a result of a long evolution, man became an erect biped with a big brain operating his tough, resilient body. His erect posture freed his forelimbs or hands for efficient manipulation of objects and allowed him to see, hear, and speak from a considerable height. Furthermore, the unusual nature of his receptors and effectors enable him to send and receive symbols or signs and to transform them into realities.

Man's major receptors, the eyes and ears, were greatly refined and became capable of sensing delicate differences in things seen or heard. In fact the human eye has been called the window of the soul. Man's major effectors, the voice apparatus and hands, became very flexible and efficient. The lips, mouth, tongue, and voice box permitted the formation of uniform sounds of great range as media of communication both accurate and stimulating. The hands with opposable thumbs and fingers were unspecialized and could pick up and manipulate, fashion, and change a great range of materials. The relatively huge brain linked these unusual receptors and effectors together, permitting language or communication through symbols and the planning and construction of mechanisms to conquer time, space, heat, cold, disease, and famine, thus enabling man to fashion new dimensions of life in accordance with his dreams.

Man's real purpose is not a struggle for survival or supremacy, not a devastating scramble for wealth, but a generous and fruitful rivalry in adding to human knowledge and creating new human values. Television education can accelerate such creativity with its living lens mirroring and interpreting the infinitely varied human scene in a wide range of symbols.

Education should be viewed as one of the basic universals or activities in the cultural pattern. A human being in a culture is either crippled or strengthened by the extent and depth of his knowledge of the basic symbols grouped around certain universals which appear in any culture. All cultures must deal with universals or activities and institutions, and it is difficult to understand them without employing some morphology.

I. Education—directed learning
Philosophy—value choices
Religion—relation of man and the universe
Language—symbols and communication

II. Health—maturation in the life cycle
Vocation—work or profession
Aesthetics—search for beauty
Recreation—play, use of leisure time

III. Technology—use of natural resources
Economics—satisfaction of wants
Social structure—kinship and etiquette
Government—ordering of human relations

The universals appear in some form in every culture. They are, however, arranged and organized in very different patterns. In every case, the key to the pattern can be found in the philosophical and religious underpinning and buttressing in the way of value choices which give direction.

(VALUE CHOICES)

Truth Beauty Adventure Peace
Vitality Wisdom Sensitivity Intelligence

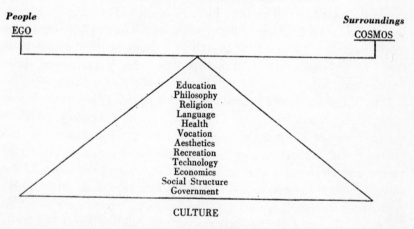

CULTURE

Education may be visualized as the critical point of a fulcrum made up of a culture's universals. This fulcrum operates as a means of balancing and adjusting people and their surroundings; that is, the ego and the cosmos, in terms of values toward which the culture attempts to progress through space and time.

Humanity is now in the stage of seeing itself not only as a rational scientific investigator; that is, the *animal rationale,* but also as the result of its own creation of symbols, its own choices of what it would like reality to be, that is, the *animal symbolicum*. What does this mean? It means that human beings have constructed a rich and varied culture or way of life through their creation of symbolic forms, whether in language, mathematics, engineering, or art forms. They can choose their own direction toward force or freedom, toward humanization or mechanization, toward stratified or classless society. Humankind can do this mainly because it has steadily created and expanded a system of universal education that can also be individualized. The powerful, symbolic forms must be given to all the people and on a high and undiluted level. Civilizations of the past have failed, and we will fail in our period of mid-passage if we do not recognize this fundamental fact.

Education is a universal in all culture patterns; for without it no culture can either survive or progress. Every culture must provide for experiences that are capable of making the individual a participant in the culture pattern, that is, for education or a process of directed learning which socializes or trains each person to take his place as a responsible and competent adult in the society. Education may be defined as directed learning that provides for both the nurture of personal growth and for the transmission and renewal of the culture. Furthermore, education is defined as lasting from birth to death and encompassing both formally directed learning in the schools, and informal learning in the family and other social nuclei, as well as in mass media of communication such as books, periodicals, newspapers, radio, and television. Televised education can be a vital synthesis of all directed learning.

Only in the last hundred years has any real progress been made toward universal education based upon mass media and democracy, which is the only way of life providing sufficient freedom of maneuver for the human spirit, with the concept of the dignity of each individual as paramount. Universal education transmits and renews the values of the culture pattern for everyone's well-being and enjoyment. It can also provide for the fullest flowering of the individual's talents and abilities. Universal education requires that everyone should be educated as far as his talents and abilities permit and that any elite should consist of an aristocracy of talent.

No civilization can survive or progress unless it has a philosophy of wise value choices, an internal logic which it understands and believes in and which gives direction to all of its activities, including religion, kinship, food-gathering, communication, education, and so on. The culture must have an understanding of the purpose and inner logic of its own way of life; it must have competence in the basic symbols of knowledge and the techniques necessary to its survival and progress. Furthermore, it must provide for change and for long-range thinking.

A wide range of experts from various disciplines seem to agree that our greatest problem today is learning not only to avoid fragmentation, but also to adjust ourselves to operating on a planet with world-wide loyalties. Lowie, the anthropologist, points out that, "In a general way all such problems may be reduced to a simple formula. Man was primarily, and has been for thousands of years, accustomed to live in tiny political units with a correspondingly narrow sense of moral obligation."

The mathematical biologist, Pierre Lecomte du Nouy, feels that human beings are learning to be architects of their own true and cosmic evolution into a huge organism, which may be called humanity. He insists that we are "craftsmen of our own evolution," because we have acquired a conscience and a concern for the future; but this transcendent and flowing destiny for humankind is possible only if we educate ourselves and our children in a basic integrity, which would mean that all mankind can be trusted. To him, ethics are paramount, everyone must be trained in a good and noble life and all other universal needs follow in its train, and the good life must certainly include thinking of the entire planetary-humanity as one engaged in a common undertaking.

Education, then, must meet the challenge of humanity's widening horizons with a universal education based upon the symbols of truth, which everyone has an opportunity to learn. In order to reach this objective, education must continue its long struggle to raise the professional standards of all educators.

Television and Teacher-Student Values

Televison is a catalyst in college instruction, stimulating the students, instructors, and administrators in their approach to the problems of improvement of instruction, and forcing them all to analyze and explore the unique nature of the university or college culture pattern. This catalytic action is manifested in many ways. We seldom, as professors, see others teach, and there is a real lack of exchange and cross-fertilization in ideas between various disciplines and fields. Television can play a significant role in such interchange, speeding up the quality of instruction as we learn from each other. Instead of working like modern monks in our separate cells, we may learn more from each other. In addition, when students see superb instruction by a superior teacher, the repercussions will be felt in every part of the university structure from research and publication to salaries and teaching schedules.

We know much less than we should about the college culture pattern. Some studies have been made, such as Logan Wilson's fine analysis of the professor, called *The Academic Man*. Then there are the works of Cowley, McConnell, Hofstadter, and Hardy. We need to know more about the full sociology of knowledge, the conflicts between the social groupings of scholars and of students, and the way in which cooperation can be achieved.

Operational problems are set up not only by the newness of the television medium, its limitations, and its strength, but also by the various impacts of human society upon it. What we do in educational television is to a large degree conditioned by the flow of events in general television, which is setting up new patterns and affecting everybody. I think the point should be made at the very beginning that in educational television we should keep our approach on a high intellectual plane, for anything worth having requires effort. Perhaps TV has tended to underestimate the capabilities of Americans, who have been changed by universal education from the pattern of old Europe. There are changes astir in the land now, and it may be that the people are running ahead of the leadership. The saga of the paperback books is a case in point. Our textbooks are splendid, but they need to be expanded by wide creative reading, field trips, films, and other experiences.

The problem is above all one of insight into a symbolic communication and the fact that education is directed learning, that ethical objectives are paramount, and that higher education is not amoral but has value choices. Do students learn more when they really are given a grasp of principles, a chance to see why things occur? Hogben, Robinson, Conant, Sarton, and others have agreed in their adventures into the humanization of knowledge.

Above all, it should be pointed out that television is a team project, and research needs to be done on a team basis concerning: (1) the roles of the administrator and policymaker as tied into a TV project; (2) the roles of the teacher in writing, creating visualizations, and presenting his script; and (3) the roles of the director and producer, and the large crew of experts who back up the director and producer.

The director-producer can be tremendously effective not only in designing the stage, but in helping the college professor to move over into his new role without losing his basic and characteristic methods of instruction, which can no more be slashed away without damage than a culture can forget its own past history.

When exploring television education in relation to culture patterns of higher education in the United States, it is essential to have both a philosophical research approach and an operation research approach. In other words, it is of basic importance to explore the philosophical underpinning of the medium we are working with and the hypotheses for the direction of learning which we wish to secure.

Furthermore, operational research with regard to the culture pattern of higher education is basic. We know relatively little about the college cosmos and the social pressures which exert their impacts upon it. Operational research is also required in the actual process of instruction and teaching as it affects both the instructors and the students.

A new creative synthesis of television with the fundamental professional discipline of education, with its area of knowledge and methods of inquiry, and also with the great basic disciplines, the arts and humanities, social sciences and natural sciences, is an essential and vital challenge of our times. Televised education is another great spiral upward in "directed learning," or education, which may give us more creative results than even its great predecessors. The professors and students have already assimilated the printing press, etching, lithography, graphic arts, photographs, slides, recordings, radio, and 16-mm. sound film as ultimates in their times into the teaching process. Television is a new ultimate in the communication of ideas and conceptual thought which offers us new horizons in education.

CHAIRMAN: Thank you, Professor Moehlman.

Our three brilliant speakers have scrupulously observed our time scheme. As a result, we have some time left for discussion. I'm turning the gavel over to John Ivey for the balance of this session.

CHAIRMAN IVEY: Are there any questions you would like to direct to this morning's panelists?

General Discussion

DAVID G. MONROE (University of North Carolina): Dr. Ivey, in our political science course we have been concerned about running out of senior teachers. We have about 15 to 20 sections of this course at the freshman level, and 14 out of 16 sections are being given by graduate students. I hear some of our students saying, "I never get to hear the real teachers until I am a senior." Because of this situation I was especially interested in your observation that our job should be directed to the students; do you think that television is a method by which the voice of our senior teacher can be spread to our freshmen and sophomores?

CHAIRMAN IVEY: Probably the great benefit of television has to be calculated in terms of total university productivity rather than in terms of individual professorial productivity. This means that in using TV we are going to have to rethink the role of the professor, who is a "tri-schizophrenic" of some sort, if there is such a thing: he does research, teaching, and certain other service jobs.

It might be well to think that we need professors specializing in one of the three or four roles they are currently playing. Some distinguished people would do research primarily and lecturing occasionally, either live or by kinescope. Others would work primarily with the students, assisting them in their learning processes, once those are adequately identified; and then we would have a third group of professors working on the informal level of the student community as counselors.

The use of television will have its greatest impact if we first define the different roles that need to be played in the university community and assign people to these roles in such a way as to use their talents most effectively in the entire university. I think that the professor has more to gain by this rethinking of his roles than does anybody else. He may think that television is something that threatens him, but if it were being used as we are discussing it, he would have more time for research and for doing that kind of teaching that is meaningful.

SHEPARD A. INSEL (San Francisco State College): Dr. Ivey, how far would you be willing to go to increase the possibility of students' initiating their own learning?

CHAIRMAN IVEY: If you accept the premise that learning has two dimensions (one is what the student can bring to the learning process through his inherited capabilities, and the other the characteristics that he acquires in terms of the behavior of learning), I feel that the center of gravity ought to be on the self-starting and initiation of the students, with the professors making the universal selections they have to, broadening student horizons, and helping them choose paths. This may be idealistic, but certainly no more wasteful of time than some of the methods we are using now.

H. BURR RONEY (University of Houston): Do you have any other points of view on this transition, Dr. Ivey?

CHAIRMAN IVEY: First, somebody is going to have to come forward who has vision and courage to plot a series of model universities which would be possible if televised instruction were used without reference to the present culture system. If the transition were made here and there, and the results were apparent, then each institution wanting to effect such a transition would have to gauge the tolerance of its constituency in terms of desirable moves toward this realization.

We have only nibbled at this problem. We haven't been looking at the university as a complete organization. We have said, "Let's raise academic standards." So we put in an honors course; that's only a value system inserted in the community of students. Somebody else says, "Let's try television." So we put in television, and it works in the same structure that previously was used and despised.

We have bits and pieces of approaches to the problem, but none of them is considering the university a total organism. This rethinking is badly needed, I believe, in terms of its implications for both teaching and finance. If it were done, I think that a lot of administrators would find that they could run a higher quality operation at a lower cost than now, and at the same time be spreading the university's services to all the students and to the community at large.

VERNON DAVIES (State College of Washington): I am wondering if there is need for research in that area of student response quite apart from what goes on while the courses are being televised. What kind of response takes place after class when the student is studying alone or with other students?

MR. BLAKE: It is a common observation in university life and in formal conferences that the hard work of learning doesn't go on in the papers that are read as much as it does in the three B's—bedroom, bathroom, and bars. That is where people do the testing-out of what they believe. Once in a while they speak to the person who said it in the first place and they may trample on it, but this is after a lot of thinking has gone on. You often sit around and talk with a book also. That's no good. There is a communication going on, but it doesn't have outside correcting and feedback. There is a tremendous amount of feedback that students take advantage of that is unrelated to what the professor does.

MR. MOEHLMAN: The French take care of that situation well; they give the graduate students a room they can go to any time. There they meet and talk over their problems with other graduate students. It is quite clear that American students have their ways of getting together too. We haven't studied this area of outside feedback very much.

WILLARD JOHNSON (United States National Student Association): The United States National Student Association has attempted to study the effect and impact of college culture, Dr. Ivey, on a climate of learning and the ability of students to move into an area of academic programming. We're interested in determining the level of student sophistication in terms of educational programming.

Many of you know that there has been resistance to this kind of programming on the part of student governments. I'm happy to find so many people on our side of the fence at this conference. NSA would be interested in making some kind of integrated study, using our own resources, in cooperation with those of you who might be able to tap it from the other side.

CHAIRMAN IVEY: I can offer you one university that would be interested in it. This is the key question I think we are facing: How much of the student learning takes place outside the classroom and under what circumstances? How can the classroom be used as a means of reinforcing it and vice versa? I think the NSA is putting us on the spot.

RICHARD I. EVANS (University of Houston): In a field study of open-circuit educational television viewing that we did under one of our grants from the Educational Television and Radio Center, we examined demographic and personality characteristics of viewers. We compared people who watch telecourses regularly with others who watch varying types of programs in educational television, and also with people who watch TV of any sort. There were few significant differences among these groups. Our study indicated that there is a great deal of incidental viewing. A lot of people who do not sign up for telecourses are watching us just the same. They seem to be highly motivated. They are watching as much as the average student and perhaps even more diligently.

Are our universities so selfish that they will design these courses for a hundred students who have signed up for them? If we are to assume that universities are humanitarian and have obligations to the public at large, I feel that our present approach misses the boat. All our tests are concerned with what is happening to the students enrolled in the courses; what about that incidental audience? We have a great chance to capitalize on our twenty-seven educational television stations to enrich the lives of thousands, many of whom may never before have been exposed to learning. This may be where a great positive cultural movement will come from.

MR. MOEHLMAN: This query raised by Mr. Evans is fundamental and we need this type of projection. It is possible to teach abstract ideas, and the general public is fascinated with them. We've done it in Houston, in Iowa, and elsewhere.

ANN SPINNEY (Fund for Adult Education): I am delighted to hear all these university and college people talking about expanding their services to the community. One thing bothers me, however: Is any special thought being given to those adults in the community who, even though they are high on the acceptance chart, might require a little different approach to education, whether on television or elsewhere? Perhaps the type of education they have acquired merely by being thirty or forty years of age might be something that could be used in planning programs for them.

ERNA GUNTHER (University of Washington): Going back to Mr. Evans' remarks, we have evidence in Seattle of the impact of our open courses. The Seattle Public Library has asked the university to let them know ahead of time what courses are being planned so that they can have on hand extra copies of books associated with these courses.

CHAIRMAN IVEY: In adjourning now, I'm giving you an additional minute for your luncheon discussions.

Practical Problems of Improving Televised Instruction

TUESDAY AFTERNOON, OCTOBER 22, 1957

Presiding: JOHN C. ADAMS

CHAIRMAN: This afternoon's session will concern itself with such questions as elements of experimental design, assessment of academic achievement, assessment of teachers, and evaluation of television recordings. All of this will be directed at the core of the teaching experience, rather than at gadgets or electronics. Our first panelist is Professor W. S. Ray of our host institution.

Elements of Experimental Design

WILLIAM S. RAY (Pennsylvania State University): Since conference time is precious, I will select only a few of the more difficult, important, and, I trust, interesting problems which have arisen in the instructional research program at Penn State. I shall highlight what seem to me to be the important aspects of a problem and then move on to another one.

The Penn State instructional research team always has been concerned with the measurement problem. Much time has been invested in the selection of measures from those already available, and we have developed and refined new tests and scales. Whenever it is practical, evidence of reliability is obtained, and the relations among the various response variables are determined. Experimentation can contribute to measurement; as a matter of fact, a certain kind of validation of measurement is achieved when it is demonstrated that reliable differences can be produced experimentally.

Control Factors in Measurement

Before going on to the discussion of problems of experimental design in instructional research, it is important that you know I am using the term *experiment* in a specific sense. I refer to a formal, planned study

110

in which the investigator imposes varied conditions on his subjects, observing the differences in behavior that result. The imposition of these conditions—often referred to as manipulation of an independent variable —is under the direct control of the researcher. Differences in behavior are revealed by the measurement of some particular response. These measures constitute the "dependent" variable.

There is good reason to emphasize this distinction between experimental and nonexperimental research. Experimental knowledge is important because it represents our capacity to control, in a very direct manner, the world in which we live. Harnessing nuclear energy, reducing the incidence of polio by inoculation, and selling breakfast cereals through advertising are instances of points of control. Experimental knowledge about the educational process is certainly of equal importance to us. The points of control in education must be discovered. Knowledge of these must take the place of unreliable inference, personal bias, and even tradition.

It may surprise you to learn that the choice of conditions to be employed in an experiment presents a problem. Consider a proposed experiment which is to evaluate the effectiveness of instruction via closed-circuit television. At first thought it may seem obvious that the experimental condition should be televised instruction, but what does this expression mean? Does it mean putting a camera and a microphone into a conventional classroom? Should the instructor be required to teach in a routine fashion as he has been teaching, or should he be permitted to revise his lectures to meet the challenge inherent in television?

What about demonstrations and visual aids? Should there be some adaptation of the course, beyond chalk and blackboard, to take advantage of the new medium? If adaptation is allowed, then the question is: How much? Should the adaptations be minor ones, or should there be a concentrated and sustained effort throughout the course? Should televised instruction be interpreted as covering the selection of a superior teacher with a flair for that particular task? How shall the students be accommodated? Should they be in a classroom with the instructor, or should instruction originate in a studio without students? Should students be assigned to large viewing rooms or to small ones?

The choice of conditions is made even more difficult when one tries to define a control situation. An ideal experiment would be one in which two or more groups of subjects were treated alike in all respects, save one, that one variation in treatment being the object of investigation. It is sometimes possible to establish conditions which come close to varying in only one respect; then, the choice of conditions is relatively uncomplicated. More often the experimental condition is complex, differing from any reasonable comparison condition in many particulars.

Consider the conditions which might be compared with televised instruction. Conventional, face-to-face classroom instruction comes to mind at once as a possibility; but what, specifically, do these words imply? Do they mean the run-of-the-mill kind of teaching that often takes place when a professor has been teaching routinely a bread-and-butter, lower-level course over many semesters, a course which may not interest or challenge him? Or should this instruction undergo extensive improvement? Is the instruction received by a group in the television originating room to be considered conventional and face to face? And when we say, "conventional, face to face," are we referring to a small class of twenty students, or to the large class of several hundred?

It is apparent that there is not just one comparison of interest to us as educators, but rather there are several. It is not likely that these several possibilities can be realized in a single study. Some priority must be established, emphasizing the limitations of a practical nature, or the interests of the university.

The choice of subjects usually is determined by the enrollment in the courses in which experiment is to be carried out. In our studies, almost without exception, the students who were enrolled in a course and who were available for assignment to the conditions of the experiment have been employed without further division into subpopulations. It is always an intriguing notion to the psychologist that the differences produced by the conditions of an experiment may vary with the characterics of the subjects used, and that when these subjects are pooled, differences between group averages may not be found. The reasonableness of this notion cannot be denied. Consequently, it is a matter of routine practice with us to compare the variances of the groups. When a given treatment does not produce constant, additive effects for all subjects, the variability of that group will be changed. By comparing group variances we avoid the difficulties of subdivision and answer, in a general fashion, the question as to whether treatment effects vary with the subjects.

For the most part, simple treatment plans have been employed in the Penn State research. Typically a design has incorporated one set of conditions, two to four in number. These conditions have been imposed on as many independent groups of subjects. The simpler treatment plans have provided the comparisons desired and at the same time have been quite manageable. There has been no reluctance to use more complex designs if they are needed. There has been rather a growing conviction that more comprehensive designs employing two or more sets of conditions may be desirable.

The Problems of Bias

The second problem is concerned with the unintended differences or biases which can be expected to affect every experiment and which cannot wholly be eliminated, nor even completely enumerated. Anticipated biases can be subjected to some degree of control. If two different methods of instruction are to be compared, it is imperative that the same instructor teach by both methods. Differences among the instructors employed may be large and the results of the experiment, if instructors as well as methods vary, may be seriously biased. Employing the same instructor in varied conditions requires corresponding classes scheduled at different times, a circumstance which may itself produce bias.

When a team of instructors is to be employed, it is tempting to divide the course into units, each being taught by one instructor, and to have the units taught in a different order from one condition to another. Although it would then be possible to have all the groups in the experiment taught at the same hour and by the same instructors, the problem of a bias being produced by the varied order of topics must be weighed.

In research on televised instruction, kinescopic recordings of courses makes it possible to use the same instructor with different classes at the same hour. We hope that, in the not too distant future, it will be feasible to make use of kinescopes on a limited scale in this fashion.

Bias may possibly result also when the same instructor varies his presentations in ways that are not intended by the research. Apart from his personal bias, however, we have been vexed in our experience by the spontaneous aberrations of an instructor in casual comments about the research. This may be an attempt at humor, but great care must be exercised so that students who are being treated differently will not become offended and thereby prejudice the experiment.

The student who serves as a subject in an experiment can be a source of bias. Students vary widely in interests, attitudes, traits, and abilities. The assigning of subjects to the conditions of an experiment is an operation of critical importance, for the bias that can accumulate in favor of one condition is tremendous. Certainly self-selection of a condition on the part of a student cannot be risked; this would yield results subject to an uninterpretable bias.

The only satisfactory solution is the assigning of students in random fashion to the several different conditions. Randomization, of course, does not ensure an unbiased comparison nor eliminate uncertainty from the final evaluation. It does, however, make possible the use of a statistical test of significance in arriving at a rigorous decision, in the sense that its probability of being in error is known. Random assignment of students to classes meeting at different hours brings another problem to the experiment. At Penn State we require a student who plans to take a course in which an experiment will be conducted to keep the two sequences open until he has been randomly assigned at the time of registration to one or the other sequence. Or we limit experimentation to those who can be randomly assigned to either sequence.

Randomization may distribute errors; it does not reduce them in magnitude. When information concerning differences among subjects is available, it is highly desirable to use such information to reduce the magnitude of these errors. Pretests of student subjects are administered, and these initial measures of differences are used in adjusting the final measures on the dependent variable. Thus, errors accounted for by the pretest are eliminated; those which remain are, in effect, randomized.

Evaluation and Interpretation

The third problem is that of evaluation and interpretation. Undoubtedly you know that statistical tests of significance are being employed universally in making decisions about the results of all kinds of experimental and nonexperimental research. These tests attempt to infer the general from the particular. There is no disputing the fact that statistical inference can be rigorous. Many of us believe, however, that it is being misused on a grand scale.

Certainly much disagreement concerning the use and misuse of statistics arises from the assumptions underlying them. There is no doubt as to the assumptions of familiar and widely used statistics. The problem is not what are the assumptions, but what function does knowing them serve. It is not the amount of statistical information possessed by the investigator, but the adequacy of the concept held by the investigator as to the implications of this information.

There are at least two ways in which tests of significance can be conceptualized, and a subtle but crucial distinction can be made between them. The first is represented by imaginary investigator A, who says, "The assumption of random sampling requires me to assign subjects to experimental conditions by a tested, mechanical device like a table of random numbers." The second concept is represented by investigator B. He says, "I know these are not random groups of subjects, but let me look at them as if they were and see what conclusions I would reach about the outcome of the experiment." Investigator A believes that the assumption should determine or regulate the conduct and evaluation of this experiment. His assumption is fulfilled in his operations. Investigator B believes the assumption should structure his view of the data. His assumption is contrary to fact.

It is a rare event today when an investigator does not use statistical inference. Descriptive statistics often are looked on with disdain, even though they constitute the most appropriate and defensible means of dealing with certain kinds of data. Everywhere one observes the compulsive and indiscriminate use of tests of significance. It is apparent that some investigators would rather be wrong than unconventional. At Penn State we are not taking this position. We are committed to what we regard as the sensible and reasoned use of statistical inference in the evaluation of our research.

CHAIRMAN: Thank you, Professor Ray. Our second paper on the general theme of assessment of academic achievement is by Henry Dyer, vice-president, Research Division of the Educational Testing Service.

Assessment of Academic Achievement

HENRY S. DYER (Educational Testing Service): What do we mean by "academic achievement"? To me it means two things: (1) the identifiable operations a student is expected to perform on the materials of a course and (2) the difference between the number and kinds of operations he can perform at the beginning of a course and the number and kinds of operations he can perform at the end of a course.

"Identifiable operations" and "difference" are the key terms in this definition of academic achievement. By emphasizing operations I am asserting that it is what a student actually does that counts. I want to think of achievement in terms of transitive verbs with objects—verbs like infer, generalize, recall, compare, analyze, evaluate, organize, criticize, and so on; and I want to be sure that I can identify these operations by referring to specific tasks that require them. By emphasizing the difference between what a student does at the beginning and what he does at the end of a course, I am asserting that achievement is a dynamic, not a static, concept. It is what has happened between then and now, not just what is happening now.

According to this definition, the assessment of academic achievement is not something that can be accomplished merely by going out and buying a test. It is a process in which the teacher responsible for a course must himself be the major participant. He may be able to get help from outside tests; he may find that the professional testers can give him useful ideas and help him to develop an effective strategy; but the real substance of the assessment job rests with him.

The first step for the teacher is to get a clear idea of just what he is trying to have his students achieve. What specific operations does he want them to perform at the end of the course that they cannot perform now? I say this is the obvious first step, but I am impressed by its almost universal omission. Almost invariably college teachers are more concerned with what *they* are going to do rather than with what *their students* are going to do. The prospect of doing it in front of a TV camera is hardly calculated to reduce the teacher's interest in his own performance.

Courses are organized. Television equipment is installed. Instructors plan how to present their material and perform in front of a camera. The show goes on with much activity. But nobody seems to have given much attention to what it is really all about. Nobody has tried to write down in the syllabus—if there is one—just what it is that students are supposed to be able to do as a result of having been exposed to the instructor and the syllabus. Oh, there is a hope that the students will be impressed, that they will learn something, remember something from the course, and in a vague sort of way it is felt that this will do them good; that is, it will make better thinkers or better citizens of them. But there is very little disposition to get down to cases, specifying what kinds of student performance are deemed to reflect better thinking or better citizenship.

This is hardly surprising. Stating the goals of a course in such terms takes more energy and imagination than most professors have time for; there is your practical problem. It seems to me that we must find the time required for carrying out this first step, which provides the necessary base for any sound assessment program.

The goals of achievement fall into three broad classes: informational goals, proficiency goals, and attitudinal goals. The informational goals refer to those items that students are expected to know and give forth on demand by the time they have completed the course. It would appear that these can readily be described by listing the topics, subtopics, and sub-subtopics that the course is expected to cover. But this is only half of the story. A fact in human knowledge is not just the name of something standing all by itself; it is a subject and a predicate. It is not just the name "sodium"; it is the sentence "Sodium is a metal."

Most teachers would, I think, disown the idea that the only kinds of goals they have in mind for their courses are informational. They would argue quite properly that information is one of the goals, and a necessary one, but certainly not one of ultimate importance. They argue, but their arguments are too often confounded by their own examinations which demand facts and facts only. One of the hoariest criticisms brought against objective tests is that they test only for factual information, while essay tests get at the higher aspects of learning. This would be a cogent criticism except for two things: first, a well-constructed objective test need not be limited to the measurement of factual information; and second, essay tests are too frequently graded solely by counting the number of relevant facts that each student churns up.

Most of what I think of as "the higher aspects of learning" are contained in what I have called the proficiency goals of academic achievement; that is, proficiency in various kinds of skills, both manual and mental—manipulative, problem-solving, evaluative, and organizational skills. Taken together, they add up to effective thinking and sound execution. But to be useful as guides in the assessment of achievement, they must not be taken together; they must be elaborated in considerable detail and expressed in terms of the multitude of different kinds of specific tasks a student is expected to perform, and in terms of the specific kinds of operations he must follow in performing them.

Unless the proficiency goals are elaborated in this fashion, they may be too easily overlooked or forgotten. There have recently been a number of experiments in the teaching of a laboratory science with and without actual laboratory experience. The typical setup is for an experimental group to receive instruction by television or otherwise, with demonstrations of laboratory work substituting for experiments performed by the students themselves. Control groups are given the conventional laboratory work.

Experiments of this kind have, on the surface, appeared to show that laboratory experience contributes nothing to the student's achievement. But this result could have been predicted in advance in view of the fact that the proficiency goals peculiar to laboratory instruction were overlooked from the outset. The only measures of achievement used have been those related mainly to informational goals that have little or nothing to do with what goes on in a laboratory. Under these conditions, the finding of no difference in achievement between the two groups is essentially meaningless, since the relevant variable has not been taken into consideration.

It is admittedly no easy matter to define all proficiency goals in terms of student performance. One can flounder in trying to analyze the types of performance that form the components of creative thinking or skill in evaluative judgment, with the result that nobody has yet been able to produce a satisfactory method for assessing achievement along these lines. The problem, however, has been attacked in some interesting ways; and in the course of time it can be licked, provided teachers will get down to cases and define what they really mean.

When we consider attitudinal goals, we are talking about intangibles. Everybody applauds these goals but nobody seems to know what to do about them. How do you define such goals as love of music, a sense of social responsibility, or enthusiasm for abstract ideas in such a way that you will recognize them when you see them? How does a student demonstrate that he appreciates good literature? We have our dodges on matters of this sort; we count the books he takes from the library, we measure the amount of leisure time he gives to reading, we engage him in conversation, trying to judge from the amount of fervor in his voice how far along the scale of appreciation he has come. We ask him outright on some sort of rating schedule how well he likes Shakespeare or T. S. Eliot. But we know full well that these devices are based on exceedingly tenuous inferences that in our hearts we do not trust.

An exception to the generally unsatisfactory attempts to get at student attitudes took place here at Penn State. You have already heard about it, the case where students were given generous samples of both televised and conventional instruction and then were permitted a genuine choice as to which type they would take the remainder of the semester. The general principle is clear: you define attitudes in terms of live decisions that make a genuine difference in what an individual will or will not do.

I have spent what may seem a disproportionate amount of time discussing the goals of achievement and have left little time to talk about actual ways of assessing progress toward those goals—a fault of those of us who are in the testing business. As I have suggested earlier, teachers are busy people who are unlikely to find the time they need to work out the goals of their instruction, or to devise valid measures for assessing achievement. What are some practical compromises?

Although one is unlikely to find any standard test that fits the goals of a particular course or school exactly, by studying such tests question by question, the teacher may find one that comes reasonably close. This question-by-question approach also helps in deciding which questions should be eliminated in assessing the performance of one's own students.

Standard tests, when they can be adapted, have two important advantages. First, a great deal of care has been lavished on the preparation and try-out of each question to make sure that it is unambiguous, that it is an effective discriminator between good and poor students, and that it is of the right level of difficulty for the group at which it is aimed.

Second, two or more parallel forms of a standard test are usually available, so that one has at his disposal the means for accomplishing a highly important part of the assessment task; namely, that of measuring the student's performance twice—at the beginning of the course and again at the end.

Most tests being set up today emphasize proficiency as well as informational goals. They are made up of questions which require the student to perform various mental operations well beyond the simple one of remembering facts. They are getting at problem-solving and reasoning processes of various sorts.

If a teacher wants to measure those aspects of achievement peculiar to his own instruction, he must supplement standard tests with tests of his own devising. To this teacher I would suggest two guiding texts: *Taxonomy of Educational Objectives,* by Benjamin S. Bloom and D. R. Krathwohl;[1] and *General Education: Explorations in Evaluation,* by Paul S. Dressel and Lewis B. Mayhew.[2]

The multiple-choice test, popular though it may be, has by its own nature some severe limitations. Far be it for me to cast aspersions on this method of getting at students' higher mental processes, but the tendency to think only in terms of these paper-and-pencil tests is holding back the development of new and better methods for assessing educational achievement.

[1] New York: Longmans, Green & Co., 1956.
[2] Washington: American Council on Education, 1954.

To break away from this mode of thinking, we should consider how some of the situational tests used by psychologists can be adapted to the measurement of academic achievement. These are still in an experimental stage of development and have technical problems, but they seem to have the potentiality for sizing up aspects of human behavior that can never be reached by paper-and-pencil devices.

At the Educational Testing Service we have worked up a situational test in group problem-solving which appears to tell us not only how efficiently a group of students can solve a problem, but also how well they have learned to work together, how they respond to group control, how they react to each other. It is this sort of approach that will carry us closer to an adequate assessment of what I have called the attitudinal goals of achievement.

Experiments with televised instruction should be conducted in two phases, pilot and formal. The pilot phase, run on small groups of students for at least a year, should be used for two purposes: (1) to get experience with instructional methods and, as far as possible, to discover and remove the "bugs" in these methods; and (2) to develop and try out all the means by which academic achievement is to be assessed when the experiment enters the formal phase.

Too often large-scale experiments have started out with little consideration of the methodological difficulties that may crop up and with no clearly worked out plans for evaluating the outcomes. The result is that much of what is being done leaves us with only confusion and controversy at the end.

I think it is possible to develop plans and instruments for assessing achievement concurrently with developing techniques for producing achievement. It requires only patience and a willingness to make sure before plunging in.

CHAIRMAN: Thank you, Mr. Dyer. Mr. Erickson, have you a question?

CLIFFORD G. ERICKSON (Chicago City Junior College): What did Mr. Ray mean when he said that using the method of variance and covariance to equate groups would eliminate the randomization element in the randomization design?

MR. RAY: I suggested that, when you have random groups and a pretest of student ability, it is possible to have the dependent variable adjusted with respect to the pretest, and that this has two desired consequences. One is that it reduces the magnitude of errors: it eliminates those errors that would be accounted for by the pretest, and the remaining errors are, in effect, randomized.

My complaint was directed toward those techniques of matching which eliminate randomization. There are certain matching techniques which do not eliminate randomization, but restrict it in a fashion which we can take account of in the analysis. For example, the randomized block design is the kind of design in which the restriction placed on randomization is considered in terms of a loss of degrees of freedom. Matching of group means and variances, on the other hand, destroys randomization and, while it is intended to increase precision, actually leads to less precise evaluation.

MR. DYER: Don't you criticize using a matched-group technique in any case?

MR. RAY: The randomized block design is something referred to as a matched-group design, but in that usage the word "group" means something different from the matching of experimental groups on the basis of means and variances. If I want to do an experiment, it might make sense for me to choose subjects as much alike as I can. If I have three conditions, I choose three subjects as similar as possible, assigning them randomly to the three conditions.

This constitutes a randomized block, sometimes referred to as a matched group. I need replication of that. I need another triplicate and still another and still another in which I have attempted to establish a matched group and randomized the individuals within this group of conditions.

This reduces the errors affecting the experiment because I am a single, small error; these individuals are chosen to be as much alike as I can get them on the basis of measurement. When you take two groups and juggle them back and forth until you get the means nicely lined up, there is no statistical model. There isn't any function which describes the variabilities of means treated like that. It doesn't exist. I couldn't begin to tell you how the differences between means would vary with that kind of behavior on the part of an investigator.

We plan to carry out an experiment in mathematics next semester in which an experienced teacher on television will be compared with graduate assistants teaching small sections. One very real problem that we ran into was the welter of feelings pro and con with respect to educational TV; many of our colleagues were not willing to accept a comparison of the experienced teacher on television with some less experienced teacher instructing by conventional methods. They wanted the method checked out.

RICHARD I. EVANS (University of Houston): There is more than that to the problem. There is a bias-sampling operation required. We know that certain students will gladly take a course by TV; others won't. Even while holding the instructor constant, the students' motivation—drive— has to be accounted for; one student is taking the course by TV because he wants to, and the other student who is biased against instruction by television will react in a natural way. The real impact of TV will be different. There are other variables when instruction is held constant, such as motivation variables, and so on.

MR. RAY: As I pointed out, we have used students in the course who could be assigned randomly to the groups. This allows for the possibility that the treatment does not affect all students in the same way. For example, the student who likes the idea of TV may improve. The student who doesn't like television may go down. The fact is that we don't have any evidence that this is so.

CHAIRMAN: Our third speaker, who will continue this development of practical problems in improving televised instruction, is Mr. H. H. Remmers of Purdue University.

Assessment of Teachers

H. H. REMMERS (Educational Reference Bureau, Purdue University): The coming flood of students in colleges, the parallel growing shortage of qualified teachers, and the advent of television constitute the setting of my assignment here. The basic problem is that of teaching larger numbers of students with relatively fewer teachers. The problem is complicated by "revolutionary changes . . . in American education," to quote from the report of the President's Committee on Education Beyond the High School. Speaking of an unparalleled demand by Americans for more and better education, the Committee's recommendations are:

that there be vigorous and objective exploration and application by faculties and administrators of methods of increasing the effectiveness and productiveness of the teacher, including electronic devices such as television, instructional procedures which place on the student more responsibility for self-education, adaptation of the sizes of classes to accommodate most efficiently their varying objectives, the lessening of nonteaching duties of faculty members, and the provision of assistants for duties which take the professor's time without utilizing his highest talents.[3]

The Committee also recommends that graduate schools "make special effort to devise ways of creating interest in teaching on the part of their best students and . . . devise new programs for the preparation of college teachers."[4]

Implicit in these recommendations are the problems of assessing teachers, both practicing and prospective. Narrowly interpreted, this makes my assignment in the present context a discussion of assessing teachers with respect to their effectiveness in teaching by means of television. Fortunately for a broader interpretation, Mr. Kumata, in his *Inventory of Instructional Television Research,* cites a study by Kelly and Conrad, in which they conclude that good classroom teachers are also good television teachers.

While there is much talk of experimentation with television, Kumata observes that actual performance has far outstripped evaluation in instructional television programming, a fact which he attributes chiefly to a "tendency for research to be an afterthought to instructional television efforts." Except in a few studies, he finds a true partnership between performance and evaluation does not exist.

I shall not involve myself in the controversy between those who see in television a major part of the solution of our vexing problems of higher education and those who see it as another audio-visual gimmick of slight value as an aid to education. I have no doubt that with or without experimental validation, television will be extensively used.

Taking our cue from Kelly and Conrad's conclusion that good classroom teachers are also good television teachers and from Kumata's note on the lack of dependence upon research in other fields, let us look at the problems of teacher assessment.

What do we know about teacher effectiveness? Unfortunately, the literature available on this subject is inconclusive. After reviewing this wealth of literature, Barr, who has spent a significant fraction of his professional life carrying on research on teacher effectiveness, concludes:

[3] President's Committee on Education Beyond the High School, *Second Report to the President* (Washington: Government Printing Office, 1957), p. 18.
[4] *Ibid.*

"The ultimate measure of teacher effectiveness . . . will be found in changes produced in the pupils under his direction." But a practical procedure for measuring has not yet been developed. The development of more adequate means of measuring the total changes in pupils will contribute to the success of this approach.

What Barr said two decades ago requires no essential emendation today. Evaluating teachers through student changes involves the problem of ensuring that any such changes are due solely to the influence of a particular teacher and not to other teachers or other factors. Changes in students may come about through one, several, or all of a variety of factors. Some of them are: the general ability of the students; special mental abilities of the students related to particular types of achievement; past educational experience; instructional material available to the teacher; students' socioeconomic and cultural background; teacher's teaching load and extracurricular duties; the general attitude toward work characterizing an individual student, class, or school; the quality of instruction in other areas of the curriculum; the student's achievement of valid educational objectives other than those measured by the test or other devices that are used (the teacher's real worth and influence may not be reflected in student information and knowledge as much as in student attitudes and adjustment); the effect of other mass media of communication; the effect of associating with peers; and differences in teaching objectives among teachers being compared.

In valid experimentation all such factors need to be controlled. Thus, while it is a simple matter to conceptualize teacher effectiveness in the abstract, its operational definition is not only difficult, but will vary from person to person.

Teaching and learning represent highly complex communication systems. We need answers to some of these questions in the light of the foregoing observations. What types of student achievements are found in classes taught by different teachers? For what kinds of students are such achievements shown? How are the achievements of different kinds of students related to different conditions and environments? What does the teacher do that is related to the various kinds of achievements demonstrated by students in various kinds of situations and environments? What kinds of teacher experiences and personality factors are related directly to the kind and quality of teacher behavior revealed in relation to students? What processes of selection and education develop teachers with personality factors and behavior patterns shown to be associated with effective teaching behavior?[5]

With improved experimental designs and modern electronic data-processing machines, the inconclusiveness of previous research can, I believe, be changed to give us firmly established conclusions, if we are really willing to pay the price in time and money.

A second approach is to measure and evaluate attributes of the teacher assumed to be related to teacher effectiveness in producing desirable changes in students. These characteristics of teachers (knowledge, skills, attitudes) can be measured by a large variety of available tests, attitude scales, rating scales, and other observational techniques.

At the college level the only relatively widely used technique has been student ratings of instructors. This technique has constituted a kind of feedback often desired by teachers. Having some three decades ago perpetrated such a rating scale and having the opportunity as well as the will to experiment, I reached a number of conclusions:

A considerable number of those who have used student ratings believe this procedure is useful for facilitating the educational process; knowledge of student opinions and attitudes leads to the improvement of the teacher's personality and educational procedures; there is some evidence that student opinion is positively related to achievement as measured by examination of students; if twenty-five or more student ratings are averaged, they have as much reliability as the presently available educational and mental tests.

Some other conclusions are: Grades of students are not in general closely related to their ratings of the teacher; while the effect on student ratings of a generalized "halo effect" attitude toward the teacher has not been isolated, it apparently does not exist to an extent sufficient to invalidate the ratings of separate aspects of teaching methods and of the course. Evidence indicates that students discriminate reliably for different aspects of the teacher's personality and of the course, and between different instructors and courses.

There is little, if any, evidence showing that a relationship exists between student ratings of teachers and the judged difficulty of the course. In a given institution there exist wide and important departmental differences in effectiveness of teaching as judged by student opinion. The sex

[5] For those who wish to obtain answers to some of these questions and others in this problem area, see Donald T. Campbell, "Factors Relevant to the Validity of Experiments in Social Settings," *Psychological Bulletin,* July 1957, pp. 297–312.

of the student raters and of the teacher bears little or no relationship to the ratings. The cost in time and money of obtaining student opinion is low. The teacher's popularity in extraclass activities is not appreciably related to student ratings. No research has been published invalidating the use of student opinion as a criterion of teaching effectiveness.

Teachers with less than five years' experience tend to be rated lower than those with more than eight years of teaching behind them. Whether the rating student be a freshman, sophomore, junior, or senior has no effect on his ratings, except that those of graduate students tend to be higher than those of undergraduates. Students are more favorable to student ratings than are instructors, but more instructors than students have noticed improvement in their teaching as a result of student ratings. Mature alumni of ten years' standing agree substantially with on-campus students in their evaluation of teachers. Students agree substantially with the teachers' colleagues in their rating of teachers as teachers.

Television has made an extreme change in the arcanum that has been the college classroom so far as nonstudents are concerned. The teacher on TV is now operating in a goldfish bowl, where his actions can be observed, classified, interpreted, and related to student behavior—with, we hope, the required experimental controls. Television obviously gives us a first-rate opportunity to study actual teachers as well as prospective candidates for college teaching. Nor will the bulk of the observing be limited to students; "experts" can now be brought in to help in this complex matter.

If we now revert to the original need to find ways and means of teaching more students with relatively fewer teachers, then other possibilities exist besides the use of closed-circuit television viewed in classrooms.

On the premise that social and other activities on a campus are educationally valuable, college dormitory rooms might all be equipped with television sets, so that students could be taught a sizable part of their curriculum in their rooms insofar as TV is able to make this possible. Enough money would be saved on classrooms that would thus not be needed to equal or exceed the cost of the television receivers.

With subscription television having just been given the green light for a three-year trial period, the instructional programs could be broadcast by this method, and students' fees for such instruction could, in effect, be collected a lesson at a time. This would also serve as an automatic "attendance" record.

Quite possibly the teaching machine devised by B. F. Skinner of

Harvard University, that was displayed at the meetings of the American Psychological Association last September, can be adapted for all curricular content that can be presented in the symbols of language in print. Most factual and conceptual content of present college curricula could conceivably be "taught" under the optimum learning conditions that Skinner claims for his device.

The visual aids to learning that we call books are going to continue to be available, despite dire forebodings voiced by some educational Cassandras that TV will produce generations of illiterates. There is very persuasive evidence that those who complete correspondence courses generally do so with a high degree of achievement. Most of the cognitive and some affective functions believed to be developed by college curricula can be implemented by this means, possibly again at significant financial saving to higher education.

What is highly valued in a culture will be assiduously sought after by people in the culture. To the extent that our culture truly values higher education, it will find ways and means to achieve it.

CHAIRMAN: Thank you, Mr. Remmers.

At this point, we expected to have an address by Dr. Harry Newburn of the Educational Television and Radio Center. I am sorry to have to report that Dr. Newburn is ill in the Penn State infirmary. Even so, we shall hear his paper. It will be read by Glenn Starlin, who for some time was associated with Dr. Newburn at the center.

Evaluation of Televised Recordings

D. GLENN STARLIN (University of Oregon): When a program is recorded on film or kinescope, it attains a semipermanent character. The chances that it will be used again now range from fair to good. This makes evaluation a necessity, even an obligation. The problem of selection of educational materials of every sort is troublesome. Teachers and administrators are swamped with pamphlets, free lists, books, films, and now kinescope recordings.

The Educational Television and Radio Center at Ann Arbor has more than an academic interest in this problem. Already it has a backlog of something like a thousand hours of educational programming, which must be assumed to have considerable educational value. Some materials are dated, others not too well produced, according to present standards, and some probably miss the mark in educational terms. The great bulk of the material, nevertheless, is educationally sound, its scholarship excellent, its production competent and often creative. Its technical quality is more than acceptable.

The following criteria, on which assessment of recorded programs should be based, is suggested by the Educational Television and Radio Center:

1. Does the program have an enduring educational value? It is not always easy to answer this question categorically. A discussion of the 1956 presidential election may be hopelessly dated in terms of its original topical interest, but it may have acquired value as a historical document.

Naturally, there is the question of content obsolescence. In this year of Sputnik and Asian flu, the pace of change in science and medicine needs no reminder. Scholars in the social sciences and humanities also remind us that their fields are far from static. Good teaching, however, leaves open the door for scholarship and recent finds. This is true of the high-quality teaching on most of our educational television programs. Enduring educational values are more likely to exist in programs which deal with important ideas, issues, or problems. It makes some sense to say that excellent teaching and sound scholarship furnish controls against content obsolescence.

2. Does the program have a measurable educational impact? Broadcasters must take this rather largely on faith, but when the program is preserved for formal educational distribution, this becomes a key question. We believe too little of this type of program research has taken place. Such a measure of educational impact should be done on three levels:

a) Content gain: Here, we have reference to no more than the measure of academic achievement based on the identifiable substantive points in the program. Written tests are implied.

b) Consequence: Clearly attitudinal or behavioral change due to a single program is likely to be limited. The consequences of any course or program series in this regard are a long-term, cumulative matter. Effective learning, however, implies involvement or participation. We should try to discover points of peak interest, strong negative reactions, and intentions as to follow-up—such as telling someone about the program, organizing a discussion, reading a book, asking questions—or we should try to determine in other ways in what degree the viewer has been an active rather than a passive participant. In assessing such efforts, subjective rating scales, depth interviews, or group discussions might all have their role.

c) *Check of production techniques in relation to learning:* Interesting problems arise at this point. For example, the center has a series called, *People Are Taught To Be Different.* It is sound anthropology presented by a qualified professor. However, certain concepts are represented or reinforced by modern dance sequences, spelling out the concept visually. Do these interesting dances contribute or detract from the academic objectives of the series?

Perhaps from the foregoing remarks you can appreciate the degree of concern with program research that is felt by the Educational Television and Radio Center. Financial grants have been awarded to Michigan State University, University of Illinois, Syracuse University, and University of Wisconsin for special studies in this research area.

3. *Is there a place for the program in the curricula of the schools or colleges?* Curriculum placement can be casual, haphazard, and amateurish. Just how much help is it when a bibliography, a pamphlet index, or a film guide says, "Program X, H.S. Level. Good for social studies. Girls and boys will enjoy equally."

Placement must be entrusted to professors, not just in curriculum but in special areas of curriculum. Assessment of program should include identification of learning objectives, content emphasis, and precise spots in the school program where it is useful. This should be as specific as a unit or topic in a given course. Furthermore, the rating should give the teacher real leads as to planning. Will the program merely enrich or diversify the approach? Will it basically instruct? Will it do the main job of developing a concept or presenting a coherent instruction of substance?

At the Educational Television and Radio Center, the objective of our professional screening is to assess the material's value as an educational resource for our schools and colleges. Actually the processes should be reversed and this type of analysis should be made prior to production of the film or kinescope. That is our special aim. Beyond that, what we want to know is how we can best adapt this electronic teaching tool, which we call television, to the learning process; we want to make optimum use of the new method of providing learning experiences for the educational growth of people.

CHAIRMAN: Thank you, Mr. Starlin. Please convey our thanks and best wishes to Harry Newburn.

The four papers you have just heard are now open for general discussion.

DALE B. HARRIS (University of Minnesota): I would like to reflect a bit on this "no significant difference," which is a finding of thirty or forty years' venerability in educational research as applied to methodology. Educators have been damned repeatedly for concentrating on methodology. Therefore, it is interesting to reflect that we feel so driven in our present studies to focus on methodology rather than on the variance in students. I think our research is demonstrating that the bulk of the variance is in student performance and not among methods. Some of that is motivation, and some is cultural background.

NEAL E. MILLER (Yale University): There is a point I would like to make in relation to the comparison between the instructor's teaching on television and his teaching in the classroom. I suspect that his effectiveness in the nontelevision class was improved considerably as a result of all the effort he put in to organizing his TV instruction.

RICHARD A. WATERMAN (Wayne University): We have run into some trouble at Wayne trying to get permission to use visual material published in several prominent magazines. We were developing an open-circuit, noncredit course and wrote to the editors for permission to use this material. They turned us down.

ARMAND L. HUNTER (Michigan State University): Since you were going to use the material on open-circuit and for educational purposes, you didn't have to check with editors or seek clearance in the first place. You won't run into any problems in using such material as long as you identify the source. For clarification, let me refer you to Dr. Fred Seibert, who has investigated and written a statement of copyright and clearance for television and broadcast purposes of educational and instructional material. You can secure this mimeographed pamphlet by writing to Dr. Seibert at Michigan State's School of Journalism.

Panel Discussion of Significant Concepts of Televised Instruction

CHAIRMAN: The next order of business is the presentation of five papers relating to the topic, "Significant Concepts of Televised Instruction." The first speaker is Dr. Dale B. Harris of the University of Minnesota.

Problems of Long-Range Outcome of TV Education—
Panel Discussion

MR. HARRIS: There is little doubt that as numbers of students increase, many colleges will be forced into the large-class system quite generally. There is also little doubt that closed-circuit television can handle twelve hundred students much more effectively in a visual manner than can a lecturer at the head of a large auditorium.

Television instruction up to now has concentrated on the formal lecture. While some circles believe that the lecture is one of the least effective educational procedures, I believe that it can be greatly improved by television, becoming once again the well-organized, disciplined experience it was a couple of generations ago.

Television instruction forces attention to the objectives of higher education. We must develop conviction concerning our teaching, knowing whether our goals are liberal, general, or technical. We must avoid any temptation to engage in the sensational techniques or gadgetry of commercial television. We must give serious thought to all education and to all means for informing and edifying the citizen.

A week or so ago, Walter Lippmann observed that the real demand of the new Soviet satellite on the United States is not that we attempt to outpace the U.S.S.R., but that we examine our own culture and its values to see why we have fallen behind in advancing the frontiers of knowledge. Just what value do we place on learning, the university, and the person of the teacher in our comfortable, appliance-centered and consumption-oriented age?

As teachers most of us value the question, the discussion, and the postclass conference as proof of interaction with students. We know, however, that a student may be interacting vigorously with us, though never twitching an eyebrow. Two devices for investigating covert participation, which this speaker has not yet seen discussed, are the content analysis of student notebooks in TV and control sections, and the use of "interaction sheets," which pose questions to the student and permit him to raise questions with the instructor to be analyzed after each session.

In another dozen years freshmen will be coming into college with experience in television instruction in every grade they have passed through. Some problems need consideration because of the cumulative effects of experience. Twenty or more years of the discussion and planning technique used throughout the elementary and high school years have developed college students facile at posing and discussing problems and in handling knotty issues in the student forum. Where students are permitted to do so, these techniques carry into the college classroom. Observers from abroad remark on the great skill of American youth in discussion.

What will be the outcome of a trend in education that may encourage greater passivity? Should this become true of TV instruction, the outcome might add to the reported mediocrity which is presumed to characterize contemporary culture. I note three problems that need attention from the point of view of both speculation and direct research: What will be the effect of bringing into education a technique that is firmly established as entertainment in the mind of the child? If master teachers are used to carry the lecturing burden, what will be the long-range effect on students of better and fewer teachers? What will be the effect on the student of increased exposure to verbal symbols, with some reduction in the manipulation of materials?

Every child who views television today gains a rich stock of words and phrases descriptive of personality and character. He is exposed to psychological dramas, real and unreal, of good quality and bad. Will we give him the necessary background of direct experience so that in his years of higher education he is more than a glib verbalist? Will he be able to react with personal meaning to the great drama, the great literature, the great issues of man's spiritual and intellectual quests?

CHAIRMAN: Thank you, Dr. Harris. Our second speaker is James C. Olson.

What Will Encourage Faculty Acceptance?—
Panel Discussion (continued)

JAMES C. OLSON (University of Nebraska): Assuming adequate funds and a high order of administrative imagination, the colleges and universities will never be able to take full advantage of the great potential of television unless the members of their faculties accept it as a legitimate and worthwhile teaching tool, exhibiting a determination to use it for all it is worth.

Faculty members as a group probably have been exposed to television less than most groups in our society, and the reasons why antennae have been slow to appear on academic homes are not entirely economic. Many who have been exposed to television are inclined to equate it with the trash which flickers across the nation's television screens too many hours a day. Even those who take advantage of the considerable quantity of worthwhile programs available on the commercial channels refuse to admit that the medium has any utility for teaching. Finally, those who admit that it has utility for teaching are inclined to limit its usefulness to an extension of the institution's primary mission rather than to an implementation of it.

Scholars are essentially conservative in their approach to teaching. Appreciative of the intrinsic importance of their subjects, they tend to continue methods which have worked fairly well in the past, to eschew new methods, new devices, and new techniques in the rather well-substantiated fear that they may detract from, rather than facilitate, the presentation of their material, or at best waste time, and have as their sole virtue the fact that they have not been tried before.

This conservatism, wisely exercised, has served to stay the hands of those who, if given free rein, would deflect our educational institutions from their established mission by too much tinkering with our teaching. Willfully exercised, however, it has degenerated into reaction, which has prevented our educational institutions from fulfilling their obligations to a free society.

The utility of television, even of the commercial variety, in education beyond the classroom has been dramatically and repeatedly demonstrated. Its utility in classroom teaching likewise is an established fact. What is needed now is a general acceptance of this fact and the will to act upon it so that colleges and universities may make full use of the technological advance that offers them their best chance of fulfilling their obligations in these days of mounting enrollments and costs and shortages of adequately prepared teachers.

I do not know what will produce faculty acceptance. It will require a high order of administrative leadership to convince the conservative and restrain the radical, and to demonstrate to our faculties that in television we have a powerful instrument to assist us in doing the job we know must be done.

An important aspect of this leadership will be the establishment of satisfactory methods by which faculty members who teach by television may be compensated. Teaching by TV, at least in the present state of art, is hard, demanding work; and if teaching is to continue to hold those satisfactions that will draw our best minds to it, this must be meaningfully recognized. The all-too-frequent practice of considering work in television as justifiable overload is wholly unsatisfactory. Compensation by means of reduced loads seems desirable in theory, but in practice it poses many problems, particularly at the departmental level, which make it unworkable. Direct monetary compensation is always attractive, but if teaching loads are based upon producing the optimum effectiveness of the teacher-scholar, one might question the desirability of providing for overload by temptation.

This leads perhaps to the most important of the leadership tasks required—that of devising satisfactory formulae for integrating teaching by TV into the total teaching program. The demonstrated effectiveness of television in nonclassroom teaching should make it possible for many institutions to extend their services in this area, but this very effectiveness will make it even more imperative than ever before that administrations come to grips with the problem of deciding what portion of their financial and faculty resources they can devote to this activity. In the area of classroom teaching, the nature of television will make it more imperative than ever before that faculties and administrations do more basic thinking than they have about what really is important in education.

Teaching by television is no panacea for the ills—present and prospective—of American education, but for certain of these ills it is so specific a remedy that the doctors will be well advised to learn how to use it.

CHAIRMAN: Thank you, Mr. Olson. Our next paper is that of Vice-President J. W. Ashton.

Adult Education—Panel Discussion (continued)

J. W. ASHTON (Indiana University): Although there is great stress currently on experimenting with teaching by closed-circuit television in an effort to meet the needs of the increasing numbers of students, we should not forget that one of the greatest potentialities of educational television is in the education of adults. Here is a great challenge to educators who are working in television.

With the steady growth in leisure time, except among the managerial and professional classes, and the general spread of the concept of continuing education beyond formal schooling, the opportunity to develop educational programs over television becomes momentous for educators. In all our hurry to get thousands of students on the end of a coaxial cable, we must not neglect this increasingly large outside audience with a desire for improving their understanding of the world in which they live.

To teach such an audience with the television transmitter is not always easy. The university set in a large metropolitan center has a readily available audience if it can develop programs that arouse interest. An institution like Indiana University, however, located in a community of about 30,000, with the nearest city fifty miles away, must consider carefully ways and means of best utilizing its resources and extending its audience potential. It has seemed unwise for us, as a state-supported institution, to develop programs for that small segment of the state that our equipment could reach. Instead we have worked with the local commercial station and later with most of the other commercial stations in the state.

Our basic problem, in terms of both our educational and our public relations interests, is to provide substantial service to the citizens of our state. This is the more important for us in that we have a system of university centers scattered strategically throughout Indiana, offering two years of college work plus a small amount of graduate work in selected fields. We believe that this work can be reinforced by effective television teaching. Our problems, then, have been to extend our instruction across the state and to provide faculty time for developing educational programs.

We have had less trouble in reaching wide areas than in meeting the faculty time problem. Through a grant from the Fund for the Advancement of Education, the university procured kinescope equipment; this has enabled us to circulate among the major TV stations of the state kinescopes of the best programs prepared by our radio-television staff. This may be expanded as time goes on and our resources increase. At first we shall probably use noncredit courses for this network, but we hope that credit courses may be offered eventually.

We have arranged for release from regular teaching time those teachers who prepare series of TV broadcasts. But our real problem is to persuade departmental chairmen and some of the administrative staff that the preparation of these educational TV programs represents a substantial contribution to teaching and scholarship.

In short, teaching by television at Indiana University has yet to become academically respectable. There is still a real problem of making clear the creative and scholarly possibilities of effective television programming for teaching.

CHAIRMAN: Thank you, Mr. Ashton. Our fourth paper is by Professor David S. Brody.

Teacher Preparation—Panel Discussion (continued)

DAVID S. BRODY (Oregon College of Education): A great deal of the emphasis on the potential contribution of television instruction has stemmed from a concern for the most effective way of permitting existing teaching staffs to reach greater numbers of students. Important as this use may be in meeting the demands of an ever increasing enrollment, another contribution that television can make calls for much greater emphasis—the use of TV for the improvement of college instruction as it relates to the professional preparation of the graduate student planning on a teaching career.

Once knowledge of subject matter was regarded as the primary requirement for college teachers. This view assumed that when an individual achieved the level of maturity necessary for college attendance, he had enough inherent interest to master subject matter content, without requiring the specific implementation of instructional methodology.

On the other hand, a great deal of stress has been placed upon the importance of instructional methods and the teacher-pupil relationship at the elementary and secondary levels, the assumption being that *how* a subject is taught is integrally related to the learning process.

Although the technique emphasis has been mainly on communicating knowledge and developing skills, it is generally accepted that the effectiveness of a technique cannot be evaluated independently from its effect on motivation. That teacher attitudes influence the motivation of students has been accepted without question, but to a large extent teacher attitudes have been regarded as distinct from techniques. This has been true primarily because these attitudes seemed to be noncommunicable.

Current research on group processes, however, has shown that it is possible to subject teacher attitudes to experimental analysis in terms of the effect upon a student's learning. Attitudes can be regarded and manipulated in part as techniques. Thus, the unquestioned ability of some teachers to motivate students in the college classroom can be profitably investigated from this point of view.

Good teaching demands a mastery of subject content, but in addition, it entails an attitude of interest and warmth toward the student as well as toward the course material. This requires skill in the presentation of ideas and concepts so that they acquire meaning in terms of the student's experiences. This skill includes sensitivity, patience, and a basic respect for the student. These qualities as they are demonstrated in a good teacher cannot be conveyed merely by giving advice on how to teach or explaining what to do; they can be acquired in part, however, through guided observations of the teacher at work.

To this end the TV camera can perform a useful function, providing as it does a technique for sensitizing the teacher to what is actually taking place in the classroom. Its unique contribution is to be found in the observational facilities that are made available in the study of the teaching process. Such facilities make it possible to employ many of the approaches to an understanding of interpersonal relationships that have proved highly effective in the training of psychotherapists. Just as the one-way vision mirror and the tape recorder provide an excellent means of observing the therapist-client relationship, so the TV camera provides a similar means for observing the teacher.

In many ways the television camera has even more promise, since the kinescope ensures a permanent visual and auditory record of what takes place as the teacher presents his subject matter and interacts with the student. Consequently, the possibilities for clinical analysis and research become almost limitless.

Through the study of the television picture, a teaching problem may be "staffed" in the same way that a case in a medical setting, a behavioral clinic, or a social agency is staffed. The use of TV in staffing a case offers the distinct advantage of having the actual teaching situation continually available for observation and study. It provides an unusual opportunity for self-observation and for acquiring a perspective on one's teaching that is not possible otherwise.

CHAIRMAN: Thank you, Professor Brody. I now wish to introduce Dr. Warren Seibert.

Criterion Improvement—Panel Discussion (continued)

WARREN F. SEIBERT (Purdue University): By now we are aware that there is no such thing as the perfect criterion which we can use in studying the effectiveness of televised instruction or even conventional instruction. All the criteria we find seem to exhibit some shortcomings.

Improvement of these criteria may come to us in two ways. First, we can devote more time and consideration to the preparation of tests and other indices by which educational television is to be gauged. These tests and indices should be planned so that they more nearly reflect student accomplishment along lines that coincide with course purposes or objectives. Second, we should consider and exploit opportunities to conduct retention or other follow-up studies upon student groups that have received television instruction.

There are, I believe, a number of very good reasons for being concerned about criterion improvement. First, student achievement is not unitary and does not proceed forward as a wave. Instead, various students accomplish various course objectives at different rates of speed. We need to identify those things that instruction is aiming for, order them in importance, and proceed to the development of means for estimating a student's progress toward these goals. Having done this, we will face fewer discrepancies between how we judge a student as an undergraduate and how we judge him at some later point in his life.

Second, we must show more concern for the lasting residue that instruction produces in the minds of the students. Currently, television research is almost wholly a matter of examining the immediate performance of students who have received such instruction. We know that there is not necessarily a one-to-one correspondence between a student's standing at the end of the semester and his standing at some later, more relevant point in time. It is merely making a logical statement to say that television leaves more, the same, or less residue than other methods of instruction. We don't know which, and we won't know until we have examined this question. The differences in residue or retention are not likely to be dramatic, but it is the little differences that will count.

Third, I wonder if I won't encounter a critic of television some day who will say, "You may think that television is working all right at the end of each semester, but I can tell you that the students with television in their backgrounds just don't have it when it comes to the advanced courses." And I shall answer either, "I knew that before you did," or "I'm sorry but we have some strong evidence which is contrary to what you have just said." It seems that those directly concerned with instruction television should be making certain now that the second answer will be the more likely one.

We can approach this problem of criterion improvement in a number of ways, but the important point is that otherwise inadequate criterion measurements will not acquire any respectability just because they happen to be used in connection with retention studies. With the help of instructors in past television courses, it will probably be possible to plan and develop examinations that can be used with students who are one semester or more removed from the television course under consideration. In other cases, nationally marketed and standardized examinations may be obtained and used. Besides using tests, it would be well to examine student performance in related, subsequent courses and to examine student drop-out rates and such other indices as may be available.

In summary, it is the lasting effects of instruction that matter most. Until we know something about the endurance of televised instruction, we are doing work less than our best and less than should be expected of us.

CHAIRMAN: Thank you, Dr. Seibert. Are there any questions or comments?

General Discussion

REV. HERMAN MULLER, S.J. (University of Detroit): I share the concern of several speakers at this conference for the potential twenty- to sixty-five-year old students available in open-circuit educational television. We want to meet the needs and wishes of this group.

CHAIRMAN: These early morning broadcasts in New York City bear your findings out also.

MR. HARRIS: I hope that this conference or some other meeting will face up to the problem of adequate compensation for the television instructor. I think we should set up reasonable standards.

CHAIRMAN: This question has come up at every conference. So far the prevailing feeling is that there is no single, direct pattern emerging. The literature and information on this problem is coming together now and it will be taken up in the course of time.

F. GLENN MACOMBER (Miami University, Ohio): We are going to study the question at Miami University this year and try to make an assessment of the load requirements for teaching by television as well as for teaching in other large-group type of course work.

CHAIRMAN: I suggest that you contact faculty participants here who can give you some of the answers.

EUGENE F. GREWE (University of Detroit): Could the American Council on Education sponsor a study of this nature?

CHAIRMAN: I can't answer officially for the Council. We have done our best to be a clearinghouse where information could be pooled and central issues confronted. I am sure the Council's Committee on Television would welcome your posing that question.

Tuesday Dinner Session

OCTOBER 22, 1957

Presiding: ARTHUR S. ADAMS, President,
American Council on Education

The conference reconvened at 6:45 P.M. in the main dining room of the Nittany Lion Inn, the Pennsylvania State University.

CHAIRMAN: Our principal speaker this evening is Dr. Clarence H. Faust, a man who is fully committed to all that is worthwhile in education. Ever since the first stirring of interest in televised education, Dr. Faust has been concerned about the merits of the medium and the values to be gained from linking it to education.

A wise and thoughtful educator, he has also been active in the development of libraries. At one time, he was dean of the School of Humanities and Sciences at Stanford University. He was on the staff of the University of Chicago, the institution from which he received his doctor's degree. He was serving as president of Stanford just before assuming the post of president of the Fund for the Advancement of Education. Most recently he has also been named the vice-president of the Ford Foundation.

He is my good friend and I can tell you that he thinks deeply and wisely about the matters that concern all of us at this conference. Just this afternoon he told me that he is constantly being challenged in his thinking from three different levels of education, since his three sons are engaged in education, each at a different level. I am confident that he will have the right answers for us tonight as he addresses us on the subject of educational television. Dr. Faust.

Educational Philosophy and Television

CLARENCE H. FAUST

Vice-President, Ford Foundation
President, Fund for the Advancement of Education

I AM STRUCK by how far we have come in educational television during the last five years. I cannot but recollect that when I was in college radio was the most tentative and precarious kind of enterprise, and television wasn't even thought of.

In fact, the first radio I ever heard was one that my roommate and I in college had acquired. It was an old Quaker Oats set. I don't know whether any of you remember these sets or not. It consisted of a Quaker Oats box with a roll of wire around it, a little slider, and a very ticklish crystal on the top. For an aerial we used our bedspring in the dormitory room, and when, for the first time, we heard faintly through our earphones the words "KDKA Pittsburgh," we thought a new age had opened.

That television should ever be born or that it should ever have educational significance was as far from our thoughts, further from our thoughts, I suppose, than the notion of rocket trips to the moon are these days.

We have indeed come a long way.

Educational philosophy and television is a truly open-ended subject—wide open, indeed, at both ends. What educational philosophy? And what kind or use of television? So I must begin by attempting to establish a reference point for some conception of the nature of education.

I would tax your patience outrageously if for this purpose I tried to present a comprehensive philosophy of education. And, in any case, the variety and the diversity of educational philosophies are so great that I could hardly hope to formulate a consensus from which we could jointly appraise the possibilities of educational television.

Let me try instead a brief statement of what seems to me—and I venture to hope, may seem to most of you—to be the essence of education, in the hope that it may provide a basis for considering the possible

142

values and possible dangers of this powerful means of communication in our day.

What justifies this endeavor to appraise television, as I see it, is that education simply cannot afford to disregard a new means of communication. For one thing, education depends so heavily upon communication —oral and printed—that it cannot afford to brush aside any new means of accomplishing it. And furthermore, given the growing and critical problem of numbers of students in our schools and colleges—over 40 million this year—we cannot, in good conscience, refuse complacently to examine any new means for meeting their educational needs. We must not be in the posture ridiculed in a newspaper cartoon which appeared just after the launching of Sputnik. The cartoonist had drawn a Stone Age savage, clad in skins and grasping a heavy club, obviously his means of killing game and defending himself against his enemy. On a hill above him was a contemporary pictured in the act of launching what appeared to be the first arrow from the first bow. The man with the club was represented as saying with respect to this new invention, the bow, "Well, anyhow, the thing has no practical significance."

Just as foolish as dismissing without consideration the new means of communication that television provides would be the unthinking or ill-considered adoption of television. In a careful consideration of the educational possibility of this new medium of communication, the question of how television looks from the vantage point of our educational philosophy is fundamentally an important one, and the question is simply this: Given the ends or purposes of education and a view of the appropriate means and processes of education, what shall we think of this newly discovered, newly developed means of communication?

What I think we might agree upon as the essence of education came out for me in an arresting way during a recent conference with several Asian educators who had come to this country to look into the American educational system. One of our Asian visitors began the conference by making two assertions and then posing a question. His first assertion was that America had achieved such progress in the last 150 years as, in effect, to make the rest of the world relatively underprivileged and underdeveloped. His second assertion was, "We in Asia think that this progress is, in large part, the result of your educational system."

He then asked: "What is the secret of the American educational system which explains the rapid rise of America in the world?"

The reply which a group of us formulated was something like this.

We said that the secret of the American educational system, if it could be called a secret, lay not in its particular structure nor even in its particular content, methods, and processes, all of which have changed greatly during the past 150 years. It lay rather in our commitment as a people to universal education, to equal educational opportunity for all, and, more fundamentally, to certain convictions that underlie this commitment.

We are committed to universal education, we said, not merely out of some sentimental, humanitarian concern for mankind, nor even from general abstract principles of democracy. From the beginning it has been the conviction of our leaders of thought that America's best hopes depend not on her natural resources but upon her human resources, and that the essence of her human resources—and this leads, it seems to me, to the essence of education—lies in the capacities of human intelligence.

So far as the capacities of intelligence could be developed, a people would progress and become strong. We have been convinced, too, that intelligence is not the unique property of an aristocratic group, is not a racial characteristic, and does not depend upon economic or social status. Consequently, we have believed that it is essential to provide equal educational opportunities for all—although we are still struggling to realize this ideal fully—so that the possibilities of intelligence could be most fully realized, both in the interests of individuals, who are the primary concern of democratic society, and in the interests of the society itself.

Our convictions on these matters have been so deep in our general consciousness that the phrase "from log cabin to White House" has become a cliché. In our view of the best possibilities of individual human beings and of the most urgent needs of society, the development of man's capacities of learning to think well for himself has been among the highest concerns of society and certainly the highest obligation of education.

I mention this incident in order to suggest that the essence of education is the development of intelligence, the development of powers of thought, the development of the capacity for reflection, and the development of human reason and its products, knowledge and wisdom.

The task of our schools and colleges, then—not merely one of their tasks, nor one of their major tasks, but the task of education—is the fullest possible development of capacity to take thought, to reflect, to weigh and to judge, to foresee, to choose among alternatives, in short, the capacities of human intelligence.

I should not wish to be technical in my statement of the matter, even if I were capable of being so, nor to state my thesis in terms of a particular philosophy or psychological system or position. What I have in mind might be put quite simply. It is that men possess, if not uniquely, at least in a unique degree, the capacity to reflect and to take thought, the capacity to bend their minds back upon their experience, their feelings, their ideas, the capacity to analyze and generalize, to foresee, to hold in imagination what does not now exist in reality, and to select among alternatives, and it is the function of education to develop this cluster of capacities to the fullest possible usefulness.

The essence of this process of education is not communication from the teacher to the students, but the stimulation of profitable reflection in the student. And the essence of the educational process is the stimulation of minds by other minds or the stimulation to engage in that internal dialogue by which conflicting ideas come to confront each other in the learner's mind so that in some measure the resolution we call knowledge or wisdom takes place.

The processes of effective education, therefore, are basically the processes of discussion at its best, disciplined dialogue on important questions, or to put it technically, if you wish, the processes of dialectic. The best processes of education involve the interplay of minds on important questions, the challenge and the counter-challenge directed to the clarification of problems, the adequate resolution of them; in short, the acquisition of knowledge and of wisdom.

In all these modes of educating intelligence, the supremely important thing is what might be described as internal dialogue, the learner's discovery of conflicting points of view, of conflicting evidence, of experiences pointing in contrary directions, and the resolution within the student's mind of these conflicts or the equally important educational experience of the student's finding himself unable to reach a resolution and thus coming to perceive those limits of knowledge beyond which, presently at least, lies the large circle of the dark unknown. For surely an awareness of the limits of dependable knowledge itself is an essential part of wisdom.

This activity I have described as the essence of education—this activity of the learner's mind in which facts are clearly apprehended, ideas are formulated, facts and ideas are related, conflicts of facts and ideas are faced, and judgments are reached—may take various forms. Let me mention four of them.

First, it may occur when a challenging lecturer excites the attention and interest of students, arouses their minds to activity in weighing what he has to say, stimulates them to seek understanding, to arrive at conclusions, to estimate the degree to which the judgments they make are to be held as tentative or conclusive.

Second, educational dialogue may involve the student and a book from which the student gathers not only information but ideas. He is led to mull over what he reads, to weigh it, to reach judgments of his own.

Third, educational dialogue may involve not the lecturer merely or the book, but students and a teacher who is expert in the conduct of discussion and the confrontation of minds. Such discussion, indeed, may be among the finest hours of a student's education. With the skillful assistance of a more mature and informed mind, the student is likely to clarify his thinking, to pursue profitable lines of inquiry rigorously, to meet the challenge of the ideas of his fellows, to take increasingly sure steps toward knowledge and wisdom. The teacher who can direct this process effectively is surely operating at the very highest educational level.

Education is not limited to these processes, those in which the lecturer communicates orally, the book communicates silently, the formal discussion groups carry the art of fruitful thinking to its difficult and exciting heights.

There is a fourth stimulus of thought and one perhaps too frequently overlooked. I believe that all of us in reflecting upon our own experiences as students would recall the importance of good talk among students themselves, where the process of a discussion may be less orderly, less fully informed, less efficient than in the classroom, but where we began to discover and take an appropriate delight in the play of our own minds without the guidance of our elders, and to which the exciting beginnings of our own sense of intellectual independence may, in good part, be traced.

If what I have said points to what is at least ideally the essence of education, then what, in the light of it, may be said about educational television? What role can television play in the systematic stimulation of fruitful inquiry and reflection, the stimulation of this internal dialogue which is the very essence of education?

Let me confess at the outset that I began, in looking at television, with what I suppose is the usual classroom teacher's feeling about it; namely, that this mechanical gadget could have very little educational value. There were several sources of this feeling. For one thing, a conception of education as an interplay of minds with minds, not minds and machines; and, for another, a strong feeling that most of what I had seen on commercial television screens had no conceivable educational value. Then it began to dawn on me that education was already heavily indebted to at least one great mechanical aid—the printed book. The book was indeed the first great visual aid to education.

Let me put it more concretely. Suppose that we were to attempt education on a scale we have undertaken in America without the benefit of any books. Suppose, for example, that every high school teacher of American history still had to manage as teachers did before printing; that is, by employing what he or she had set down in his or her notebook from the lectures of professors of history in colleges and universities where they had studied and using this as the basis for lectures to students who, in turn, wrote down in notebooks what they derived from lectures, this being the whole source of their knowledge of the subject.

Suppose, as in the days before printing, neither teacher nor students had access, except through a few rare and precious hand-lettered manuscripts, to the documents in American history or to the views of those who had spent a lifetime thinking about them. Suppose, in short, the printed books did not exist.

At its best, the dialogue I have described as the essence of education, obliged to proceed without the stimulus of a printed text of any kind, would be tragically limited, and it would seem impossible under these circumstances to dream of achieving education of high quality for the millions of young people who ought to know something about the history of our land, our achievements, our troubles and our failures, and the various interpretations by wise and thoughtful men of our experiences as a people.

It seems to me that it is in this light that the role of television in education has to be appraised. What advantage for the stimulation of thought and the development of intelligence does it have? And what are the limits of its effectiveness? Like the printed book, it may enlarge indefinitely the scope of the effect of the best minds as an element in the educational process, everywhere and in every hamlet in the land. It has some advantages over print which, as one reflects upon it, is, after all, a lifeless and unpromising means of communication—black marks on white paper. It makes possible, in a sense, a return to the original idea of the university where students gathered in Paris or Bologna to see and to hear, to be instructed, and to be stimulated by the best men of their times.

It has, confessedly, some disadvantages by comparison with print. What the book made possible, as compared to oral communication, as Professor Riesman has recently suggested in a very interesting lecture entitled "The Oral Tradition, the Written Word, and the Screen Image,"[1] was a greater independence of mind for the reader. The reader may select what he is going to read. He is in less danger of being overwhelmed by the personality of the teacher or being pushed by the pressure of the audience of which he is a part into lines he would not take independently.

The book, as Riesman puts it, "helps liberate the reader from his group and its emotions, and allows the contemplation of alternative responses and the trying on of new emotions."

The question for television, then, it seems to me is this: as we examine it in relation to books as a means of stimulating independent reflection and in relation to the educational activities that involve direct personal relationship of teachers and students, what role does it have in education?

Perhaps what I have been saying can be brought to a point for your consideration and criticism, or approval or disapproval, by sketching some aspects of the role of television as it seems to me, if it is wisely used in the American educational system.

First, let me say that television is neutral, like the printed book, capable of conveying the worst as well as the best; and second, that I am not thinking of it as the whole means of education. There will always be the need for the teacher who serves, to use Socrates' phrase, the function of the midwife bringing knowledge to birth in individual minds. But given our commitment to universal education, given our commitment to equal educational opportunities for all, television could follow up the advantages we have had from the printed book by making generally available as teachers our wisest, most thoughtful, and most effective people in every field of knowledge, making them available to be seen and heard as well as merely to be apprehended through the coldness of type.

[1] Antioch, Ohio: Antioch Press, 1956.

Lectures that students might travel from all parts of the country to obtain under a brilliant teacher in one university and that could at best be available only to the handful of students that his voice could reach might, through television, be made available to young men and women in every corner of the land.

In the second place, an almost firsthand knowledge of anything going on in the world, now available only to a few students and research scholars who are on the scene, could, through television, be made available to every inquiring mind in this country. The debates in the United Nations, the way life proceeds in a Korean or Indian village or in a South African tribe could, if captured on films and made available over television, be available to every student everywhere.

Let us look at one or two of the fields of knowledge where television might be of great advantage. I sat some years ago with a group discussing the possibilities of television for a college course in the social sciences. One member of the group was President Charles Johnson of Fisk, in whose untimely death American education suffered a great loss. President Johnson pointed out that television might fill what is now a vacuum in social science courses. On the one hand, he said, we have the lecture and the textbook which serve to clarify certain concepts and to order ideas about, for example, the conditions of the slums in our great cities. On the other hand, we have the possibility of field trips in which students see these conditions firsthand. The difficulty with the lecture and the textbook, he said, is that students may not perceive the complexity and the play of variables in the actual situation, because inevitably these media present a situation from one point of view and perforce oversimplify it. The difficulty with the field trip, on the other hand, is that of a sheer confusion of elements in the actual situation so great that it is hard for students to discover what is essential and to clarify their own thinking about it.

He thought television wisely employed, including the development and use of selected films, might provide great assistance in acquainting students with some of the complexities of the actual without overwhelming them with its confusion. Thus it might at once direct a student's attention to the complex nature of things and at the same time leave him free to develop the originality and insights that he ought to develop for himself.

Let us look at a second way in which television might be useful, in this case, in the natural sciences. A recent project suggests the great possible value of this instrument for developing the student's capacities for original and profitable and independent thinking. A group of distinguished research physicists under the direction of Professor Zacharias at the Massachusetts Institute of Technology has been working on a physics course for high schools. They have been troubled by the fact that high school physics courses do not reflect the most advanced contemporary conceptions and insights in physics. They were confident that these could be presented intelligently for high school students. With the assistance of wise and experienced secondary school teachers, this group of research scientists has developed a course for the high school. The course will involve films presenting the most effective teachers on various aspects of physics, filmstrips presenting experiments of various sorts, monographs, and teachers' guides. The whole course can be made available through television to high school students anywhere in the country. It may well, indeed, be found useful as an introductory college course in many institutions.

It is worth remarking that it was the prospect of the film and television presentation which justified the very large amounts of time which Dr. Zacharias and his colleagues have taken and will continue to take from their own research activities to build this new course. These men could hardly be expected to respond to a plea to teach a class or two of high school students, even in the best school system in the country. The possibility that their efforts would reach hundreds of thousands of students is sufficient to command their time and their energy.

We have a dramatic example of how such plans may work in the television course offered last year in the Pittsburgh schools, which through films is being offered to some 75,000 students in this country. The distinguished professor who taught that course could hardly have been expected to give it the time and effort required if it were to be presented only once to 30, 50, or even 100 students. It was the possibility of capturing the work on film and presenting it over television that enlisted him in the large efforts he gave to it.

Obviously, the way in which television can function effectively as an ingredient of the educational process will vary from subject matter to subject matter and at various levels of education. Its role in the humanities —my own particular field of interest—will differ from its role in physics and in the social sciences. Here, as in other fields, it may make the best lecturer available anywhere, but it may also do some special and very important things that could not otherwise be done. It may, for example, make possible the presentation of a poet, Robert Frost or T. S. Eliot, to students anywhere. Certainly the appearance of Robert Frost by way of television in the fifth-grade classrooms in the Pittsburgh schools the year before last must have been a great educational experience for students.

Again, television may fill a vacuum in courses in drama. The teacher of plays has the text of the play in the classroom, but the text is like the musical score for a symphony, and it is almost as difficult for students to interpret the printed text of a play, to visualize a stage, to see actors upon it, to hear their tones and intonations, and to see their movements as it is for most of us to pick up a symphony score and hear the notes and harmonies of an orchestra. Here again television can perform a tremendous role. The juxtaposition of parts of plays or varying interpretations of plays by superior actors on television by way of films would make it possible to introduce into the classroom the element that has been missing in the teaching of literature. Through television, moreover, the holdings of the great art museums, the performances of great orchestras could be available in the remotest rural schools.

What we need as educators to do, I have been trying to suggest, is to reconsider the ingredients of the educational process, the lecture, the textbook, the original masterpiece or great book, the class discussion, the laboratory experience, and television, with a view to putting these elements together in a way that would enable us to carry through our hopes for providing as many years of education for all of our population as American parents and students demand and as our times need, while at the same time improving the quality of education, introducing into it elements which could not otherwise, by any stretch of the imagination, be provided generally and universally.

We could, I think, make one or two serious mistakes about television. We could seize upon television as *the* means of education, neglecting the other ingredients of educational processes that are necessary for the development of human intelligence. Or we might, and perhaps the danger of this course is more real, make the equally sad mistake of neglecting this great and powerful means of communication.

If we do the latter, I think we stand in danger of finding ourselves, given the numbers of students to be educated, with an educational system simply inadequate to our needs. We should then have reason to expect that countries now underdeveloped and underprivileged educationally, but ready to employ every new means of education, would pass us by in educational achievement. We could, to put it extremely, find ourselves in the position of the Chinese, who had a powerful education system at a time when Western Europe was still in a state of barbarism, but permitted that system to freeze in its content and method until it became inadequate to the needs of the Chinese people and was ultimately surpassed by educational developments in the Western world.

There are, as I see it, three important forward movements that television might enable American education to make. First, by enlarging the scope of our ablest teachers it might do a great deal to raise the salary ceilings for teachers and to elevate the status of the teaching profession— surely two highly desirable results.

The chief difficulty with teachers' salaries is not that the beginning salary is too low, but that teaching does not offer as good a prospect for advancement in compensation as the other professions. We might reasonably hope that both the salary and the status of the teacher who is able through television to extend his scope far beyond present limits could be very high, and there are encouraging signs that this is, in fact, possible. Moreover, by redeployment of teaching resources, the student-teacher ratio might well be so greatly increased that much higher salaries would be possible generally. I am sure such changes in salary and status would have no small influence upon the attractiveness of teaching to our best minds.

In the second place, television may be one of the means for mustering our educational resources to accomplish what seems otherwise a hopeless task. As I said at the outset, there are today more than forty million students in our schools and colleges. If we attempt to provide one teacher for every thirty students in the elementary schools, one for every twenty-five in our high schools, and one for every twelve or fifteen in our colleges, it will be utterly impossible to find enough good teachers to raise education to anything like an appropriate level.

A reorganization of our devices for education, including such things as placing more responsibility upon students for their own education, pruning the curriculum of the proliferation of courses, and the use of television, seems our best hope of mustering resources to provide education of high quality for as many years to as many students as colleges will be called upon to provide.

Finally, the matter of quality must be, above all, our concern in appraising the possibilities of television in the light of our educational purposes.

If our purpose is the development of intelligence, if the essential function of education is the development of the mysterious ability of men to reflect, to take thought, to judge, and to weigh, then we certainly need to look hard at the new means of communication available in our time. We need to consider what new possibility exists because of television for confronting the students with the most exciting minds of our day, what new materials otherwise not possible in the curriculum may be introduced by it, and not least of all, what curricular reforms will result when we begin to re-examine and readjust our means of education.

I am convinced if we do this, we should find in this new instrument a means of enlarging the scope of our ablest teachers, a means of bringing situations and events all over the world into the educational process, a means of bringing the products of arts and sciences into every classroom and every hamlet and, in short, an instrument for making our schools and colleges more effective in preparing the next generation to meet more intelligently the problems it will face in this critical time for America and, indeed, for mankind.

CHAIRMAN: Thank you, Dr. Faust. I now wish to introduce the participants who have been responsible for the planning of this conference and to whom we owe a debt of gratitude for the success of their diligent efforts, which are proving so fruitful in our behalf. [Dr. Adams then introduced the following: President John C. Adams, president, Hofstra College, and chairman of the Committee on Television, American Council on Education; Mr. John Weiss of the Ford Foundation and the Fund for the Advancement of Education, who served as consultant to the Program Advisory Committee; Dr. Ray Carpenter, Pennsylvania State University, who coordinated the groundwork on the campus and the conference agenda; Dr. John E. Ivey, executive vice-president, New York University; Mr. Leslie P. Greenhill of the Pennsylvania State University staff; Mr. Reed Ferguson, director, Conference Center, the Pennsylvania State University; and Mrs. Dorothy Smith, secretary to the Council's Committee on Television.]

CHAIRMAN: Your work at this conference has been consciously, deliberately addressed to the question of teaching by television. I think all of us recognize, however, that it is useless to talk about teaching by television if we do not have the television channels. So it seems to me that this is an appropriate moment in the conference to give recognition to the work of two organizations involved in activities germane to teaching by television. One has been concerned with the reservation and preservation of the channels allocated by the Federal Communications Commission; the other has been concerned with those many technical details which do so much to make or mar effective teaching by television.

Just this afternoon, I was talking with one of you who pointed out that a director had forgotten to change the camera at a crucial moment. Again, I can understand that if a kinescope is not reproduced on the right kind of film, the most stellar performance imaginable by an instructor becomes merely a snowstorm on the screen. Therefore, it becomes apparent that what we do in educational television is a team effort. If we do not have that team effort, that joining-together of connections of mutual support, we haven't really achieved that which we are capable of achieving.

So, I would like first to ask Mr. Ralph Steetle to speak to us. He, as you know, has been intimately concerned—from the very beginning—with the reserving to education of the channels we have at our command today.

Reservation of TV Channels for Education

RALPH STEETLE (Joint Council on Educational Television): The decision to reserve television channel assignments for educational use was, by and large, not an academic decision. It was an administrative decision without the full participation of faculties. This was necessary because the setting of deadlines by the Federal Communications Commission did not allow sufficient time for extensive faculty involvement. It was an act of administrative faith that convinced the Federal Communications Commission that these channels ought to be set aside for education.

Now, whether or not those channels as yet unused will be held depends upon you. It depends upon how wisely you use television both for formal and informal education. It would be inconceivable, it seems to me, to discuss whether or not we should have education in the United States. I think you have the responsibility of making television so strong a part of education that the remaining channels cannot be touched.

CHAIRMAN: Thank you, Ralph.

It is now my pleasure, in special reference to the whole area of program production, to ask Dr. Burton Paulu, the President of the National Association of Educational Broadcasters, to speak to us.

Cooperation of Educational Broadcasters

BURTON PAULU (University of Minnesota): I like what Dr. Adams has said about the cooperative nature of educational television. If it is to be successful as a tool in education, it requires understanding on the part of administrators. It requires contributions from the content experts. It requires the work of those who specialize in program planning and production. It requires the appraisal of those who are expert in studying the results of all teaching.

CHAIRMAN: Thank you, Dr. Paulu.

Demonstrations of Teaching by Television

TUESDAY EVENING, OCTOBER 22, 1957

Presiding: FRED MCKINNEY, Professor of Psychology,
University of Missouri

Following the dinner session, conference participants went to four small TV-receiving rooms to observe a second series of teaching-by-TV demonstrations. The chairman and the teachers demonstrating their TV instruction live or by kinescope were in an adjacent originating room. Each receiving room was equipped with a microphone, an arrangement which permitted the observing audience to raise questions with the chairman and the demonstrating teachers.

The live teaching demonstrations were presented by: C. N. McCarty, Michigan State University (General Chemistry); E. C. Wareham, Jr., the Pennsylvania State University (Music Appreciation); and F. J. Bogardus, Purdue University (Mechanical Engineering). Teaching demonstrations by kinescope featured: S. A. Insel, San Francisco State College (General Psychology); Max Sorkin, New York University (French); J. M. Sachs, Chicago City Junior College (Mathematics); and Richard Evans, University of Houston (General Psychology).

Professor McCarty's demonstration showed close-up views of a chemical reaction. Professor Insel demonstrated the use of role-playing as a method of portraying personal interactions. Techniques used in teaching a TV course in music appreciation were demonstrated by Professor Wareham. Conference participants observed how the meaning of a sentence in French could be completely changed by scrambling some of the words and how avoidance of this error is taught by Professor Sorkin. The kinescope demonstration by Professor Sachs was related to locating a point on a grid map. Professor Bogardus, in his demonstration of teaching Mechanical Engineering, showed the development of the involute curve by means of a model. Dr. Evans' demonstration of teaching General Psychology via television included a student dramatization of points being taught, including a student interruption of an episode in the interest of feedback.

CHAIRMAN MCKINNEY: You have seen seven educational presentations. What are your reactions? Which ones of these programs would help the learner grow most? Which of them were adequate stimuli for educational growth? Did they motivate the student relevantly or

156

irrelevantly? Did they motivate him to participate in some way overtly or covertly? And if you believe the student was rewarded, in what way was he rewarded?

Now it is your turn to discuss these examples of televised instruction. Just ask for the mike, press the button, and I will notice your signal and cut you in.

ROOM 19: On Mr. Insel's film, I would like to ask if the roles were played by students?

MR. INSEL: Yes, they were all students, the two people sitting with me at the desk as well as the actors.

ROOM 11: We have often found that the responses from the students indicate that they are learning but not always the specific points we want them to learn. In the demonstrations by Dr. Insel and by Dr. Evans, I wondered how you can be sure that the students are selecting from the content that point you are teaching?

MR. EVANS: One way is to have a follow-up question-and-answer period. We actually cut into the episode quite a bit and gain immediate feedback, where this stimulates questions about various points we wish to emphasize. We structure the episode in a brief period of a few minutes. The "actors" are given a rough idea of what they are supposed to do. We recommend this procedure for a low-budget operation. These are just to help the producers and directors. We can use this procedure to stimulate feedback, and the questions that come in from viewers will give us another chance to emphasize the points we want them to learn.

ROOM 19: I would like to ask Professor McCarty what he does when one of his scientific experiments on TV doesn't work?

C. N. McCARTY: The experiments always work!

ROOM 19: You mean, Dr. McCarty, that you fake an experiment to make it work?

MR. McCARTY: Once in a while we rig it to be sure it works. If an experiment does work, we can use that as an illustration. If it fails, we can tell the students why it failed. We promise them to try it again. That is good education. Of course, experiments don't always work.

ROOM 19: How did they get the white printing overlays that were used to present the names of the professors on the TV screens?

L. GREENHILL (Pennsylvania State University): We use white lettering on a black card. The card is on one camera and is superimposed over the picture on the other camera. There are two cameras on at the same time.

Room 11: I would like to ask Professor Wareham if he believes the visual aids he used in his course on music appreciation contribute something essential to the instruction?

CHAIRMAN McKINNEY: Mr. Wareham is not here at the moment. Would you answer that question, Mr. Greenhill?

MR. GREENHILL: Mr. Wareham likes to use visual aids, but it is difficult to say exactly what contribution the visuals make to learning in the music course. In many instances, we cannot test for what some of the visuals contribute. In the case of the music appreciation course, the examination is given in two parts: one a factual part, which has to do with a learning of facts, and the other is a listening part in which students are required to identify musical selections, the works of composers, or different types of voices in different kinds of arrangements. This is approaching the kind of performance test we would like to see better developed and more widely used.

Room 11: I have a comment on the music appreciation demonstration and its value. I took lessons on a slide trombone in high school over a period of about two years, and I never did learn how a few of the parts worked. Now, in a few minutes, Mr. Wareham has taught me how they work.

CHAIRMAN McKINNEY: We'll tell this to Mr. Wareham.

Room 19: I would like to raise a question about the straw-cutting by Professor Wareham. Was that a visual aid or a demonstration? I think there is a point to be made there, because perhaps the pictures of the composers were more of a visual aid, and there we would have to evaluate whether the picture added anything. The other demonstrates something which is at a different level from straight graphic presentation.

CHAIRMAN McKINNEY: I wish Mr. Wareham were here to comment on that. Does anybody else wish to answer that question?

Room 11: I have been rather disappointed at the quality of the kinescopes and the films, the contrast between what we have seen and the technical quality that can be achieved. Otherwise, I think the demonstrations were excellent. It seems to me that the live productions were far superior to the kinescopes and the films.

CHAIRMAN McKINNEY: The men in the studio here can all take a bow.

Room 19: If Professor Wareham were here, I would ask him whether that was a visual aid or a demonstration and whether that would make a difference in his own mind. Those of us who are teaching science courses make no distinction between the demonstration and the visual aid as long as it gets the point across. I think that was an excellent demonstration.

ROOM 11: I don't think there's any point in splitting hairs over the cutting of straws.

MR. GREENHILL: I would like to propose that, since the hour is now ten minutes of eleven, we consider adjourning shortly.

CHAIRMAN McKINNEY: This meeting is adjourned.

Review and Preview: A Summary of the Conference

WEDNESDAY MORNING, OCTOBER 23, 1957

Presiding: JOHN C. ADAMS

CHAIRMAN: Good morning to you! Conferences, I suppose, are the occupational disease all of us share. But I cannot remember a conference more brilliantly planned than this one. We have had superior papers. Topflight specialists in educational television have discussed our problem with expertness, discernment, and a genuine wish to contribute to our central theme. They have broken new ground; and if they departed on occasion from television, that was in the nature of our topic, for we were looking at the heart of the educational process, at the goals of teaching and learning. I have not heard a word that was not germane to our theme during these hard-working days.

We have covered a lot of ground. Therefore, I shall call upon a man experienced in problems both of education and of televised instruction to make the summary of this conference for us. I ask Dr. John E. Ivey to give us a synthesis of what we have been doing and where we are headed.

Breaking the Barriers

JOHN E. IVEY, JR. (New York University): This is a frustrating assignment, primarily because of the tremendous stimulation that I have had here. After listening to so many meaningful ideas, insights, and projected possibilities, I went back last night to a review of the book that came out of our original 1952 conference. To be reading about what was said in 1952 in the light of what we have achieved since then brings an interesting impact of its own. Unlike five years ago, we are now well through the research and development stage of trying to prove whether or not television used for instructional purposes will work. We know that it is working. We are ready for the full-production stage.

We have done enough research to know what it will do in the sense

160

of "n.s.d.," that ubiquitous "no significant differences," and we smile, for n.s.d. symbolizes the fact that we have broken through the major barrier; we don't have to debate whether or not this instrumentality can be used as effectively as a teaching medium as the classroom teacher is being used at the present time. Mark this conference and what was learned here as the pivot of the major operational phase of putting educational television into the heart of United States education.

Five years ago there was a great sense of urgency about whether or not our facilities would be allowed to prove what has become the major significant conclusion of this conference. We not only have had research studies of great competence in this area, but we have developed new methodologies in research which can stand up with those of the psychologists and sociologists and others responsible for measurement fields.

I think we need to broaden our research base. I want to talk about that shortly. Even so, we have done sufficient research so that we do not have to go over the same old ground of replication and duplication before we take the big step in putting instructional television directly into our concept of higher education, and for that matter, into elementary and secondary education, too. My second feeling is that in order to put this n.s.d. symbol into a framework of operation, we will have to develop some new concepts, and tackle new barriers.

Institutional Barriers

The first of these I would like to call the *institutional productivity barrier*. It was emphasized yesterday that you can't develop good tests unless you know the purposes of the activity for which you are testing.

I contend that you cannot operate a university and judge your effectiveness unless you can define the purposes of the institution so that the information can be used administratively in achieving those ends. So the central idea in overcoming the institutional productivity barrier is to put educational television into the conceptualization of university purpose and into the procedures of university operation.

What are some of the things that we are going to try to do in reconceiving the university structure with television in it, things we can do because television is available and that we would not be able to do without this medium? Here are some check points. We can increase the number of students and adults we provide with meaningful educational experience. We can increase the number of faculty contributions of a scientific and scholarly nature. We can increase the number and magnitude of creative proposals for dealing with issues of local, national, and international import. We can increase the number and impact of activities designed to infuse the products of knowledgeable truths into channels of social and governmental deliberation and action.

These objectives of increased institutional productivity can only be reached through new methods of multiplying the efforts of staff, both in time and space. Imaginatively used on campus, television can provide the basis for new ways of utilizing faculty time that will contribute substantially to increased institutional productivity and greater faculty freedom and satisfaction. In the use of television as means for the university to reach out and beyond the campus to serve adults in performing traditional extension functions and many new services, only the barest beginning has been made.

There are two key figures in the concept of university productivity. First, there is the student. If the focus of university effort is to help the student become proficient as an independent learner, then the more successful the university becomes in this objective, the less dependent the student becomes on the day-to-day, formal contact with the university professor. Conversely, however, the more the student becomes an independent learner, the greater will be his need for a wide and rich variety of the tools for learning—books, films, exhibits, records, laboratories, and new types of personal contact with professors and other students. Television, both as a bridge between the professor and student—in certain well-defined areas—and as a tool for learning, would become a vital instrument for assistance to the student, and for greatly multiplying the catalytic value of the professor.

The second key figure in the concept of university productivity is the professor. Where the chief objective of university educational effort is to develop the student as an independent learner, the professor's role must be redefined. The kinds of learning situations, assistance, and tools needed by the student will have to be completely rethought. The performance of instructional staff, consistent with these needs, will have to be conceived as the effort of a "teaching team." The appropriate distinctions will have to be made among the respective functions of the full professor, the associates, assistants, and instructors, so that the distinctions by rank are functionally relevant, and carry with such distinctions, financial remunerations of a vastly greater range than is true today. The assignment of research responsibilities and time should likewise be systematically approached.

To the teaching team, television becomes a central mechanism for large-scale, flexible communication, live and kinescope, in classroom, library, and in the dormitory and/or home. This medium can save the time and effort of faculty and student alike. It can make possible the replay of lectures and other presentations at many different times on kinescopes. With television, more attention by the instructional staff can be given to the special learning needs of small groups and individual students.

These lines of reasoning bring one to the conclusion that the key to finding increased institutional productivity lies in teaching the student to become a more productive scholar and learner. This suggests a paradox: that the faculty can multiply its creative effort by spending less time in "teaching" students, and more time helping students to learn how to learn. In this setting, faculty function might be more highly specialized as to teaching, research, and public service. Its size might be smaller. Its remuneration can be substantially higher.

Faculty economic welfare is thus directly tied to faculty productivity, in the broadest sense. And, by the same token, television can become one of the chief means for increasing faculty productivity within the premises here developed. To overcome the institutional productivity barrier, with television as a major tool, is one of the next hurdles in educational planning and development.

Until we do this, we are subsidizing television out of the energies and the time of the participating professors; and in the long run, this won't bring any substantial motivation or creative thought into the problem of increasing the productivity of a university. This, you might say, is in the area of the *faculty welfare and productivity barrier.*

Learning Barriers

Do you recall the term that Clarence Faust used last night—the "internal dialogue of the student"? How do we produce internal dialogue? This may be another way of asking: How do we debate with ourselves? How do we develop methods of inquiry? How do we relate things external to the person who encourages this so-called internal dialogue?

I have a hunch that an exploration of the legitimate and effective means of learning behavior that will produce the kind of thinking and analytical processes people are going to carry away from universities and have with them long after they have forgotten the content of chemistry,

English literature, and political science, will throw us beyond the barrier in the area of retention, motivation, and other problems we have been talking about.

Now, a second barrier to be overcome we will call the *learning behavior barrier*. I am using the words "learning behavior barrier" very consciously, because I have been afraid that one of the undertones of this conference has been that learning is something people do but it doesn't have overt behavioral characteristics except as they listen, write, and talk.

I have tried to relate this idea to a number of concepts that we were talking about yesterday and the day before. We were told about drive, cue, response, and reward. Of these four concepts, drive, response, and reward can be directed better and with much more attention to learning forces external to the classroom than can cue.

We can do a great deal through the reorganization of our student communities, our faculty community, and our university culture to get at the motivation, the response and reward factors. More emphasis in our face-to-face contacts with students, in groups and in individual contacts, will enable us to deal more effectively with the cue factor of the learning formula.

Obviously, learning behavior is an acquired skill. This fact would suggest we give more attention to testing and classifying our students in terms of what their needs for new types of learning skills may be.

This would add major new dimension to our knowledge about student needs. We would still want tests of capability and achievement. My guess is that even our best ways of measuring intelligence still have a large factor weighted with achievement rather than inborn intelligence. This achievement area would be found in the premise that learning to think and solve problems is more of an acquired behavior skill than generally recognized.

If these premises are true, we can really make major progress in designing the most effective programs to produce independent learners only as we increase our fund of basic research on learning behavior. Television as a powerful medium for reaching the lone student and/or providing certain teaching functions without face-to-face contact of the student and professor will undoubtedly be more useful as we discover more about its role as a tool in the process of developing student learning behavior. More advances in learning theory and more basic research in learning behavior are the keys to breaking through the learning behavior barrier.

Then we come to a barrier which we must overcome: the *learning quality barrier*. Here we inject a qualitative factor. The center of gravity in most of our institutions of higher learning, it would seem to me—and most of the research that has been reported here confirms this—has been oriented by subject matter.

What is it that distinguishes the quality of an educational program? Here, the educational literature is full of glib and well-worn phrases. For example, one institution prides itself on producing graduates that have some magic balance between the biological and physical sciences, on the one hand, and the social sciences and humanities, on the other hand. This is the quality program for the well-rounded educated man. What precisely are the specific ingredients of this well-rounded quality program? Well, for the most part it consists of a general balance of courses in the areas prescribed. Within the "course control" approach to educational prescription the magic is supposed to take place between student and professor.

Few indeed are the institutions that have carefully defined the relevant objectives of their educational programs with sufficient preciseness that they can be tools for course-building and curriculum-building. The concepts, understandings, and values relevant to each set of educational objectives, therefore, rarely become visible as clear targets of the educational process.

Discussions of educational quality have got to be transferred from the broad generalizations to the analysis of specific educational objectives and the concepts, skills, and values relevant to their attainment. This transfer is essential to the achievement of increased institutional productivity and higher levels of faculty productivity and welfare. As fields of knowledge become larger in number and deeper in specialization, the effective and economic design of the *content* of the learning process awaits breaking the learning quality barrier.

We can and must overcome the institutional productivity barrier, the learning behavior barrier, and the learning quality barrier. Even while we work on overcoming these barriers, there are other matters in the further development of educational television on which we can fruitfully direct our thinking and action.

It seems that one of the big lessons that we have learned is that, for certain purposes, the operation of instruction through television has no limit in the number of students that can be accommodated except a technical limit of the number of students you can get in front of the television tube. In other words, the student capacity of television is a technical limitation rather than an educational limitation. If this is true, we are offered an infinite possibility for the mobilization of educational resources of the nation and the world.

In a number of papers read before this conference, and in the open discussions held here, we saw the enormous potential in televised instruction for mobilizing the educational resources of the nation and of the world. Suppose, for example, that it were possible to have a political science course in which men like Dwight Eisenhower, Harry Truman, Adlai Stevenson, and Dick Nixon would lecture from time to time via television to political science students throughout the United States. Instead of the political science students' having a limited experience with their professor, think of the experience and impact this course would have, taught over a national educational TV network, by men of this caliber! You can't do anything like this in education without television.

With television as the serving medium, you could approach the whole college curriculum in this way, working out programs that would bring the leading personalities in any specific field into the lecturing and teaching situation. This could be done live or by kinescope and geared into the teaching purposes and objectives of the institutions and fitted into their own course structure.

Here is something that we could do qualitatively with television that we cannot do without it. The larger the numbers of people you can get before a television system, the greater resources we would have to mobilize the best brains in the world to put on the other side of that tube.

Well, this I would call, then, the area of the *resources utilization barrier*. It is concerned with extending television operations beyond the needs and program resources of a single institution or small group of institutions, so as to multiply infinitely the number of students who are going to be accommodated. Almost in direct ratio to our success, we could increase the quality and variety of resources available on television.

Television and the Responsibilities of American Education

Now I would like to consider how television can help us to meet the over-all responsibility of American education, a responsibility we have difficulty achieving without television. Remember the question Dr. Arthur Adams brought up at the beginning of the conference—"what for?" What is the purpose of all this? Certainly we are not interested in gadgets as such. We are interested in students. And we are interested in the welfare of the faculty. These deep interests in students and faculty account for the concern I feel when I realize how little we know about the answers to all of those questions we have been posing. I haven't met others who can tell me the answers to how we are going to do what we must do, as we interpret the social cultural role of American higher education during the next fifteen or twenty vital years.

Here we are, faced with a world scene in which there is comparatively little vigorous leadership in mobilizing the civilian component of democracy. There is a great deal of fear, premonition, worry, and insecurity that causes us to mobilize to a certain extent the military strength of democracy, but little imaginative effort has been put into the amassing and developing of ideas and learning that are central to American democracy in a way that will make them useful in the areas of the world that are just emerging into the light.

Our institutions have not assumed this as a major responsibility. In England, France, Germany, and all of Western Europe, and even in the Middle East, the universities have a status and prestige that they do not have in this country. When you travel overseas, you get the impression that university people are closer to the main stream of events. What they say in British educational circles carries weight in Parliament.

I am afraid that higher education in this country has become so preoccupied with the operation of its own establishment that it is responding passively, if at all, to the urgent issues of the day; and as a result, we have no reason to expect any increase in prestige and status. What bearing does this have on television? I believe that this void in university prestige and status has developed because we have not brought the world to America. And we can bring the world to America through the television tube. You don't have to go to India to see the village development program and the work of American agricultural extension service personnel in helping to develop villages that are little more than mud huts with dung-plastered walls. You can bring the Indian village to America by television.

Similarly, we have domestic problems that we haven't dealt with vigorously. How many university presidents and professors rose to the challenge a few years ago when many of our concepts of the unfettered mind were being attacked in high circles? How many today will take an active, effective part in dealing with fundamental issues that, if they are not solved in the way they should be, can result in American universities' becoming little islands of intellect and culture?

I had a letter the other day from one of the constituents of New York University who was taking the executive vice-president to task because we were sponsoring a group of metallurgists who were going to Russia to study with the Russians. My correspondent apparently thought that only the Russians would gain, that they would send our people back without any information about Russia. When you talk about these matters, you get the impression that we are the ones who are bringing down an intellectual and scientific iron curtain. In certain respects our security measures are a great deal more stringent than those of Russia.

This disturbs me as I consider the future roles of our university and of American educational leadership. I feel that the institutions and the professors must play a greater role in the world of affairs, and that they should be reinforced in their efforts by a medium as promising as television.

The television tube offers us an opportunity to discuss in terms of immediacy the current issues of the day. The informal chats of the Presidents of the United States, first on radio and then on television, have demonstrated the immediate political and social effects of discussing momentous issues with large groups all over the country, when those issues were hot, when something had to be done.

This will require a new orientation of the role of higher education in American society; and this television tube offers us a way of deploying the power of thinking and reasoning in a way we haven't yet begun to tap, a way that cannot be tapped unless we think through that question, "what for?" Thank you.

CHAIRMAN: The applause shows that you feel as I do: we have just heard a penetrating series of observations on the long-range implications of this great medium. Thank you, John Ivey.

Every good program planning committee, I think, wants to start big, grow strong, and end with the best; and that is why we invited, urged, and cajoled Arthur S. Adams, the president of the American Council on Education, to speak to us on this occasion, looking back to the initial conference of 1952, and looking ahead as far as he cares to.

Review from the Fifth Milestone, and a Glimpse into the Future

ARTHUR S. ADAMS: Thank you, Mr. Chairman, for your characteristically extravagant generosity.

Ladies and gentlemen: First, I would like to express my profound thanks to each of you for what you have done to make this conference a major milestone in the development of education and of educational television.

Your attention, your preparation, your lively discussion, which I have heard in the meetings and in the halls, have made this conference what it has been. So if you feel that it has been a good one, you can thank yourselves. You made it a good one.

Since I was asked to review the developments in educational television since 1952 and to take a glimpse into the future, I'll have no difficulty in finding something to say. Remembering the 1952 conference, which also was held here, I think it is fair to say that we were all in the position of the man who was in the watermelon patch. He looked down at a hundred-pound melon and said, "I'm sure I could carry that watermelon away if I could just find a way of picking it up."

The 1952 meeting brought forth lively discussions. The points of view were varied, but as I review the record, it was one of extravagant aspirations. Over and over there were recitations of seemingly insurmountable obstacles. We didn't quite know what we were talking about, but we had great hopes for the future. That 1952 conference was a successful one, serving as a platform for the resolution of opinion and judgment with respect to what might be done with educational television.

Two problems were given major attention. The first problem was money; the second, program production. We said very little about the content of the program, although we did think about how one would use the facilities available in an institution of higher learning to produce a program.

While we were talking about money in 1952, Bob Banner, who was then the production man for Fred Waring's distinguished program, recited the sums required to produce one of Fred Waring's shows, and our chins dropped to our chests. We said, "But we don't have that kind of money." There were those who challenged Bob Banner's figures. But Bob was speaking the truth from his point of view; and it was good for us to hear about the costs of a commercial television program.

Out of that conference in 1952 came the conclusion that we ought to try. Remember this was just a little over five years ago. There was one educational television station on the air, WOI-TV at Ames, Iowa. Let me say again, I did not visualize in 1952 anything like the development there has been in these five years. It had been my hope that if a few stations—perhaps one in each corner of the country—could be established and financed and start broadcasting regularly, a great contribution would have been made. But what has actually happened? At the moment there are twenty-seven stations on the air. And there will be one more in a week or so. That makes a total of twenty-eight in five years.

Yes, they have had their troubles, financial troubles, almost of the magnitude recited in the 1952 conference. I recall so well what has happened with respect to these stations when they were in difficulties and decided to keep pushing anyway. Perhaps the most dramatic example occurred in San Francisco, where it became evident that the next week's payroll could not be met unless something like $40,000 or $50,000 were realized. The station went on the air and reported its problems. This reached the American public. It also reached the newspapers. Two days before the station would have had to close down for lack of funds, the money was obtained. When told that they might lose their local educational television station, the people of San Francisco showed where they stood in this matter.

Ladies and gentlemen, we hardly know our own strength in this field, as in so many other things. We are fearful. We are diffident. We are hesitant. But the people of the country are concerned and interested in this enterprise; they are as interested as you and I. They need only be informed.

As further evidence, which one hardly expects to find in a trade magazine of book publishers, there recently appeared in such a publication a two-page statement on educational television. Despite Dorothy Smith's built-in radar system, which yields so much information, and despite what I am able to inform myself about as I move around the United States, this fascinating item escaped our attention at the time of publication. But not for long, however, for it was brought to our attention by the Council's editorial department.

Let me quote from a "Shop Talk" item in *Publishers' Weekly:*

New York bookstores report a continuing interest in the books in the New York University course, "Comparative Literature," which is telecast over CBS Channel 2 at 6:30 A.M. Although the demand has slackened off a bit since the first day of the telecast when New York stores were flooded with requests for *The Red and the Black,* people are still interested.

Barnes and Noble had its busiest day on Saturday, September 28th. The course started on September 23rd. The store was a beehive of activity. There were long lines of people behind the three cashier checkout desks. *Life* magazine was interviewing some of the customers, and INS was taking photographs.

At the same time the New York University book store was, of course, swamped with orders for the books covered in the New York University now famous course in "Comparative Literature." As soon as the first lecture on *The Red and the Black* was given, the store was besieged by customers and its stock of books quickly vanished. Mail order sales were 25 to 30 a day."

And mind you that this is not an educational television magazine; this is in *Publishers' Weekly.*

The station covers a radius of fifty miles at least and orders come in from New York, New Jersey, Connecticut, and Long Island. The store reordered twenty-five but quickly raised its quantities to a hundred.

And then from another section of this article:

As an example of how the university's telephone lines have been tied up by this rush of business, one day at the beginning of the furore, George Roosevelt [chairman of the Board of Trustees] tried to reach Dr. Carroll Newsom, chancellor of the university. He finally sent a wire asking the chancellor to call him, as he had been trying to complete the call for three days.

Well, after our meeting here, I think we can understand the vitality of this concern. It is real. It is genuine. It is meaningful.

I closed my remarks at the 1952 conference with a rather fanciful analogy. I indicated that I felt there were two factors impinging on the members of that conference. These were the eye of conscience and the sword of decision. I meant this very seriously because I felt that if that group did not feel the impact of the eye of conscience with respect to its responsibilities concerning educational television, then no forward progress could result. And I included the sword of decision, because it was clear that decisive action must be taken if any genuine results were to be achieved.

The eye of conscience has been far-reaching in these five years, because I detect unmistakably in what you say, what you think, and in what you do, the fact that you feel a sense of conscience about what may and should be done through this medium. One of the striking things to me about it is that, although we have been talking about educational television and how it may be used more effectively, inevitably we have been led to a close examinaton of the teaching process itself quite irrespective of the medium to be used. In short, through educational television, we have been led to give concern to something we should have busied ourselves with long since. But since life was going on in its traditional way, and since there was no press of conscience, no urging to re-examine these ideas, it wasn't done until we had this new medium.

We had to find ways to use television effectively, and a good start has been made in finding them. In doing so substantial areas of further inquiry and concern have been opened up. In addition to its prime function of satisfying the educational needs of thousands of people, educational television has provided a lever which has pried open a whole area, a complex of teaching problems, which demand and deserve our careful consideration.

What of the future? I am no oracle of Delphi. I was not an adequate guesser five years ago, and therefore I cannot claim to make predictions for the future. Like John Ivey, I have a tremendous concern, not alone for the educational affairs of our immediate day-to-day activities, but for the state of the world as a whole.

In that connection, I would like to tell you a story out of actual experience. During a recent trip to Africa, I was sitting in a one-room shack on the plain of Nigeria waiting for an airplane, and, in order to use my time profitably, I was reading an educational monograph, written in a learned way, but not in what could be called a lively style. I finished it with something of a sigh. As I laid it down, a Nigerian, twenty-five or thirty years old, came up to me and asked, "Are you through with that?"

I said, "Yes, I am."

"May I have it then?"

"Yes, you certainly may but I don't think you will find it very interesting."

"Oh, that doesn't matter," he answered, "it's something to read."

It's something to read! Can you imagine the condition of people in the emerging countries of the world who hunger for something to read? Are we making the best use of the magnificent opportunities for learning we enjoy when we have educational television, when we have such a medium for furthering educational opportunities? And there are in this country, ladies and gentlemen, young men and women, older men and women, who are just as eager to learn. They want to know. The channels to those thousands, perhaps millions, are not fully opened, but educational television offers possibilities of establishing such vital lines of communication.

Yes, we have a powerful medium. We have an expectant and an attentive audience. You have made tremendous contributions in finding the way in which this medium may be used for its most effective educational purposes. You have learned about dealing with program directors and cameramen. You have realized that you have to find ways to organize the subject matter that you wish to present effectively. You have encountered a whole area of technology with which you must coordinate in order to make an impact on your viewers and listeners.

Great gains have been made, and there are even greater ones to be made. I have just said that this is a powerful medium and that word "power" suggests something to me, because I have enormous interest in small boats. In the boating world, the tendency we see nowadays is for people to buy a skiff, 14, 16, 18 feet long, which inherently has a maximum speed of about twelve miles an hour. This might be achieved with an outboard motor of, say, 7½ horsepower, maybe 10. But because people sometimes wish to have a craft that will make a big splash, they put on this little skiff a 25- or 30-horsepower outboard motor, with the result that the bow points up into the air, an enormous bow wave is created, and the stern sinks down perilously close to the surface of the water. The owner of the boat feels that he is really going somewhere in a hurry, but he really isn't going much faster than he would with the 7½- or 10-horsepower motor.

I apologize to those of you who do not share my interest in small boats, but the analogy seems to me to be clear. We have a powerful medium. We cannot expect that we are going to make better speed, that we are going to have increased performance, just by putting on more horsepower than we have had before. We must investigate all aspects of this vehicle. For instance, we must consider the distribution of weight, if I may go back to the illustration of the outboard motor. And weight, or substance, in the educational process is the curriculum. As I have listened to what you have had to say, it seemed to me that our next move must be an inquiry into the curriculum. I believe that we need to have a conference like this one which would address itself to the concerns of the curriculum in respect to educational television.

It may be that our organization of the curriculum into courses, course units, is a perfectly valid one. But I have somewhat the feeling that we are putting enormous power behind a structure that we have inherited from the past. It may be that we need to redesign the vehicle in order to carry the additional power.

I shall investigate the possibilities—and I would solicit your interest—in holding a conference that would address itself to the curriculum in respect to educational television. If you wish to express your offhand interest now, I should be pleased to have it, because we are moving into an uncharted area. As we review the record, we note that, first, we considered the technical means by which we could use educational television. Then we had a conference on credit courses by TV. This was followed by one on closed-circuit television. We are now concluding a conference on teaching by television. What more natural, then, than that we should now address ourselves to concern about the material to be taught by television?

What I am suggesting is only a first step and in no way is it to be interpreted as any negation of the broader concerns which have been lucidly expressed by John Ivey. He is thinking in an altogether valid and significant direction with respect to the place of higher education in the world, not alone in our country.

This I would subscribe to and endorse with all the enthusiasm at my command, but if we are to climb the mountain, do we not have to take some first steps? I would hope that we could begin to take these first steps, as we have taken steps during the past five years, with assurance, insight, and the enthusiasm that you have unmistakably displayed during these last five years.

Thank you from the bottom of my heart.

CHAIRMAN: That applause, Arthur, signals our gratitude for a superb windup, looking backwards, looking ahead. Would this group not wish me to take a moment to say thank you for other matters as well?

We thank you not only for the concept of this meeting, which will remain with us, but for those efforts you made in our behalf and to which a number of foundations generously responded. We thank you for drawing together all of these top-flight specialists who have worked so well on this vital theme.

Would not all of you who are guests at this great university join me in thanking our hosts? And we are especially grateful to Ray Carpenter and his colleagues, who have played such a key role in this program.

Finally, let your chairman say how grateful he is to all of you for tolerance of guillotine tactics in an effort to keep the show on the road.

Papers Supplementing Subjects Discussed at the Conference

A Prospective of Televised Instruction

HOPE LUNIN KLAPPER (New York University): Five years ago research in educational television was limited to the basic question of whether students could learn from televised instruction. That question has been answered conclusively: they can learn. They have learned. That answer, however, has opened the door to many other implicative questions.

One of the areas which is now receiving educational and research attention is the use of production devices in ETV. We are curious to know what effects derive from the fullest possible use of the medium, and our ethical background urges us not to waste possibilities by simply duplicating the traditional classroom scene on the screen. The findings of psychological and communication research lead us to believe that well-selected visual and audio material can definitely increase learning. Television gives us an opportunity to test kinds of visual and audio techniques that cannot be tested in traditional classroom situations.

Extensive use of production devices is expensive, both in time and money. We cannot afford to experiment at random. Experiments must be systematic and penetrating. This paper will briefly present three questions which relate to the use of audio and visual materials in ETV. It will present the answers suggested by New York University's recent experiment with ETV.

Do production devices make the course more interesting to the student? We have used such devices, ranging from cartoons, graphs, and pictures, all the way to dramatizations. Toward the end of our course in History of Civilization, students were asked to select the telecast which they enjoyed the most. All students selected a lecture which made heavy use of production devices.

Students in the course called Man's Cultural Heritage were given a questionnaire designed to elicit reactions to the visual and audio techniques used in the course. Their response was unequivocal. Almost nine-tenths (87 percent) check the statement, "On the whole, the production aids definitely made the course more interesting to me," and only 5 percent felt that these devices did not add to the interest of the course.

But this is in no way equivalent to saying that production devices *necessarily* make a course interesting. They offer no guarantee of student interest; this is made apparent by the very disparate reactions students had to the various courses offered on ETV at New York University. Thus, students' responses to "On the whole, liked it" showed that English Composition (14 percent), English Literature (17 percent), and History of Civilization (38 percent) were not as "enjoyed" as Man's Cultural Heritage, Term 1 (59 percent). Yet, the English courses and History of Civilization used production devices, while Man's Cultural Heritage, Term 1, did not.

These findings suggest various other implicative questions for which there are as yet no answers. Production devices can make an interesting course more interesting. Can they also make a less interesting course more interesting? Can they move a course from the "traditionally uninteresting" to the "interesting" category? And, although educators agree that interest correlates with learning, at what level is the point of diminishing educational returns reached? Since production aids are time consuming and costly to prepare, should they be saved for those courses which students typically classify as "less interesting"?

Do these techniques create more favorable attitudes toward TV? In Man's Cultural Heritage, students in the section which used production devices were decidedly more favorable to ETV than were those who had the course with no visual or audio aids. Among students taking the course without aids (Term 1), 27 percent said they hoped to take more TV courses; the same hope was expressed by 61 percent of the students taking the course with aids during Term 2.

But again, visuals and audio aids do not inexorably elicit favorable attitudes toward ETV. In the English courses, less than 10 percent of the students said they hoped to take more television classes. This response was three times more frequent among students in History of Civilization (31 percent) and in Man's Cultural Heritage, Term 1, given without aids (61 percent).

The data of the New York University study indicate that students may develop strongly favorable attitudes toward ETV even when the screen discloses merely a lecturer and a blackboard. However, for a given course, they somewhat more frequently develop such attitudes, and the attitudes are more strongly favorable, when the course does use production techniques.

One may well ask how important it is that students be "very favorably" as opposed to "just favorably" disposed toward ETV. What will the increased favorability yield? Does it promote and influence other attitudes more clearly held in high regard by educators? Are attitude toward homework, attitude toward learning and education, general attitude toward school affected? These questions are pertinent and answerable, but there seem, as yet, to be no studies which bear upon them.

Does the use of audio and video aids lead students to think they learn more or more easily? Students in Man's Cultural Heritage firmly believed that the visuals helped them learn. When asked to check as many responses as described their feelings, almost everyone in the class (99 percent) agreed that "having definitions and major points . . . shown on the screen was very helpful." Over three-fourths of the students (78 percent) felt that "production aids made it easier to learn the materials of the course," and two-thirds (64 percent) felt that "the production aids were, for me, definitely aids; they usually helped me learn." Equally significant, only 7 percent felt they "would have learned just as much had there been only an instructor and a blackboard on the screen."

The answer is clear, but the clarity in no way makes its significance less obscure. To what does this belief in the helpfulness of the production aids lead? It might increase feelings of adequacy and security, or heighten interest in the course materials, the college, or school work in general. But it might also lead to a false sense of security: because the student thinks he knows, he might study less and in the end learn less.

Although most students were certain that they learned more and/or more easily than they would have had there been no production aids, their performance does not bear out their conviction. On the midterm and the final exam, students in the "bare bones" version of Man's Cultural Heritage scored higher (a mean gain of 19.1) than did the students in the production version (a mean gain of 11.2).

While this clearly suggests that production aids do not increase learning, it is not conclusive. Many topics require investigation before we can know the effect of production devices on learning.

We have not learned, for example, which kinds of visual aids and audio devices are most effective in aiding the student to learn specific kinds of information. We do not know whether the student may not require a practice period before he is able wholly to benefit from visual and audio aids. And, oddly enough, we cannot yet know whether our tests are really valid. A lecture with production aids may well have effects not revealed by traditional tests. For example, the new techniques may lead students to think more broadly about a topic; and typical course tests, particularly objective tests, may be inadequate to sample breadth.

I believe careful and systematic research on these and related topics will greatly modify the tentative conclusion that production aids do not aid learning.

H. BURR RONEY (University of Houston): Television has been accepted by the University of Houston as a major instrument in achieving the institution's educational objectives. More than 11,000 regularly enrolled students in 61 standard college courses have been receiving instruction by TV during the past five years. We have found that television saves space, time, and faculty, and in many cases it results in what is accepted as better teaching. Present problems are not quite the same as those we faced when we began televised instruction. We now have great need for more space, more staff, and a greater allocation of time on the part of the participating faculty to their TV work. We need more and better equipment. And of course we need more money. Because of these limitations, I feel that we are not reaching the full potentialities of this powerful medium.

In the area of faculty acceptance—still something of a problem—we are expending time and energy to demonstrate that there is nothing immoral, unsound, or nonacademic in the use of TV as an educational tool. Even though we have been through these arguments many times, different and new views keep coming to light, so frequently that some of us feel we might as well take faculty resistance and need for replicated research for granted. Surely the social psychologists could help us meet this problem and thus obviate the need for wasteful repetition. There must be ways to influence faculties which do not involve impropriety. The most effective way to achieve interest and cooperation seems to be to involve a faculty member in actual teaching by television.

More significant are the problems arising from what we do not know about the application of teaching techniques to the learning process. The cold eye of the TV camera has been very revealing. As a result of the attention TV has focused on the professor, we are wondering about the actual relation existing between what we do in our teaching and what we expect to have happen in our students. Does one technique really produce more learning than another? What is the desirable balance between reading, talking or discussion, television usage, and laboratory performance or its equivalent forms of discovery and practice? Is it more important to cause students to want to learn than to supply the facts of the case? Can we increase motivation leading to the acquisition of knowledge, and if so, how? So far I know only negative answers to most of these questions.

The proper use of television is not merely to transfer old practices to a new medium. How I may feel about my teaching performance is not a valid indicator of the student's learning. We need more research on better ways of effecting better learning. The necessary basic information about learning is available; what we need is knowledge of how to use the subject matter of a particular discipline to achieve educational results that have been previously determined as desirable.

Our experience with courses in which for practical scheduling purposes lectures have had to be repeated, either live or on film, seems to indicate an important line of future development. In Biology, with each lecture available three times, twice on TV and once in a classroom, the number of students who for various reasons "attend" more than one lecture runs about 10 percent. The value of this repetition shows in their performance. In Mathematics 132, where lectures in plane trigonometry have been recorded on film, these films can be checked out by students. In recording the film, a department course came into being; each lecture was the product of the best efforts of each member of the mathematics department. Students seem to have an increased sense of their own responsibility for learning, for with the film available to them, for twenty showings if necessary, they have only themselves to blame for not learning.

Through individualized use of film, the gifted student would have an opportunity of proceeding at his own more rapid pace. Although we have not made this particular use of recorded lectures, I expect future development in this area. This would allow the faculty, as it does in our mathematics department, more time for individual counseling sessions with students who are having difficulties.

MARTIN H. ROGERS (State University Teachers College, Brockport, New York): It is obvious that the introduction of television as a teaching medium may permit a single instructor to reach more students simultaneously, but there is concurrently a question whether or not some of the instructor's effectiveness may be screened out in the process. While spreading a single instructor's influence to more students, television could dilute that instructor's potential influence.

There are uses for television, however, which tend to increase an instructor's effectiveness. The search for teaching aids and techniques for the enrichment of learning is never ending. It has uncovered and developed the instructional use of charts, models, films, slides, filmstrips, tape recordings, and the outdoors. Television is about to join the list of teaching aids which enrich learning and make teaching more effective. Like other visual aids, television is used most effectively and appropriately in the teaching of subject matter which has high visual content. It has an additional value in providing visual presentations with greater flexibility than is possible with charts, slides, filmstrips, or films. Students, sitting in a classroom, may witness televised demonstrations performed indoors or outdoors; they may observe laboratory demonstrations and scientific experiments; they may observe children studying, at work, or at play, without themselves being observed; or, illustrations and demonstrations taking place within the same classroom may be reproduced on the television viewing screen in close-up shots which have the effect of placing each student in a "front row" vantage point.

An experience with a course in Kinesiology for students majoring in physical education illustrates some of the values of television teaching. Two sections of students were taught simultaneously; one section viewed the instruction on closed-circuit television for the full semester; a second section sat in the studio and received direct instruction. The viewing group had only the television screen to observe, could hear the instructor and all the discussion which took place in the studio class, and could interrupt the instructor for questions and comments by means of a two-way communicating system. There was no personal contact with the instructor. The studio group was in personal contact with the instructor, heard the explanations, saw the demonstrations at first hand, and experienced a normal classroom situation with the addition of the presence of television cameras and a viewing screen which they could watch if they wished.

The instructor conducted the class in his accustomed manner, making no special preparations simply because of television. He required the television medium to adapt to his style rather than attempting to produce something unusual for television. The television technique thus became incidental unless there were opportunities for TV to make the instructor's methods more effective.

Such opportunities arose frequently. An articulated human skeleton was used to illustrate joint structure, movement, and muscle attachments. A close-up view (impossible for all students under ordinary circumstances) enabled some fifty students, viewing the television screen, to observe the demonstration as though each were only a few inches away from the skeleton itself. By shifting the cameras from close-ups of the skeleton to schematic drawings on the blackboard or to movements performed by the instructor or an assistant, the entire class received more varied visual impressions than would otherwise have been possible. The students in the studio section soon learned to watch the TV monitoring screen when close-ups were being telecast, in order to get the benefit of the "front row" seats.

Explanations of the mechanics of human motion frequently called for demonstrations which the cramped classroom space did not permit. Television cameras were set up at the swimming pool and in the gymnasium. The two-way communication system allowed the instructor in the studio to direct the performance of diving, gymnastic, and game skills to illustrate the desired principles. In the studio and viewing room these demonstrations were observed as though the students were themselves at the pool or in the gymnasium. The talk-back allowed questions to be asked and answered, demonstrations could be repeated or modified at will by remote direction, and the students were not disorganized, nor time lost, by moving from the classroom. It was possible to introduce this type of demonstration with about five minutes' preparation, so that many student questions could be answered by a living demonstration almost immediately. On several occasions the cameras were merely pointed out of the studio windows to pick up activities on the adjacent playground and sports fields, and the participants in the outdoor activities unwittingly became the subjects for kinesiological analysis by members of the classes in the studio and viewing room.

An informal evaluation of the student achievement in this experience revealed the following: (1) There was no appreciable difference between the studio and viewing room groups on daily assignments. (2) The three highest semester averages were received by students in the studio. (3) All members of the viewing room group clustered toward the top of the distribution of semester-average marks. (4) A third section of Kinesiology, taught in a normal classroom during the same period of time by the same instructor, did the poorest work as shown by the semester-average marks. (5) A non-physical-education major student who worked the monitor switch in the control for the semester, asked on the day of the final examination to take the exam himself. He passed the exam with no preparation other than his visual observations during the semester.

Concepts of Televised Instruction

EDWIN P. ADKINS (State University College for Teachers, Albany, New York): The fear most often expressed when college faculty members consider the use of instructional television is that the values of classroom discussion will be lost. They visualize the ideal-sized class (twenty to thirty) under favorable conditions, but they fail to consider that this kind of class, under expanding enrollments, is virtually a thing of the past, especially in a public institution. Neither do they realize fully that the supply of master teachers on the college level is not adequate and will diminish in proportion to the number of students enrolled.

With these considerations in mind, the State University College for Teachers at Albany, New York, in cooperation with the New York State Department of Education, launched a series of experiments in closed-circuit television discussion techniques during the 1956–57 school year. This experimentation is continuing during the current term and certain promising practices are observable. In a freshman-sophomore general political science course now being offered, lively and stimulating discussions are taking place three times weekly between and among the students in four separate rooms. The situation is similar to the discussion technique experiments at the State University of Iowa but differs in several important respects.

The instructor is in the studio (a classroom converted at little cost), with twelve students seated as in the usual classroom. A small microphone is around the instructor's neck; and one microphone of a larger type (Electro-Voice 664) serves the students. Two manned cameras (Dage 320) cover the instructor, the students as they are talking, and any visual aids that are being used. A director in the control room handles camera positions and selects from the monitor the picture to be transmitted to the viewing rooms. Each viewing room is equipped with two 24-inch General Electric receivers.

There are three viewing rooms, with fifteen to twenty students in each. A graduate assistant in the room acts as monitor and discussion leader. The students in each room can hear what is being said, but pictures are transmitted only from the studio to the viewing rooms.

The students in the studio are exchanged every few days, usually at the end of a topic or unit. Each viewing room has four representatives in the studio group. Seemingly, several desirable results are obtained in this way: The instructor can become acquainted with all the students by sight before the term ends. This system tends to educate the student in the total process; and when he returns to his own viewing room, his reluctance to enter into the four-way discussion has decreased. At the same time the student seems to identify himself with the students in his particular viewing room much more closely than if all members of the class were in one large lecture hall. It is also the feeling of those most directly involved that a larger percentage of the students actually participate than is usual in a large-class situation.

When a student in a particular room desires to question or comment, he informs the assistant by raising his hand. The assistant then presses a lever which turns on a red light near the instructor's station in the studio. As in the regular classroom, he may recognize the question when he wishes. By the location of the light the instructor knows in which room the question is originating. When the question has been recognized, the assistant reverses the position of the lever, an act which opens the circuit to the studio and to the other viewing rooms, and at the same time, turns off the instructor's microphone while the question or comment is coming through. When the comment has been completed, the lever is released and returns automatically to a neutral position, thus activating the instructor's microphone. In practice this has permitted fast-flowing discussion with no more pause than in the traditional situation.

An additional method used occasionally is for the instructor to turn over the discussion entirely to the room assistants for five to ten minutes. During these periods nothing is transmitted and the discussion is confined within the separate rooms. This seems to clarify concepts which might otherwise be lost to some students and tends to add to the feeling of oneness within each group.

The program has not been under way long enough to permit definitive evaluation. The most that can be said at this point is that the process being tried holds promise for the future of instructional television. Especially is this true since relatively inexpensive equipment has been used throughout.

DAVID G. MONROE (University of North Carolina): Enrollment pressures, limited financial resources, the need to extend services—all these conflicting considerations faced the State of North Carolina when, in 1953, consideration was being given to the proposed establishment of televised education on the three campuses of the Consolidated University (the University of North Carolina at Chapel Hill, North Carolina State College of Agriculture and Engineering at Raleigh, and Woman's College of the University of North Carolina at Greensboro). But in the larger sense the real concern was one of evaluating the potential values of televised education in terms of the acknowledged costs and problems involved. Many considered that educational TV was, at best, a calculated risk, for such reasons as: (1) few teachers possessed the interest in and capacity for televised teaching, (2) the uses of televised teaching were limited in subject matter and procedure, (3) the television studio could not provide the kind of teacher-pupil relationship that the classroom provides, and (4) televised education cannot hope to compete with commercial programs of larger interest to the listening audience, and backed by money and know-how.

On the other hand, there were many who believed that televised education is one of the important answers to serious educational problems that grow more critical each year. They considered that broad areas of higher education are adaptable to television instruction and that within the ranks of the faculty there are teachers having the interest and capabilities to provide excellent instruction. More particularly, they stressed the fact that television provides a real means of satisfying two important educational needs: utilizing present teaching staffs and classroom facilities to their maximum extent, that is, multiplying teaching capacity and plant facilities without the usual additions, and of extending the teaching frontiers of the faculty beyond the local campus to that of the state and beyond.

Televised education in Chapel Hill began January 8, 1955. I think we have made significant progress, both in the multiplication of teacher effectiveness on the campus and in broadening the extension program of the university off campus.

For example, in June of this year, the Dental Foundation of North

Carolina provided the School of Dentistry with a black-and-white television installation which included two cameras, a console monitor, and a two-way audio system that allows the instructor to speak and the students to ask questions. Major oral surgery was performed via TV for the first time last week. I asked Dr. John Brauer, dean of the School of Dentistry, for his opinion about TV, its uses and potential values. He wrote:

Faculty and students are enthused. The closed-circuit television affords a most favorable opportunity for the teaching of many areas in dentistry. Laboratory procedures, due to the minute details, in many instances, must be demonstrated in small groups of five or six students, when such instruction is done in the customary way. The television camera can now in many laboratory procedures present a clear, more defined illustration or procedure to 50 or 100 students than was possible to the five or six students in previous methods. This same favorable experience can be multiplied many times in various clinical operative procedures when working with patients. In reality, it permits a greater clinical experience for many students, since a particular oral surgical operation or other clinical procedure can be witnessed by 100 or more students at a time.

In terms of the extension activities of the university, TV has contributed in a variety of ways. Two of these warrant particular comment: (1) the offering of TV credit courses, and (2) participation of UNC in the North Carolina In-School Television Experiment.

For some years there has been a growing demand for extension division courses for students and others unable to study on campus. The need has been met, in part, by the use of the standard type of courses requiring the preparation of written assignments and by the infrequent assignment of faculty members to teach off campus. During the summer of 1955, the university offered its first TV credit course. Since then, eight other courses have been completed or are in progress. The total enrollment has not been large (89 students enrolled for credit, 251 signed up on a noncredit basis), but the future is promising. To date, about six hundred written inquiries have been received concerning television courses, and they are all encouraging.

The second development—the university's participation in the North Carolina's In-School Television Experiment—is one which has great promise for the future. It was made possible by a grant of $105,000 from the Fund for the Advancement of Education, matched in money or service by the public school systems of eleven major cities in North Carolina. The experiment was designed with four objectives in mind: (1) to bring to the public school classrooms via TV the services of highly qualified teachers having the resource backing of the university; (2) to teach large sections of 100 to 300 students, and thus release teachers or reduce teaching loads to permit effective reallocation of teacher time for counseling, research, and so on; (3) to utilize school buildings more effectively by using auditoriums and other larger areas not normally employed for teaching; and (4) to evaluate TV as an effective large-group method of teaching in comparison with regular classroom procedures.

Workshops were held in Chapel Hill during the summer of 1957. There, the experimental plan was organized, courses developed, teachers selected. Instruction began in the fall of 1957. About 7,000 students in junior and senior high schools in North Carolina, South Carolina, Virginia, and Tennessee took televised courses in American History, World History, General Science, and Eighth-Grade Arithmetic through the facilities of WUNC-TV. The first two courses originated from the Chapel Hill studio, the other two from Greensboro. Four commercial stations—WSOC-TV, Charlotte; WSJS-TV, Winston-Salem; WLOS-TV, Asheville; and WCYB-TV, Bristol—provided the cooperative transmitting network. This well-organized and conducted experiment attracted widespread interest and may well have set the stage for a new and much-needed approach to public school education. Our underlying problems were and are money and academic interest.

Televised education at UNC was made possible largely because of the interest and support of William D. Carmichael, vice-president of the Consolidated University. He was influential in securing the backing of public-spirited citizens, local foundations, and local industry who contributed about $1.25 million to construct the transmitter and the three TV installations in Chapel Hill, Raleigh, and Greensboro. WUNC-TV was in operation for some months before General Assembly appropriations were available for operational expenses. Of the 1955–56 biennium appropriation only $108,000 per year was for the operation of the three units. Two years later, the General Assembly appropriated about $147,000 per year for the 1957–58 biennium. I mention these financial factors to suggest that university television operates within the framework of serious financial limitations. This year, for example, the Chapel Hill studio has an operating budget of $39,000.

Paralleling the budget dilemma is the problem of cultivating a greater faculty participation in televised education. Thus far no provisions have been put into effect to reduce the normal teaching load of those instructing over television. The granting of released time to instructors offering courses for credit would be an important boon to the cause of TV: it would enable the instructor to devote needed time to the preparation and presentation of his course, and it would remove a problem of how to compensate the instructor for the added work load occasioned by TV teaching. The difficulty was eased temporarily when five teaching grants, each for $1,000, were set up for the giving of five television courses. These were essentially summertime grants: that is, the instructor would devote a part or all of his nonteaching summer schedule to the preparation of his course.

While we have a rough road ahead, television does offer some alleviation of three critical problems—a larger and more effective use of our undermanned teaching staffs, a more effective utilization of classrooms and other plant facilities, and the offering of a larger measure of services to the people beyond the campus gates.

BARCLAY LEATHEM (Western Reserve University): At Western Reserve University, after nine years of television experience, we believe the two most important problems of teaching by television are improving the quality of instruction, and stimulating viewers to active participation in the learning process.

The first problem concerns the instructor's use of television, his ability to adjust to a new medium and to take advantage of its potentials. What can the teacher do on television that he cannot do in the normal classroom situation? What can he do better? How can instructional programs be produced with legitimate attention to good showmanship? What relationship is there between form and content? If visual aids improve instruction, can we determine what kinds of visual aids are most effective? Can this information be made available to all colleges and universities engaged in televising instruction?

We believe there should be more exchange of information. Easier availability of kinescopes would be helpful. The present emphasis upon kinescopes for use primarily by educational stations is probably necessary, but universities that use commercial stations are also engaged in teaching by television and should have ready access to kinescopes for private showing to local instructors and television program directors.

An effective means of upgrading instruction would be the use of an Ampex Videotape Recorder. Its cost, however, for most privately endowed universities is prohibitive. Foundation assistance to purchase this device would enable a number of these universities to improve the quality of instruction. Selection might be made on basis of regional location, size of potential audience, television experience, nature and extent of educational television activity, and availability of dependable air time. It is to be hoped that foundations would not refuse essential aid to a few on the ground that such assistance could not be given to all.

The second problem is closely related to the first. Improving the quality of instruction should increase the active response of viewers. Because we use the facilities of WEWS, a commercial station, and reach thousands of people who are not taking courses for credit toward a degree, we have a special problem in adult education. How can we stimulate more of these viewers to change from passive to active participation in the learning process? Here again the budgetary limitations of privately endowed universities restrict experimentation. We believe the sale of home study guides would increase if the cost could be substantially lowered. We believe noncredit viewers could be given some personal attention, perhaps by having graduate students read and criticize occasional written exercises, that might encourage them to further efforts. Discussion leaders might be made available to neighborhood groups. Viewers might be invited to attend especially scheduled colloquia on the university campus. Incentive techniques might be used to encourage noncredit viewers—awards of books, for instance, to persons who demonstrate initiative and ability. These and other possible aids and incentives to learning require funds beyond the resources of all but a few privately endowed universities. Without financial assistance, therefore, solution of the problems here mentioned is unlikely, or at best will be long delayed.

Fullest use of television for instruction should include preparation of master courses in several fields. Courses could be planned that would bring to viewers famous professors from several universities, each discussing his own specialty. Such a course might present more than one critical analysis of the same topic. Through television, students attending one university would have an opportunity to see and hear professors from other universities. Moreover, subject matter could be illustrated by use of outstanding talent. In drama courses, for example, scenes could be performed by the best professional actors. The possibilities in music, art, and literature are obvious. The finest talent in every field could be used. Television would then provide an enrichment beyond present teaching techniques.

REV. HERMAN J. MULLER (University of Detroit): Beginning with the fall semester 1957 the University of Detroit has instituted a series of broadcast television credit courses leading to a bachelor's degree. The courses are especially designed for students of the Detroit area who might otherwise be unable to attend college. They are by no means meant to supplant the normal media of instruction. The five courses offered during the first semester are: Rhetoric and Composition; The Development of Western Civilization, I (From Antiquity to about 1660); Introductory Psychology; Elementary Spanish, I; The Public Life of Christ. The courses are given from one to four o'clock in the afternoon, Monday through Friday. English, history, and psychology are repeated on Monday, Tuesday, and Thursday evenings from seven to eight-thirty. In addition to attending the lectures in their homes, students are required to come to the campus once each week for a one-hour period for each of the courses taken; such sessions are devoted to discussion, oral quizzes, individual counseling, and tests.

By way of experiment, the afternoon classes are also being given to special classes over a closed-circuit setup on the campus. In these classes a twenty-minute discussion period follows each half-hour lecture. In addition, each television instructor has a special control class which is being taught under normal classroom conditions. Assignments and testing in all three categories —open-circuit, closed-circuit, and control group—are kept as constant as possible in order to afford a reasonable basis of comparison.

It is too early to make an adequate study of comparative achievement. However, the testing thus far indicates that in the field of history at least, the closed-circuit group is doing slightly better than the control group, while the regular TV group is somewhat behind the control group.

Perhaps more enlightening for the present are the results of a brief questionnaire given to the students taking the television course in history. They were asked to set down in writing what they liked best and what they liked least about the course they were taking. In the closed-circuit group fourteen of twenty-five volunteered information, while thirty-three of the fifty-two open-circuit TV group submitted their views. The summary that follows will, I think, prove interesting.

Comments related to mechanics.—One student stated that it is easier to see what is presented, while seven thought that the professor speaks more distinctly and is more easily heard over television. Three were of the opinion that the novelty of the medium arouses interest and makes class time pass rapidly. Four students stressed the point that the TV professor seems much closer to them. As one student put it: "It is as though he were speaking directly to me. This I feel creates a rapport between the lecturer and the student which cannot be attained in a classroom setting."

On the other hand, a few bewailed the fact that TV reception was not always clear. Four were particularly irked at the lack of clarity in some of the blackboard illustrations and map projections. Perhaps the most consistent complaint was that graphics were presented on the screen too briefly. Five expressed this opinion in writing, as others did in conversation. For the rest, one student found himself distracted by changes in camera angles, and one thought the lecturer's voice too harsh at times.

Comments related to effectiveness of the TV lectures.—It might be said here that the comments were most gratifying. Indeed, one student went so far as to say that as much could be gained from a thirty-minute TV lecture as from the traditional fifty-minute class period. Twenty-one students lauded the careful preparation that went into the TV lectures, and more than half of these added "more" before "careful." For those of us who like to give the students an occasional chance to ask questions and discuss a point, it will be enlightening to note that eight showed great satisfaction that uninformed students were no longer able to interrupt classes with foolish questions. Five students found it easier to concentrate during television classes.

From the standpoint of effectiveness the chief complaint of the students was that the lecturer moved along too rapidly to permit adequate note-taking. Some thought that the topics were treated too briefly. Four wanted the lectures to be lengthened, and one student thought that the lecturer at times appeared a bit nervous. (He may have been thinking of the day the TV crew scrambled the professor's slides!)

Comments related to activity of the students.—While six students were of the opinion that the television setup left adequate and even more time for student discussion, some felt that the discussions were not really discussions; six stated that questions which could not be asked immediately were forgotten. Again, three bewailed the inability to compare their achievements with other students, four disliked the lack of personal contact with the teacher, and two found it difficult to adapt a medium used for passive enjoyment to active participation in learning. Precisely for these reasons several students praised the TV system for demanding and developing more responsible study habits and greater intellectual maturity on the part of students. It was remarked that students in the closed-circuit group were more alert than is usually the case in a regular class.

Comments related to the use of visual aids.—There was a general overtone of satisfaction among the students concerning the use of visual aids. Seventeen especially noted the fact that television permits a greater use of such aids. A few also mentioned appreciation of the more detailed syllabus and study guide which was given them. The adverse comments were limited entirely to the mechanical defects which have already been listed.

General comments.—The University of Detroit telecourses were designed for students not otherwise able to avail themselves of a college education. One lady of the class expresses pretty much the sentiments of eight other students. She writes: "I long wanted to continue my college studies but could not spend the time away from home. With telecourses the impossible has become a reality." In similar vein one of the men remarked that television courses enable "the married man with a family to continue his education toward a degree while requiring a minimum amount of time away from his home and his family." He added: "The system provides the answer for men with responsibility like mine, and I feel the University of Detroit should be complimented for meeting this real need." The business men and women in the group were particularly happy that, after a hard day's work at office or shop, they did not have to eat a hasty dinner, dress, and then drive an hour or more to school only to arrive home utterly exhausted at ten o'clock or even later.

For the teacher, who has labored so strenuously with arrangement of materials, graphics, maps, slides, and run-down sheets, there is the consolation that certainly not all his work is being done uselessly. Moreover, he becomes even more aware that visual aid techniques used in class do not always work out too well on the television screen. Wall maps, for example, which rely so much on color for distinguishing areas may be utterly useless on the black-and-white screen.

Finally, administrators who have had the courage to expend added thousands of dollars can take pleasure in the thought that the money has not been spent in vain. True, the number of people who at present are able to avail themselves of the new telecourses is limited, mostly because of lack of converters and special antennas. With the increasing popularity of educational television, however, there is every hope that programs such as those offered by the University of Detroit may prove to be a real blessing for the community in which they are conducted. Such programs can never take the place of the traditional classroom. They can, however, be a valuable substitute where such is necessary.

VERNON DAVIES (State College of Washington): One-way teleteaching defined as televised instruction with communication between students and teacher absent or severely handicapped, may readily descend to the level of "spoon-feeding." This assertion is founded on some basic premises: (1) A principal aim of a liberal education is to help students achieve a sense of self-direction and individual responsibility in their pursuit of learning; (2) such a sense of self-direction and responsibility can be achieved only through the recognition and development of individual abilities and differences; and (3) the adequate and creative development of individual abilities and differences can be achieved only in a nonroutinized, nonequalitarian teaching situation.

Any attempt to place greater responsibility on students must involve some departure from, and/or supplementation of, one-way teaching. The validity of this becomes evident when one contrasts student and instructor roles in one-way teaching. In such a situation the instructor assumes the active and authoritative role. While the manner in which he teaches may be influenced to some extent by what he may learn of student reactions, the important and relevant decisions are conventionally made by him. He takes and carries the responsibility.

The submissive and passive role of the students derives from the usual expectation that they do no more than watch, pay attention, complete the assignments, and ultimately be examined on what they have retained. Their principal burden is to sift out, as best they can, what they think the teacher thinks is important and memorize such for replication in the course tests. The responsibility they assume is assigned rather than self-generated, and, therefore, independent, self-reliant search for knowledge is not stimulated.

Unfortunately, the usually passive role expected of the students in one-way teleteaching is not the only characteristic leading to an underdevelopment of self-direction and independence. In such instruction everyone is normally treated alike, which is inimical to self-reliant learning. Some persons can learn to carry out functions or do things for themselves with virtually no help from others. At the other extreme are those who develop independence with great difficulty. Effective development of responsibility must, therefore, take into account the very real differences existing among students. The tendency is for mass instruction by television to give little or no recognition to such differences except in the allocating of course grades. The brilliant receive the same instruction as the dull. The weak are treated in the same way as the strong unless they are somehow able to obtain special help.

Since communication tends to be a one-way affair, the teacher tacitly assumes that it is of no importance for him to learn from his students. Whatever their felt needs, anxieties, and desires, he has no need to find out anything about them. The sole function of the hours spent "on the air" is to negotiate an exchange of information from the person who possesses it to a group of persons, located at a distance, who lack it, with an occasional effort being made to persuade or entertain. It is thus a one-man demonstration.

All of this permits the teaching of a course to be highly equalitarian and routinized. Students, while differing greatly, are taught as if they are identical, and the decision making is almost wholly restricted to one person. This description seems to be typical of a good deal of televised teaching and much other instruction at the college level. It is appropriately referred to as "spoon-feeding." Of course, calling it by a derogatory name does not make it bad. Nevertheless, many leading educators and university groups are looking on it with increasing reservation and misgiving. As one example, Clarence Faust, president of the Fund for the Advancement of Education, has recently criticized the active-teacher, passive-students type of teaching. He states that "Nothing seems so much to impress foreign scholars who visit institutions of higher education in this country as our failure to put sufficient real responsibility on undergraduates for their own education."[1] Of course, to speak of "putting" greater responsibility and actually causing it to happen is something else again. We feel sure President Faust would also agree that student

[1] *The Key Reporter,* April 1957.

responsibility is something that must be patiently developed. It cannot be willed into existence or brought about by changing media of instruction. A lecturing instructor who spoon-feeds in a classroom will not necessarily achieve better results by having his instructional activities transferred to a television studio. Instead, with the help of a skilled technical staff, his teaching may be made even more palatable and lulling to passive listeners.

The discussion up to this point has been largely critical and negative in tone. The purpose has been to stress the view that televised teaching is no more immune to spoon-feeding than is ordinary classroom instruction. However, it would also appear to be true that televised teaching may be made as effective as other kinds of instruction in stimulating responsible, self-reliant learning. Space limitations will not permit an outline of specifics, but a statement of some general principles appears possible, if education through the media of television is to escape the limitations mentioned above: (1) Methodological procedures in the televised instruction should be consciously and directly aimed at encouraging "do-it-yourself" education, which is at the opposite end of the continuum from spoon-feeding. (2) The sources of information available to students are numerous and varied, including books, journals, museums, newspapers, commercial television and radio, participant observation, and the use of interviews. In view of this, the instructor using television should studiously avoid developing the compulsion that if he is not continually purveying information himself, he is derelict in his duties. (3) As an integral part of a course taught by television, an instrumentality should be devised that is sensitive and responsive to the felt needs and problems of enrollees, so that they will be motivated to seek help in achieving responsibility in the learning process. (4) Finally, instructors teaching by television should, where necessary, redefine their role in the direction of being guides and helpers rather than being merely suppliers of information or interesting performers.

FRED MCKINNEY (University of Missouri): I submit that television can help revitalize education because its use will cause more teachers to raise questions about the variables in good teaching. It cannot be employed without disturbing some of the longer established practices in higher education which are less appropriate in present-day classrooms.

Let us explore briefly some of the essential elements in effective education and how educational television may implement their effectiveness. We may assume that the best education occurs when the student is ego-involved in the educational process or when the student is actually engaged in a trial and error process of some sort. We may assume further that this occurs best in small, intimate groups and with a leader with whom they can identify in some way.

It is hypothesized that close-circuit educational television used with small groups (in addition to a presentation from a studio group) holds possibilities as an aid to meeting the impending shortage of effective teachers. In addition, it has characteristics which, if properly exploited, can enable class activities to promote the motivations of the student. ETV has possibilities in the future for retaining in higher education intimate groups and student ego-involvement, even if it is necessary to use well-chosen and supervised students as leaders and resource persons in the small groups. It will probably be necessary also for the studio lecturer to meet all the students in small, informal groups for brief discussions. Over a two-and-a-half-year period this has been found successful in teaching a class-wide course at Stephens College. The small student groups which are made possible through closed-circuit TV have an educational value in their own right. Properly planned, there is the possibility for development of an *esprit de corps* which can enhance the educational endeavors of the group members. In addition, this may be a means of giving the superior student more responsibility as a resource person, and giving the average student a vehicle for working through an adjustment.

ETV seems to allow better classroom use of demonstrations and illustrative charts for large numbers, and more intimate use of such activities as role-playing skits, special interviews, and projective material to promote discussions and class protocols, all of which make for more vivid teaching.

ETV, furthermore, has possibilities for producing student gains beyond increase of knowledge of course content. These noncognitive increments, it may be assumed, have always been important elements in the teaching situation when students have judged a teacher as outstanding. These noncognitive effects of teaching may include personal insights, attitudes which lead to the student's better perspective of himself and his world (increased curiosity, greater understanding of others), and other activities which catalyze personal learning.

Concepts of Televised Instruction

HAROLD P. SKAMSER (Michigan State University): There seems to be a strong and definite trend toward increased use of television for college instruction. This is particularly noticeable in the closed-circuit television now being tested on many campuses throughout the land.

From a limited experience with broadcast and closed-circuit television, the following observations have been developed: (1) An advantage of closed-circuit television is its ability to make an outstanding lecturer or teacher available to a large number of students. (2) A considerable number of students are given an over-the-shoulder look, even though they are seated great distances from a demonstration, an operation, or a procedure. Every student gets a close-up. (3) The many types of visual aids can be used easily and made visible to all. Experimentation with films, slides, filmstrips, charts, posters, models, blackboards, and the like disclosed that all could be used successfully. (4) In a viewing room, usually somewhat darkened, remote from the cameras and the teacher, there are very few distractions; only the television screen can be the focal point of concentration in the area. This seemed to lend a considerable advantage. Tests and other devices at Michigan State University indicate that the students learn better and more effectively under these conditions.

Some conclusions have been reached concerning the disadvantages of television:

1. In the camera room there are many distractions. The students' attention seemed to flit from the lighting to the screens, to the instructor, to the equipment, cameras, and auxiliary aids, and so on. In fact, sometimes the lighting interfered with the viewing on the screens.

2. It was further agreed among those in our own little experiment that there was not much point in putting a mediocre teacher on television. There are several reasons for this; among them, the students subconsciously compare this professor with professional television shows, involving similar personnel who are doing something of an educational and informational job. Because of differences in talent, equipment, manpower, and so forth, the comparison is usually odious. Also there is no great reason for multiplying mediocrity in teaching.

3. Another difficulty and disadvantage which we found was that the scale or proportions of detail and lettering must be very carefully controlled so that such detail is not lost on the screen. Further, it is our opinion that there should be enough screens to be viewed so that no one student is thirty, forty, or fifty feet from a screen. Perhaps small groups of twelve to fifteen around each screen would be ideal. We believe that using one or two screens for one hundred or two hundred students is false economy.

It is our impression that perhaps the only way that colleges and universities can meet the demands of the growing number of students is to provide more closed-circuit television teaching in the next ten to fifteen years.

W. C. McNally (Miami University): In three semesters of presenting Human Physiology by television we have found that the majority of students do not like televised instruction, but rather than take a class with a teacher of lesser or unknown reputation, many elect to take the television instruction.

During this time there was no extra conscious effort to present the television course lecture materials in ways which would particularly appeal to students. It is true that the work was more carefully outlined and the outline diligently followed. The outline did not follow that of the textbook. Since many of those enrolled are freshmen, and since very few will take additional work in the biological sciences because of curriculum arrangements, it was felt that following a definite outline would be more helpful to the students. The outline was put on 2″ × 2″ slides. Care was taken to not crowd the material on any of the slides. The appropriate slide is shown at the beginning of each lecture. First a summary of the previous work is called to their attention, then transition is made to the next point, and finally the subject is developed logically. At the end of the lecture the outline is used again and attention called to exactly where we are.

Slides of the textbook illustrations are made and used, as well as slides and diagrams of other pertinent materials. We have found that demonstrations by television enable more students to observe the details much better than in a conventional class, except for those in the two front rows. We have shown the difference between oxygenated and unoxygenated blood and the action of the valves of the heart as if each were in line with the window in the aorta and with the window in the right auricle.

In our conventional classes, we have a laboratory exercise during which we expose the beating heart of an anesthetized dog. We show the influence of vagus nerve stimulation, changes in blood pressure resulting from different body positions, effects of changes in the blood volume, effects of various drugs, and of direct stimulation of the heart by electrical stimuli. Of the 35 students in the laboratory, perhaps a dozen who are nearest the dog can see the details, but by means of television all can see equally well. When the exercise is performed via television, it is impossible for each student to pick up the heart while it is beating, to experience the odor and the spurting of the blood when an artery is cut, but we feel that many of the anatomical structures and the action of the heart can be seen exceptionally well.

Our students feel that the lack of student-teacher contact is the biggest disadvantage in teaching by television. It is a very real objection, both from the students' and the professor's point of view. The opportunity for that bit of encouragement given to the good or exceptional student, or to the unknown, is lacking. The student has a point in not knowing what the instructor is like, how he reacts to a class situation. I feel that this is true, even though the marks at the end of a semester for those in my television class and in a conventional class show no significant difference.

The human physiology course meets for three lectures and a one- to two-hour laboratory per week. The professor does all of the lecturing and meets one of the laboratory sections. The other laboratory sections are handled by assistant professors, each of whom has had teaching experience. It is planned that the professor will take over laboratory sections other than his own from time to time. This contact, it is hoped, will be very helpful and somewhat revealing to both student and professor.

Also planned is a series of student-teacher conferences to help overcome the lack which is met by the conventional class. It seems that large lecture classes are no better than is television in the student-teacher relationship.

FRANK S. TRUEBLOOD (Los Angeles City College): My experience in teaching by closed-circuit television is limited to one class last semester, when I had an experimental class of 100 students in a one-semester course in general physics. This course is required at Los Angeles City College of all students who have had no previous training in the field of physics and who plan a major requiring either two or four semesters of physics. Of the 100 students in last semester's experimental group, about 40 percent indicated that this course would be their first and only course in the subject. I suspect that of the 31.8 percent who dropped out of the course, most were among this 40 percent, since the homework was directed more toward the needs of the engineering group. Indications are that our new group this semester will run only about 15 percent instead of 40 percent of nonphysics majors.

Mathematics through algebra is prerequisite for this course. The basic requirements for completion of the course are eight to ten homework sheets consisting of problems, thirteen to fifteen experiments performed in the three-hour-a-week laboratory, and five examinations plus the final.

My purpose is not to extol the virtues of television, nor do I wish to convey a negativistic attitude. After all, this is still classified as an experimental project on our campus.

I consider the most significant problem in my experience with this first experimental class in physics to be the seemingly impersonal relationship between my students and myself. There seems to be a sort of synthetic or artificial contact. It was an odd experience to have students speak to me on campus, students I didn't recognize and possibly in some cases students I had never seen, and I do not know how many pass me by without even a nod of recognition. This lack of personal contact is somewhat compensated for in the laboratory where the group is necessarily small—about 30 students in our case.

We have eight to ten Physics 11 laboratory sections scheduled, and they include students from other Physics 11 classes as well as the television group. Last semester I was scheduled for only one of these labs (25 students), but only about half of the group were from the television class. These small groups, of course, are a help in solving this problem of personal contact. They are certainly a help for the more timid student—at least he can talk over his difficulties with *somebody*. My personal feeling, though, is that I am losing contact with this type of student even though he may not be losing contact with me.

This problem was recognized almost at once in all our first classes in television, and at the suggestion of our producer additional microphones were placed in the large listening room. These microphones make it possible to hear the students ask questions directly and eliminate the need to relay the question by way of the monitoring system which we have available.

This question-answer system is only a partial solution to the problem. Even though the system worked to perfection—and I do not doubt that with proper training and experience both televising and receiving instructors could work as a coordinated team to achieve near-perfection—there would still be an element of artificiality about it.

The students still ask a question of a picture and the teacher responds without seeing the student's reaction or sensing the feeling of the group. To solve this phase of the problem, it has been suggested that both instructors, the one televising and the one receiving, be selected from the same department. (Last semester we used a receiving room teacher from another department.) This then makes it feasible, after a demonstration or the development of a basic concept, to turn off the set and have each teacher conduct, say, the last fifteen or twenty minutes of the class period more or less as a normal class. This we are trying with our new class this semester and so far it seems to show some interesting possibilities.

There is still the problem of the timid student in the large group, and it may be resolved by dividing the large group by means of movable partitions or even using smaller rooms. This, of course, brings ETV down to the level of another audio-visual device to enable the same number of teachers to do a better job. Our director, Dr. John Lombardi, has intimated that if this does turn out to be the prime advantage of television in the schools, even at greater cost, it may well have established its place in the educational system.

The statistics from last semester's experiment on the comparative values of a large group receiving televised instruction versus a small nontelevised control group have not as yet been released by the director of evaluation and research, but I find an interesting difference in the two groups in regard to their response to 100 questions covering the material presented during the semester.

Of the televised group, 68 percent represents the highest percentage of the class that missed the same question, while for the smaller group taught by me with much more of the give-and-take, personal relationship, one question was missed by every student in the group, one question by 95 percent of the group, and eight questions by 80-90 percent of the group. Does this imply that the give-and-take of a small class may not be superior after all to the organized planned presentation via television? I wish to draw no conclusions from these percentages except the possibility suggested by them, which further study might reveal.

As far as the medians on the examinations for the two groups are concerned, there seemed to me to be no significant difference. And on the questionnaires filled out at the end of the semester, I am told that 35 percent of the students said they felt that they knew the TV teacher about as well as the teachers of other large classes.

Another possible solution to this problem of lack of personal contact may be in the scheduling of the class in split sections. That is, schedule, say, two of the three hours on television and schedule the other one hour per week (the familiar quiz section or recitation section) in smaller groups using several teachers. I think this would be of particular advantage to television because it incorporates the advantage of the planned, organized presentation via television with the informal give-and-take of the small group. By incorporating the meeting times and places in the schedule of classes, both types of presentation would be guaranteed instead of accidental. I say accidental because I find it very difficult to break a presentation at the proper time to allow fifteen or twenty minutes for discussion at the end of the period. Twice now I have planned to do this in my present television class and have run over the allotted time.

I believe the statistics for last semester's experimental classes are to be released this month and will become available upon request in the near future by writing to Mr. Harold B. Owen, Television Education Specialist, Los Angeles City College, 855 North Vermont Avenue, Los Angeles 29, California.

Our studio, I am told, is unique in that the instructor has full control over each of four cameras. This control is accomplished by the use of four push-buttons located to the left of the instructor's desk. Thus, the instructor can switch to blackboard, cards, himself, or camera 4 for anything special, say, a part of a movie film or the whole film if desired, a close-up of small instrument dials, or even moderate magnification or vertical projection. Of course, we have to plan ahead for camera 4, as our technician requires time to set it up for the specific purpose for which it is to be used.

OLIVER M. STONE (Case Institute of Technology): Closed-circuit television provides new and interesting possibilities as a medium for bringing laboratory procedures and equipment into view in remote classrooms. However, if this new teaching medium is to become a significant factor in the more efficient and economical use of instructional staff time, it must be extensively used in the ordinary classroom situations. It is imperative that the unique advantages of the medium be explored and exploited to their fullest extent.

One obvious advantage is its flexibility in presenting visual material. This is highly important since about 85 percent of all learning comes through the sense of vision. It is generally recognized that teachers at the college level have not utilized the visual aspect in education to its fullest extent. This suggests that it may be possible to increase the effectiveness of instruction by the use of television and at the same time effect a saving of instructional time.

Some other advantages can be listed as follows: (1) some forms of visual material which are inherently small, such as instruments, gauges, and electronic equipment can be magnified many times when shown on a 24" television screen; (2) mobility to show the various details of the object is easily accomplished; (3) models and graphic material can often be produced more economically in a small size and then magnified on the screen for easy viewing; (4) there need not be duplicates of the various visual material (as is often the case under conventional teaching methods) to accommodate a number of sections meeting at the same time; (5) these considerations in turn reduce the space necessary for storage.

In teaching graphics courses it is particularly desirable to make use of visual material. The underlying principles and the procedures that are followed in the graphical solution of problems can be more readily demonstrated than verbally described. Also facility in the interpretation of shape and space relationships, that are suggested by the flat drawings, can be developed in the student more easily through visual material. Models and objects such as instruments and machine parts are particularly effective in a television presentation. Demonstrations which utilize the chalk board, tear sheets, graphic illustrations, and projection equipment including the Vu-graph can also be very effective.

In order that television may become more effective as an educational medium, the problems most urgently in need of solution seem to fall under the following classifications:

1. *Psychological*

   Improvement in acceptance and attitude toward the medium by both students and faculty is needed.

2. *Technical*
   a) Improve present equipment to get clearer and sharper pictures; larger screens and, especially, color would be major improvements.
   b) Improve the operation of the camera, including lens selection, so that the visual material and the speaker would be more effective.
   c) Improve the general and special lighting of the visual material.

3. *Preparation of the visual material and the presentation*
   a) Attractiveness of the visual material from the design standpoint greatly increases its effectiveness.
   b) Size of letters, weights of lines, and contrasts with backgrounds must be such that the visual material can be easily seen and perceived.
   c) The entire presentation must be well planned and progress in a logical and orderly manner.
   d) The verbal presentation must be forceful and interesting.

It is my opinion that the acceptance problem will be largely solved when the technical and presentation techniques have been improved. Technical improvement is constantly being made in the equipment that becomes available. More experience should solve the camera operation and lighting problems.

The most significant problem, and perhaps the most difficult one with which those of us who are teaching by this medium are concerned, is the presentation. Experience will be of great value. However, I believe that constant research and evaluation of the various presentation techniques, together with the exchange of information in meetings such as this and through publications, will greatly increase the effectiveness of educational television.

Where two-way communication is employed (as at Case Institute), I believe that three sections of about twenty-five students each is the maximum that can be handled effectively in a single presentation.

Critiques of Televised Instruction: Chemistry

Robert D. Brown (University of Alabama): I should like to confine my remarks to the use of television for instruction in the natural sciences, especially my own field of interest—chemistry. Although there are problems encountered here which are common to other disciplines, there are others which are unique.

Perhaps the most significant problem encountered is that of recognizing and understanding the potentialities of TV in chemistry instruction. There is no specific answer to this because every lesson presented, especially one involving demonstrations, has its own particular problems. This is further complicated by the personality of the teacher who, upon beginning a TV project, should ask: What are *my* capabilities for teaching *my* subject?

It is not necessarily true that a good teacher will make a good television teacher. Parenthetically, one may add that television will not make a good teacher out of a poor one. However, there are some simple techniques that must be followed by the TV teacher. He must strive to look at his audience which means looking at a small circular opening a few feet away, and he must limit his pacing back and forth so that at least he will remain within camera range.

This personal aspect of the problem can be solved only if the would-be TV instructor has the willingness to learn and adapt his methods to the limitations of the medium. This willingness must be combined with active conscious efforts of adaptation. Perhaps the most effective way to do this is to make kinescope recordings of the beginner's lessons, first with his knowledge and later occasional ones without his knowledge. These should be studied carefully to see what improvements are possible.

As for the potentialities of the medium per se, these obviously must be compared with those of the teacher or lecturer in classroom or lecture hall. As an illustration of this problem, it does not seem at all desirable to use closed-circuit TV unless a lecture room of sufficient capacity to reach as many students in several repeated lectures as might be reached in one TV period is not available, because it usually takes more effort to produce a TV lecture than it does to give several lectures on the same lesson or subject. Digressing further to express an opinion, I think that only where distances are great and one wishes to reach widely separated audiences would one use TV at all. There may be exceptions: in some instances closed-circuit television has been used with apparent success in giving laboratory instructions to many sections all of which are doing the same experiment at the same time.

These are general problems of production, transmission, and reception which are now well recognized and I shall not comment on them any further. I do wish to mention some of the specific problems one encounters in presenting a chemistry lesson.

As an example let us take a lecture-demonstration in which hydrogen sulfide is produced and used to precipitate some of the metallic sulfides. To ensure success, every step must be worked out in advance, every piece of equipment must be gauged to the scope of the television camera—because if the camera misses everyone misses. True these are technical, but nevertheless very real, problems and must be taken into account. Also, few TV studios are properly equipped to do scientific programs, although this can certainly be remedied.

Another limitation is color. I purposely selected the above example, because unless we use color TV, not yet widely available, we miss the brilliant colors of the precipitates, colors actually specific for certain elements. In other examples where we are restricted to the impartial black and white of ordinary TV, we lose the association values of "blue copper sulfate," or the pink of a "phenolphthalein end point" in titration, and so on. There is another technical difficulty associated with this problem. Some spectacular reactions produce strong light which cannot be handled by the cameras, so that much care has to be exercised in this respect. This may be solved by the use of elaborate light filters, but even then much of the effect is lost. Generally speaking however color transmission is not an insurmountable problem. But what of smell? How can one send the "captivating" odor of hydrogen sulfide, ethyl mercaptan, or butyric acid over the coaxial cable or microwave relay? Or the pungent fumes of ammonia or hydrogen chloride, and so on? And also involved may be a sense of feel as much as a sense of smell.

We know that sound offers no problem, and that color is no longer a technical problem but rather one of economics; and Huxley in his *Brave New World* dreamed up the "feelie," but the possibility of a chromatic talkie, feelie, and smellie seems rather remote. Indeed, certain laboratories over the country have distinctive odors because of the type of research that has gone on in them, and without the intriguing aromas of the chemistry laboratory much is lost. It is a loss we will have to endure although we could send out simulated smells as part of the lesson plan with instructions to smell this midway in lesson 9 and take a whiff of this one at the end of lesson 12!

Finally there is the matter of the laboratory. It needs close supervision and, moreover, is the place where the student learns by doing. It is evident that there is no real substitute for this kind of experience. This is not to say that much of the conveying of ideas cannot be accomplished by TV; however, it is only an adjunct, it only prepares one for the activities of the laboratory, and this we must recognize if serious omissions are to be avoided.

In conclusion, it appears that if one sets out to teach a natural science such as chemistry by TV, it is imperative that he learn first the capabilities and limitations of TV, and second how to adapt his teaching methods to it. Both can be accomplished by experimentation and objective evaluation. If this is done there is much that TV has to offer. My experience leads me to conclude that, although in some instances it can prove superior to conventional methods especially where large audiences are concerned, in others it cannot compete. Therefore, the wisest attitude is to consider television as an adjunct to other methods. If this is done, it can prove a very useful device.

W. BERNARD KING (Iowa State College): Frequently, when reviewing the literature on the educational aspects of television, one reads such comments as (1) "On the whole, television students have done as well as other students, and at times somewhat better," (2) ". . . television students in a signal corps course did just as well as nontelevision students when paired according to aptitude and information scores," and (3) in a general chemistry course offered at the Iowa State College during the fall quarter 1955, students receiving ". . . instruction by closed-circuit television did 'just as well' as did the control group." A "just as well" performance is not adequate. Televised instruction must do a better job than the typical classroom teaching to justify the cost in dollars and the cost in wear and tear on the professor.

Institutions of higher learning are confronted with the problem of televised education, not merely with educational television. It is our duty as representatives of our institutions to determine *those specific areas in which television and related mediums can make their greatest contributions*. This would appear to be the most significant problem facing televised education. Development will come once the discoveries of those specific areas are made known.

Following are a few suggestions as they pertain especially to the subject of general chemistry.

1. *Select essential topics and develop them into films of the highest caliber. When appropriate, demonstrate laboratory techniques.* What a difference there is between the veteran and the novice merely in shaking a test tube! Unquestionably an experienced teacher in front of a camera can do a far superior job in manipulations than can a graduate assistant in front of a section of students, crowding to find a vantage point. Making these superior films will require money, planning, imagination, good script writers, good sign makers, good experimenters, good camera men, good speakers, and a world of patience.

2. *In addition to films covering essentials, some should be made for the express purpose of developing an interest in science.* Maybe this is wishful thinking, but what a pleasure it would be to see students reading chemistry books and other books on science because they want to, and not because some professor says, "This is your assignment; study it."

3. *The films must not be lengthy*, possibly thirty minutes as the upper limit. If superbly done, a twenty-minute film would certainly accomplish far more than a fifty-minute lecture of the common variety. But having excellent films is no guarantee that students will benefit from them. Students must be prepared and conditioned for instruction by TV. They should be cautioned that TV education is intended to teach, not entertain. The ability and determination to listen and observe is all important. The day's topic should be studied ahead of time. Students realize this after a while.

4. *Provision should be made for showing a film several times during the week and possibly before final examinations.* Such a procedure would be helpful to the poorly trained student. It would also give the major professor a better opportunity to visit the classes of the graduate assistants and be of real help.

5. *Textbooks surely will remain the source of most of the information.* The laboratory should contribute in developing a real interest in science. It can do this if the time is spent solving laboratory problems rather than in performing experiments that do little but gather stagnant data. Can there come a day when a student does his laboratory assignments in the absence of a teacher? Opportunities to ask questions and a chance to use the vocabulary of the chemist are still essential. Can we expect proper development if the

student has no one to talk to about his problems? Television, movies, kinescopes, or whatever the medium is, can, when painstakingly produced, make a real contribution in the lecture hall, but it is doubtful if they can replace the teacher, even the lowly assistant in the laboratory or the recitation room.

C. N. MCCARTY (Michigan State University): Several important problems confront the teacher of a science, such as chemistry, when he attempts to teach via television. From the standpoint of the chemistry involved, the most significant disadvantage at the present time is the lack of color in transmission by television of chemical demonstrations. Color and color changes are of utmost importance in many chemical reactions; a black-and-white image is therefore obviously inadequate. As color television becomes available at a price within the budget of most colleges and universities, this objection will be eliminated.

To many lecturers an important disadvantage is the restriction imposed because of the limited field of view of the television camera. During a conventional chemistry lecture the instructor often walks from one place to another at a large lecture table to point out and to emphasize various details of demonstrations, models, and other visual aids, or to use gas, water, and other utilities which are needed for his experiments.

During a televised lecture, on the other hand, he finds it necessary to remain in a restricted area long enough for students to assimilate information. When he moves to a new location or points to another chart or visual aid, he must allow sufficient time for the camera to follow, and time for the students to examine and absorb the new image. These restrictions of space and time impose upon the lecturer an awkward lack of mobility and a reduction in the amount of subject matter which can be discussed in a given period of time.

Another related factor is the smaller amount of "usable" blackboard space for presenting a given concept. An area only about five feet square is covered by the normal field of view of the television camera at a distance which gives a sufficiently large image for visual clarity. Such an area is quite inadequate for writing most chemical equations. A possible partial solution to the problem is the use of more than one camera and of multiple monitor sets which present different pictures simultaneously. Naturally new problems of planning, training of camera men, rehearsal, and increased cost are thereby introduced.

The criticism most frequently heard from the students and one which is difficult, if not impossible, to overcome is the loss of personal, live contact with the instructor which the student gets in a conventional lecture room. Students feel they do not get to know the instructor and, hence, lose an important part of the college experience. Even with talk-back microphones, students are reluctant to interrupt a lecturer who is not in the same room. Questions in the minds of students go unanswered, and the lecturer is never made aware of the fact that some of his statements have not been made clear. To many teachers, facial expressions, the "feel" of the class, and the questions asked are an invaluable measure of student understanding and of the need for further repetition or example. It is difficult to conceive of this problem being solved by an attempt to overcome the natural shyness of many young college students through training in the use of talk-back microphones.

L. O. Morgan (The University of Texas): In the University of Texas the general chemistry course is quite large because of its status as a required course for all engineers and students majoring in scientific fields. The number of faculty members and teaching assistants is limited and most of the latter have had no previous teaching experience. In order to strengthen the laboratory portion of the course certain measures are being taken. One of these is the experimental use of television as a supplementary teaching aid.

The premises upon which the television experiment is based are that (a) more students may be reached by a single, well-qualified instructor; (b) the medium is well suited to the presentation of close-up views of laboratory experiments; (c) the material presented to a large number of individuals is more closely controlled and more uniform; and (d) the need of the part of the student to assimilate and use the information immediately provides a powerful incentive to pay attention to the material presented.

The premises proved to be well founded on the basis of our experiences over the past year in a preliminary trial of the techniques. The trial was not designed to give quantitative information on student performance when taught by television but rather to discover and evaluate qualitatively the factors of greatest interest for future consideration of the methods employed. Points to be considered more carefully in further trials include: (a) time factors in experimental work, (b) accident rates, (c) long-term retention of specific experimental details, (d) retention of supplementary information.

At the present time we maintain an open mind concerning the over-all benefits of the use of television in this way. We do not now see it as a means of reducing our total manpower requirements, nor do we believe that it is suitable as a substitute lecture device. It is possible that a revision of the traditional lecture-laboratory method of subject-matter presentation would provide a more suitable framework for the use of television in teaching chemistry to the college student.

Kurt C. Schreiber (Duquesne University): During the last academic year Duquesne University conducted an experiment in teaching organic chemistry by television. The choice of subject was not arbitrary. Organic chemistry, perhaps unlike any other subject, normally depends on the continuous use of the blackboard throughout the lecture period. The test, therefore, was whether the restricted use of the blackboard would make it impossible to present this subject over TV and what techniques could be devised to minimize the use of the blackboard. Since this represented Duquesne's first experiment in teaching via TV, we were also concerned with the question of the student-teacher relationship.

Let us outline first the problem of the blackboard. The total blackboard area available in a large lecture room cannot be reproduced on the screen with the writing at the same time readable; thus, only a small portion is normally shown on the screen. This is not serious when a relatively small amount of writing is presented during the lecture. However, when the teacher writes continuously, the only way the cameras can keep up is to pan with the teacher. This presents a definite strain on the student who is a slow writer. While in the regular lecture course he can fall behind and still continue to copy from the blackboard even though the teacher has gone on to other reactions, in televised instruction he must copy as fast as the material appears on the screen. Many students, for this very reason, find that they concentrate better when receiving TV instruction than normally. But others find the pace too fast for them.

The second problem concerns the sometimes large structural formulae of the organic chemist, which often must be written with special care to fit on the screen and be readable.

To minimize the use of the blackboard, four to six charts were prepared for each lecture. The material on these charts was given to the students in the form of mimeographed sheets. Sufficient space was left for the student to write in additional comments as he saw fit. You might say that this represented a prepared notebook. The length of time spent in going over these charts varied from four to ten minutes. On many occasions the discussion of the material on the chart was interrupted by supplementary equations put on the blackboard. The charts (28 inches by 22 inches) were made by writing with black ink (1-inch lettering) on light grey cardboard. Even though this technique helped considerably in the presentation, the restriction on space was severely felt by the instructor throughout the course and particularly during the last few weeks when the more complex organic compounds were discussed.

Despite the problems presented above, the limited testing of the students taking the course indicated that their knowledge of organic chemistry was in no way impaired through television teaching.

In this experiment the class was divided into two groups, one group being in the studio with the teacher, while the second received their lectures via the television screen. The second group was in contact with the instructor through an intercom system. Even though the students were frequently urged to make more frequent use of the opportunity to ask questions, it was noted that both groups were more reluctant to ask questions than in the normal classroom. On direct questioning the students indicated that they were loath to interrupt since the TV lecture was such a complicated production.

During the second semester other techniques were tried in order to give a closer student-teacher relationship. Two groups were rotated at regular intervals, thus giving all the students a chance to attend class face to face with the teacher and also to give the teacher a chance to become acquainted with the members of his class. It is the opinion of this writer that a three-week rotation system would work satisfactorily.

It has been my practice in all my lectures to establish contact with the students by asking questions during the lecture. With the use of the intercom system it was possible to continue this procedure, and to draw the student in the receiving room closer to the teacher. He, too, was part of the lecture and not merely a passive receiver on the other end.

In my opinion further techniques will have to be developed to close the gap in the student-teacher relationship to make television teaching more widely accepted.

Critiques of Televised Instruction—(continued)

HARRIS W. WILSON (University of Illinois): In the spring semester of 1956–57, I presented the first in-class television course at the University of Illinois. The course was Rhetoric 101, the first-semester freshman credit course in English composition. The instruction, consisting of two thirty-minute programs each week, originated in the university television studio, WILL-TV, and was received by one class of twenty students in a separate classroom building. The instruction was also available on home receivers within the radius of WILL-TV's signal.

A 21-inch receiver was set before the class, and for two of the three weekly class meetings the class received instruction by television for thirty minutes of the regular fifty-minute period. In the remaining twenty minutes of each of these two periods, an instructor who had been present in the classroom during the telecast amplified or clarified the television instruction. The entire fifty minutes of the third period of the week was used by the in-class instructor for impromptu themes, hour tests, etc. The televised portion of the course began at the fourth meeting of the class and continued for twelve weeks of the regular sixteen-week semester course. The in-class instructor had sole charge for the remaining three weeks of the course.

The course created, as far as I could detect, only casual and passing interest among those not directly involved. No objective studies were made of student response, comparison of grades with those of regular classes, effectiveness of presentation, or other aspects of the experiment. Consequently, the following observations are entirely subjective.

It seemed to me that the students benefited more from the television class than they would have from an ordinary composition class because of increased interest and the more effective presentation of certain portions of the subject matter. Interest ran high throughout the course, a fact I know from both the in-class instructor and from personal interviews with the class members. How much this heightened interest derived from novelty, however, I do not know. Also, I have no doubt that such matters as grammar, spelling, punctuation, and mechanics were presented more effectively on television—at least initially—than they are usually presented in the classroom. This was due partly to a greater conscientiousness by the instructor in his preparation, partly to the aid of television personnel, who are trained in visual presentation, and partly to the camera itself, which provides an automatic focus of attention.

From the point of view of the instructor, I felt no diminution in stimulation in speaking to the camera instead of the class. This may again have been largely due to novelty, or it may have been my keen realization that my efforts were exposed to the entire faculty and community if they chose to watch. I would not have dreamed of going before the camera without being completely prepared, or even overprepared in the sense of having more material at hand than I could possibly have used. Consequently, I reached my full potential as a lecturer much more consistently, I am sure, on television than in a regular class.

My in-class instructor was a young man in his second semester of college teaching, his first experience in teaching this particular course. I am certain he must have profited from watching an instructor of over ten years' experience in action, although he did not express himself strongly to me in this matter. But a potential value, at least, of televised courses would be the instruction of inexperienced teachers.

The element I missed most profoundly in the experiment was the lack of face-to-face contact with the class. I was surprised to learn, for instance, how much I depended on the facial expressions of my students to determine their comprehension of my instruction. Also, I missed the direct questions, both mine and theirs, to emphasize and clarify particular points. Finally, I missed the time that questions and answers give the instructor for the collection of his wits before he proceeds to a different phase of his subject.

The nervous and emotional strain imposed upon me by this television experiment was considerable—a good deal greater even than what I can remember of my first teaching experience. Some of this was undoubtedly due to my awareness, as I have mentioned, of my colleagues' ability to observe me. Another pressure was my complete and sole responsibility for the presentation of the subject matter—organizing the course, devising visual aids (I had an art student's help in making the aids), and attempting to adjust the instruction to the progress of the class. A major irritation, which might seem minor to one who hasn't experienced it, was the intense heat from lights, especially in late spring. I have finished programs with not only my shirt but also my coat drenched in perspiration. It is extremely difficult to perform effectively under such intense physical discomfort.

I seriously doubt that the course in writing can ever be presented over television exclusively. The criticism of the student's writing and the supervision of his attempts to improve his writing seem to me much too personal and intimate a process ever to be done with full effectiveness at a distance, and this personal reaction and control is the essence of the good writing course, either basic or advanced. Consequently, the televised course in writing must always make provision for this personal relationship, and it is exactly in this relationship that the instructor's experience and knowledge are most important.

But it would seem to me as foolish to maintain that television has no part in the freshman composition course as it would be to claim that television can carry the entire burden. Enthusiastically supported and wisely used, it can contribute immeasurably to the quality of the freshman writing program. But from my experience of last spring, I would insist that to be completely successful, televised instruction must be a cooperative effort. One man cannot do it alone.

ERNA GUNTHER (University of Washington): Closed-circuit television can be used in part to alleviate the problems of large classes in some areas of instruction. Whether students express a liking for TV in the classroom or not, their tests show that they are on a par with those who have direct teaching. It is realized, of course, that other factors, including study habits, are involved. Once students become accustomed to the novelty of this mode of instruction, their reactions may change.

Closed-circuit teaching in science can bring an intimacy to demonstrations which could only be achieved by endless repetition of the experiment before very small groups. The teaching of techniques in dentistry is also being successfully accomplished. The television technician in charge of the closed-circuit teaching at the school of health sciences at one university has expressed great satisfaction with the results in dentistry and wishes that the medical courses would use his services more than they do. Closed-circuit demonstrations are also used in nursing and in public health. In dentistry the entire class—present in the room where the instruction takes place—hear the instructor with little amplification. Four monitors are provided for 65 students, and often they can follow on their own models the process the instructor is carrying out. This type of participation seems an important factor in the learning process. The demonstration is the introduction to the laboratory period.

Closed-circuit television can also be used profitably in the teaching of languages, especially when the course stresses the speaking of the language, rather than reading knowledge or grammatical analysis. Speaking a language well involves not only the ability to make the proper sounds, but cadence, rhythm, and gesture. These can be transmitted by television. Furthermore, if two people carry the program together, the student not only hears the correct thing to say, but also the response. The criticism often leveled at language courses is that they "go too fast," especially if the broadcast is a short half-hour. The instructor, anxious to cover a certain amount of ground, forgets the repetition he indulges in during the longer class period.

In all television presentation the passivity with which the student receives the instruction is important. He must learn to work as actively with the instructor on the screen as he does in the classroom. This is especially true in mathematics courses where problems are set and solved by the instructor.

It is often mentioned that in auditorium-sized classes, the students do not all clearly see the instructor, cannot follow his facial expression, and sometimes know him even too little to recognize him on the campus. Well-placed monitors would correct this. Since the opportunity to ask questions is so rare in these large classes, the advantages of television far outweigh the loss of discussion. Generally questions are asked only in the quiz sections anyway.

Open-circuit television as a teaching medium has the same problems which have manifested themselves in many kinds of extension classes—a need to satisfy the serious student and at the same time to cope with those who have an interest without the necessary background. However, public telecourses serve also the function of the extension division of bringing subjects before the public, so that their success should not be gauged by the number of registrants for credit. They fulfill the same purpose as the noncredit discussion courses offered by many schools. Incidentally, the telecourses also introduce faculty members to the public, which in a state-supported school is an important public relations factor.

Both of these fields of television offer areas for exploitation, but their exponents must be aware of the limitations which each technique sets. Closed-circuit TV cannot take the place of classroom teaching, and telecourses cannot be substituted for the college campus. They are both supplements to improve programs and extend their effectiveness. The spirit of television is more informal and spontaneous than film and, even when in kinescope, it maintains this feeling. When used in teaching, TV depends more on the transmission of content than on dramatic presentation and therefore can carry out the true principles of education.

College Cultural Patterns and Their Effects on Learning by TV

RALPH C. LEYDEN (Stephens College): Before we develop a pattern in the use of television that limits our sights to what we are now doing in education, we must ask ourselves, *"What can we do in the education of young people that we are not doing now, at least not so successfully as we would like to?"* It is particularly important that we ask this question concerning our programs in general education at the lower-division level.

Presumably our major goal in general education is to equip the student with fundamental information and to develop in him the ability so to handle the basic facts and concepts of sociology, science, humanities, and the like, that he can make positive contributions to the life of his times. We have been busy with the first half of this goal, disseminating information, but in large classes we have found little opportunity to let students wrestle with themselves and one another in learning to handle the facts and ideas presented to them. Consequently, we have tended to give them the digest of our own conclusions which have resulted from our own study and our own discussions with others. John Stuart Mill in his essay "On Liberty" reminds us that "If the cultivation of the understanding consists in one thing more than in another, it is surely in learning the grounds of one's opinions. Nor is it enough that he should hear the arguments of adversaries from his own teachers. . . . He must hear them from persons who actually believe them."

The educational process should provide a place for the kind of experience Mill is talking about. So I repeat my question, "What can we do in the education of young people by using television creatively?"

Can we bring the community into our classrooms, vitalizing the learning through presentations of men and women in the civic, business, and cultural life of the community? Can we consider new realignments of subject fields which may bring back into education a greater sense of the relatedness of knowledge? Can we provide special noncredit offerings in any of several fields for students whose backgrounds are inadequate, thereby benefiting the student and relieving the teacher from taking class time for supplying the background or for review? Also important, can we, through use of television, devise new combinations of the lecture and discussion methods that capitalize on the strengths of both methods? By such experimenting can we discover better ways of increasing student learning and involvement? Can we discover ways of maximizing attention to individual differences? Can we utilize the more advanced students by having them assist us in working with beginning students and thereby stimulate both groups to broaden and deepen their understanding? Can we broaden our own backgrounds in general education by sharing the responsibilities of new courses which realign the familiar subject matter?

Some attempt to explore these possibilities was made during the last two years in the course Ideas and Living Today at Stephens College. Other colleges would no doubt have different needs and different solutions. We felt that a new course should be added to the curriculum that would introduce students to several fields of knowledge in such a way that they would begin to sense the basic interrelationship among the various disciplines. We wanted students, and faculty too, not only to have the advantage of the teaching of stimulating and broadly educated lecturers but also to have the opportunity to explore together the implications and applications of what the lecturers had to say. We thought of these lecturers as "living textbooks." Also, we wanted to use an interdivisional faculty in order both to stimulate the common intellectual life of the campus and to acquaint them further with the general education program to which they made their contributions from their specialized fields. We concluded that by employing the medium of closed-circuit television, we might be able to accomplish some of these goals.

During the first two years we chose visiting lecturers from varying fields of learning, but each with a strong background in the liberal arts. We urged each to draw upon this background through frequent references to fields other than his own specialty for illustration. Each condensed his material into twenty-minute lectures, always providing more material for discussion than the remaining thirty minutes permitted to be explored. Students were assigned to over fifty different classrooms equipped with receiving sets. Members of the faculty, representing all divisions, volunteered and were assigned as discussion leaders of these groups.

In selecting lecturers during these two years we gave first consideration to a man's ability to teach, and left him free to choose what he would emphasize. We of course tried to select lecturers who would be likely to emphasize differing fields of knowledge—sociology, philosophy, psychology, politics. But remembering their presentations, I feel that by even naming these fields now I am giving a greater sense of restriction of subject than was actually the case.

Of course we experienced many difficulties. Neither the entire faculty nor the entire entering class who took the course were completely enthusiastic about it, especially during its beginnings. But it has been interesting to note that questionnaire studies show the course has steadily gained in approval from students both during their year of taking it and, interestingly, during the following year when they were not associated with it. The participating faculty likewise have spoken of the experience as the best in-service training in which they have ever participated, and the great majority who have participated continue to volunteer.

During the current year we are using both visiting lecturers (for short periods) and members of our own faculty. We have at the same time brought greater variety and greater unity into the course. Centering the first semester around the subject of The Nature of Human Expression, we are including series of lectures on Introduction to Learning: The Humanities, Language, and Mathematics; during a second semester the series of lectures will center on the topic The Nature of Human Environment, and will include contributions from sociology, psychology, and science. Further, we are experimenting with using hand-picked second-year students as assistant discussion leaders in some sections, with twenty-two students in them instead of the usual fifteen or sixteen.

I cite this example of our course, not so much to tell of what we are trying to do as to illustrate how the answering of some of the questions which I have posed has been attempted. The experience is difficult, often frustrating, but has been rewarding enough that our faculty voted to continue the course as a regular, but constantly experimental, part of the curriculum. Other institutions which feel the need to ask "What can we do in the education of young people that we are not doing now?" will seek and find other solutions.

HAROLD WHITEHALL (Indiana University): My own experience with television has been rather fortunate in that I have been released over a commercial station, WTTV of 100-kw video and 50-kw audio, and I have had the usual reactions—some of the best letters from people who frankly did not originally intend to be listening to educational television at all. The farmers' wives, the farmers, the industrialists—those are the people whom I could never even approach in an ordinary university teaching career, but whose reactions to what I have to say have been most rewarding, and I think, on the whole, most worthwhile.

This brings us, I think, to another point about educational television. We can have closed circuits; we can have UHF; we can beam a course to students who are working for the purpose of getting a grade, but I see in the future of educational television something completely different. For the first time, perhaps, in the history of the universe there is opportunity for those who can learn and want to learn to do so. I suppose that human culture started about 5000 B.C. when people first learned how to write. They learned to write in syllables—an extremely complicated process—that involved cuneiform and hieroglyphics, and thus the visual and the oral first came together. Unfortunately because of inevitable complexities, the whole *modus operandi* of writing and reading was confined to the few individuals who had the talent and the gift for learning to transcribe. Inevitably, education became a priesthood matter, exercised by priests as some kind of priestly mystery.

Then around 1600 B.C., during the remarkable Hyksos revolution, people learned to write what we would call alphabetically. Where this happened is not very important to my present purpose, but probably it occurred on the coast of Syria in the Asian town of Byblos, "the place of the book." It was almost certainly the invention of some genius who, in the interest of trade, found that this kind of writing could serve the purposes of trade.

But what was a gain in convenience was a loss in pictographic qualities. The video was sacrificed for the audio. Since that time, many things have happened. We know from the third book of the *Confessions* of St. Augustine that he was quite amazed when he found that Father Ambrose could read without moving his lips. Now this particular revolution was an extremely important one. We think today in terms of the written word. We read our newspapers and assume that people have always been able to read silently without moving their lips. But as St. Augustine says, if I might paraphrase his words a little more forcefully than he himself did: "This is a revolution which will shake the world." It was a revolution which actually shook the world. Think of the medieval scholars reading and transcribing their texts in their carrells and repeating each word individually and writing it down phonetically. It is only since the invention of printing around 1450 that the habit of silent reading has allowed us to use silent reading in education.

Now reading alone is not satisfactory. It has ambiguities. Many recent scientists have been quite capable of learning the strategy of expression which is demanded by reading. After all, language is basically speech. Reading is secondary. And we must realize that after all it was only about two hundred and fifty years ago that we first learned anything like a satisfactory punctuation system for English. We must realize that reading—although in a way very satisfactory in the sense that it is not evanescent; it can be repeated; people can read over and over again—is by no means the perfect system of communication. Moreover, literacy as we understand it is relatively recent. It is only in the last one hundred and fifty years that we have even visualized the possibility of an education based upon reading. Let us admit that real literacy as such is on the one hand very good, from the standpoint of a given individual; on the other hand, it lays too much stress on those factors which, from the late eighteenth century onwards, we have come to consider as the proprieties of written expression.

To all these things, television, it seems to me, provides a provocative and perhaps a future corrective. On television alone one can associate the visual with the audible. Now I happen to be an audiophile myself, and am not particularly concerned with the videophile. I think that one of the lessons that we have to learn from educational television, to judge from my short experience, is that we can overestimate the video part of ETV, and underestimate the audio. I am sure in my own mind that an impelling lecturing style, without any particular gift for the visual, is far more important than the exhibits—the made-up possibilities of the video.

I know that our generation, unlike preceding generations can respond to the visual. Nonetheless, in my experience the driving lecture style, the ability to talk without rehearsal, to talk with spontaneity and with some kind of feeling for the individual member of the individual audience whom you are addressing—these are the real bases of educational television. The timing that the lecturer or teacher gives the lecture is of paramount importance.

In my experience, I can give them everything I have got, in the phrases I have got, without recourse to talking down or watering down the verities of my scientific information. The spontaneity of the occasion is extremely important in television. What more can I say? I have enjoyed it. Television has sharpened my teaching technique, it has given me technical resources I never previously dreamed of, and it has given me a feeling for the individuals of each class I teach as individuals, not as mere members of an anonymity to be graded.

JAMES F. SHORT, JR. (State College of Washington): The urgent need to reserve educational channels, to put them into operation, and to experiment with the production and evaluation of closed-circuit courses may have led us to overlook a fundamental fact about television and its social effects. This fundamental fact is simply that television is a social force, with great implications for education. It is a social force quite beyond our efforts to bend it purposively to the end of formal, or even informal, education. To some, it may seem that our conferences are a little naïve in this respect. We are a little like a group in James Watt's time *might* have been had they gathered to discuss what was to be done with the steam engine!

Yet, this need not discourage the efforts of our conferences. It is a challenge—a challenge to understand this social force in its educational impact. For, who can say what *might* have come out of a conference of James Watt's contemporaries? Certainly we are not going to *do with* television all that we might wish, but we can seek ways and means of utilizing it most effectively and of understanding its impact on the educational processes in our society, both formal and informal. It is toward the latter end that these few words are addressed.

We seem to be doing the first job well, but though we are aware of the existence of the latter, very little research seems calculated to give us answers to problems in this category. I have in mind such important questions as: How is commercial television influencing the formal educational process at all levels? This concerns both students and teachers and their relations, as well as the curriculum and the broader aims of education.

What are children of all ages (from two to ninety-two) learning from television, informally? Surely this is important to know if we would understand the educational impact of television and its potential usage in more formal educational efforts. How has television influenced preparation for, and expectations with reference to, the classroom? Can we build upon this impact in the classroom, with or without educational television?

Can commercial television, as well as educational television, be used more effectively in formal education? The radio and motion pictures, and national news magazines, have been used to some extent (how much we don't really know). How about television? Can programs with formal educational value be sold to commercial sponsors? We already have some good examples—*The Search* series, "Mr. Sun," and numerous dramatic and musical programs.

What are the implications of television in terms of student conduct, attitudes, and aspirations? What about social consciousness and political awareness, and family and community relationships, recreation patterns, and many more?

Each of these areas has implications for education, some more direct and obvious than others. It behooves us to be aware of them and to take them into account, lest our best-laid plans miss the mark out of failure to understand them. It may well be that some of the barriers referred to in this conference can be overcome only after some of these questions are answered.

EUGENE F. GREWE (University of Detroit): A university has been described as a community of scholars. Not the least important part of a university education is the interplay among these scholars. This interplay may be informal—over coffee cups; extracurricular—in meetings of Greek-letter or subject matter organizations; private—in conferences with teachers or advisers; or purely academic—in classroom or in seminar situations. But wherever and whenever it occurs, it is in this interplay that a kind of education takes place which can take place in no other situation. Its essential feature is the student's active formulation and expression of ideas which can be immediately challenged and modified in the direction of truth. This activity must not be lost sight of in any plans for collegiate education via television, no matter how well televised courses may work in other key educational functions.

In the current University of Detroit experiment, students in the daytime program may enroll in five credit courses—the regular first-semester program for students pursuing the Ph.B. degree (a non-Latin A.B.); students in the evening program may enroll in three of these five courses. But whatever the program, all students attend a fifty-minute quiz and/or discussion meeting for every course once every week. We have found this weekly campus visit essential to the effectiveness of our program.

In these sessions the students—of all ages, by the way, and of widely varied backgrounds—meet each other, learn to acclimate themselves to the amenities of classroom situations, and have opportunities to make those personal, intellectual, and social adjustments which are part of the development of educated persons. Without such opportunities, an individual may continue to be as provincial, ungracious, and uncommunicative as a self-educated hermit.

Wittingly or not, spokesmen for televised credit courses, in their enthusiasm for the obvious values of television in education, have frequently given the impression—or have allowed others, unchallenged, to give the impression—that educational television will soon make it possible for anyone to earn a bachelor's degree without leaving his hearth except for registration and one or two examinations per course per semester. The *Detroit News,* for example, spoke editorially of students earning a bachelor's degree through televised courses alone. Our president, the Very Reverend Celestin J. Steiner, S.J., has repeatedly stated that television was to be used for only the lecture and demonstration parts of courses, and then only in those courses in which enrollment is large enough to make televising them practicable and which are of such a nature as to lend themselves to television.

But the position of advocates of televised college credit courses is misunderstood not only in the public press but in our colleges and universities. Many of our colleagues are deeply concerned about the possibility—very real in their minds—that "TV graduates" of their schools may be an essentially different and inferior kind of person from former graduates who were educated in conventional classes. They are concerned about the possibility of their being forced to teach on television despite their own sincerely felt objections to the medium and their own evaluation of their lack of aptitude for such an assignment. Furthermore, many feel that they are in a very undesirable position: they may wish to refuse such an assignment but hesitate to do so for fear that such a refusal may make them *persona non grata* in a school which had previously held them in high regard.

In the light of the foregoing misconceptions and difficult situations, it is my belief that a group of people who have had firsthand experience in teaching via television—for example, the group attending this conference—ought to take the lead in formulating some kind of statement of policy covering the teaching credit courses via television. While I realize that the following suggested statement may strike some as controversial, I submit it in the hope that it may prove a suitable basis for discussion and that it may lead to an acceptable statement which could conceivably be one of the more significant items to come out of this conference.

Some parts of the proposed statement may be more readily appreciated if we consider for a moment one final observation. Although teaching by television has in some instances already been shown to be clearly effective, there is little question that there is still considerable need for further experimentation. The chief impetus to experimentation has been and is the indisputable fact that within the next decade or so college enrollments will increase by close to 100 percent. While such a prospect is almost staggering, it may be well for us to keep in mind that it is not essential that we prove (1) that, through the use of television, we can cut down on the use of campus buildings by 100 percent or (2) that where we now need fifty experienced teachers for certain multiple-section courses, we will soon need only one.

Let us think in terms of a freshman English course, like the one I am now teaching, chiefly via television. If we can show that instead of needing a class-room for three fifty-minute periods a week for each class, we can, through the use of television, get by with only one fifty-minute period a week on campus for each class, we will have made possible a saving of 66.7 percent in classroom space. This would make possible a theoretical increase of from 1,500 to 4,500 freshman English students without adding a single classroom to the campus. If we can show that instead of needing, say, fifty experienced teachers for about one hundred classes, we may, without losing effectiveness, require only twenty-one experienced teachers and forty teaching fellows, we will have made a significant contribution. If we could at the same time pro-vide a thorough in-service training program for these teaching fellows, our contribution would be even greater.

In short, the cause of televised credit courses will be furthered best, not by implications that the whole of collegiate education as we know it today must and will be changed, but by reasoned judgments about the best possbile use of television within the framework, basic methodology, and fundamental purposes of collegiate education as it has proved to be successful through the years.

With modifications and additions thought necessary by the group, then, the following might be a statement of policy which would be welcomed by many in America today, both in and out of the category of professional edu-cators:

1. No student should be granted a certificate or degree from a college or university for course work done only via television. Students obtaining certifi-cates for the completion of two years' work may have no more than 75 per-cent of their courses via television. Students obtaining degrees may have no more than 50 percent of their courses via television.

2. With the exception of those courses which have satisfactorily fulfilled college standards and requirements in the past by using only the lecture method, without quiz and/or discussion meetings, credit television courses should be so arranged that students will meet at least once a week in con-ventional quiz and/or discussion groups.

3. The academic standards to be maintained in televised credit courses must be the same as those in conventionally taught courses bearing the same title, course number, and credit hours. Assignments should be of the same nature—purpose, scope, type, and number. Wherever possible, final examinations should be identical with those administered to students in conventional classes.

4. In view of the many problems involved in teaching televised courses—personal, academic, technical, and professional—a teacher may without prejudice to himself refuse to teach his course(s) on television.

5. After carefully conducted experimentation, the decision to offer a

specific course via television should be made by the members of the department which regularly teaches that course.

6. The department offering a televised course should have final authority to decide the content of its course, although it should defer to the judgment of the television staff in decisions regarding the best technical means of communicating the material.

7. All televised courses must be given by bona fide members of the department responsible for offering the course.

8. The view that 29.5 minutes of televised instruction is of necessity at all times to be construed as the equivalent of fifty minutes of classroom instruction is not to be accepted as unalterably proved. The nature of each course and subject matter should be carefully examined, and the final decision that 29.5 minutes or more than that amount is needed in a given case should be made by the department teaching the course.

9. Details relating to the use of kinescopes and to the computation of the teaching load of persons teaching courses via television should be thoroughly examined and discussed by a committee consisting of college or university administrators, teachers who have taught televised courses, and representatives of an organization such as the American Association of University Professors; and recommendations for standard procedures and loads should be published in the very near future.

Concepts of Televised Instruction

FREDERICK J. BOGARDUS (Purdue University): The spur of advancing technology and of the world political situation is forcing us to seek ways of improving the *quality* of our product, the graduate engineer. This comes at the same time that population and sociological trends are burdening us with increased quantities of our raw material, and industry is demanding of us a greater output. Further, the quality of our raw material does not appear to be improving to any great extent, and there is little promise of any general raising of the standards for high school graduates.

Consequently, it seems that one of the major problems facing educational television in regard to the field of engineering, at least, is how to obtain this increase in quality in the face of powerful influences operating in the opposite direction. It may be assumed that this is a problem primarily facing the large state university since the major increases in size will take place here.

The situation in nontelevision classes is far from ideal. For example, assume twenty divisions of freshman chemistry—a three-hour lecture and three-hour laboratory course. How many schools have top-quality personnel available to handle one hundred twenty contact hours of freshman chemistry per week, plus all the higher-level courses? Inevitably great variations in instruction creep in, due, perhaps, to inexperience on the part of the younger staff member, disinterest of the older professor who longs for contact with upperclassmen or graduate students, or lack of coordination and motivation within the department. Double the enrollment, and the problems multiply.

Here, then, is an opportunity and a challenge to instructional television. It is fine to say that we can handle twice as many students through TV, but what will be the result of that handling? Will we turn out masses of factually trained, "handbook" engineers, who are little better than glorified technicians? Or can we stimulate ever larger numbers to think for themselves; can we motivate them to accept an increasing degree of self-education; can we arouse the spark of initiative and creativeness so essential in the profession of engineering?

It seems to me that here is the crux of the matter:—Can instructional television accomplish this improvement in quality which is so urgently needed?

There are many facets to this problem, only a few of which can be mentioned here. For example, the use of instructional television exerts a leveling influence since all students are exposed to the same instruction. How can this instruction be paced so as to stimulate the better student and still not lose the slower man? What will be the attitude of the administration toward changes in the failure rate which may accompany such endeavors? Will the necessary time and money be provided to prepare instruction so as to take advantage of television as a visual aid and reduce the effects of its inherent limitations?

Improved quality certainly can come from elimination of poor instruction and using only the top-grade teachers. Under television our best teachers become even more valuable and should be rewarded accordingly.

Now, how are we to know whether we are obtaining this rise in quality, or not? Is our present scheme of testing capable of distinguishing between the number of facts crammed into the head of the embryo engineer and his ability to solve problems, to exercise judgment? It seems rather futile to attempt to evaluate the effects of television on the basis of existing tests unless those tests are designed to measure changes in the area so loosely called "teaching the student to think." There should be little concern over checking the acquiring of facts, for we have been doing this for years. But there should be real concern, perhaps a complete revamping of our testing procedures, over our ability to measure truly the more intangible, and yet more important, aspects of engineering education. Unless we set up means for accomplishing such measurements we will continue to debate and express opinions without the solid foundation of factual information.

Such testing problems are not peculiar to instructional television but are accentuated when we are faced with attempting to make an adequate evaluation of its effects. An interesting exposition of the need for improvement of examinations is found in "Changing Conceptions of Examining at the University of Chicago," by B. S. Bloom, a reprint from *Evaluation in General Education*, edited by Paul L. Dressel.[1]

[1] Dubuque, Iowa: Wm. C. Brown Co., 1954.

The challenge is here. Can we do the job and can we tell when and how well we have done it?

M. W. FLECK (University of New Mexico): The opinions here expressed are the result of experiences in teaching by television at the University of New Mexico. Some of these opinions concern weaknesses of the medium, and other ideas are concerned with weaknesses of the philosophy pertaining to teaching by television.

There seems to be a lack of coordinated thinking as to what the medium can do in depth—from the first grade through university-level teaching. It seems to me this constitutes a major weakness in thinking about television in an educational program. Readers of this paper must realize the writer's views may necessarily be provincial.

It is my firm conviction that there should be correlated offerings horizontally to avoid compartmentalizing in education. This is a weakness not restricted to television. Modern society is complicated, and an educated person should have some knowledge of the interrelationship of various disciplines. Compartmentalizing education turns out college-trained people who are poorly educated. Television would seem to be an excellent medium for this horizontal distribution of knowledge.

There seems to be a general notion in some places that only rote-content subject matter can be handled on television. It should be possible to present programs which could stimulate thought as well as presenting basic ideas. The goal of education, no matter how imparted, should be more than imparting information. This is not to argue against education being informational, too.

Television should develop more and more good documentaries which will explore what has been thought as well as what has been done. Thus far there are only isolated instances of such materials.

It is my opinion that every good teacher should have an opportunity to teach at least one course by television. It is a rejuvenating and stimulating experience. In the classroom situation the teacher teaches alone after having prepared the lesson by himself. In the studio the teacher is surrounded by gifted people, a circumstance that cannot help but have a salubrious effect on the sometimes jaded lecturer. An idea may have its origin with the teacher but it is the group of gifted people in the studio who make it possible to put the idea across to a viewing audience. An effective presentation of knowledge is the result of teamwork, even though it is the teacher who has the knowledge of the subject. The necessary communication between the teacher and the television staff is of great value to a teacher.

Even though television can expand a teacher's potential greatly for a large number of reasons, there are also limitations to the medium. Some of the limitations are undoubtedly very real, and others are likely to be fancied ones. But television is probably no more limited in its way than the classroom has been for twenty-five hundred years. It has been suspected that laboratory situations had to be created because of the inadequacies of the classroom. It is the laboratory which enables a student to touch, feel, and smell and thus learn through several receptors.

Television can be a good educational medium because it can reach an individual, or a group, isolated from a classroom. It is limited because it cannot go beyond the studio. It is beneficial in bringing better understanding to the isolated student because of its ability to bring him more and better teachers. But for the isolated student there can be no group learning situation, and the immediacy of impact with the instructor is lost.

Television makes it possible for the student to see detail better because the lens enlarges better than does the eye. But the student may lose the over-all scope because the lens is not as expansive as the eye. It is not possible for the isolated student to have any choice of material, and it may be that while attention is being focused on detail the student may be distracted in thought. It is believed, however, that some of these limitations of the medium can be avoided by a teacher whose experience enables him to anticipate difficulties.

CLARK GRIFFITH (State University of Iowa): The principal problem, it seems to me, is one of maintaining a balanced attitude toward television and what we can expect it to accomplish. We need to be aware that, in and by itself, this method of instruction is not really a cure-all for anything. Novelty alone will not carry the experiment a great way, just as mere showmanship is never going to prove adequate in any kind of teaching situation. The opportunity of reaching larger numbers of people is surely desirable. But it is not a panacea, any more than merely good acoustics are the guarantee of a successful classroom lecture. And inevitably, of course, at least a little *is* sacrificed in teaching by television. The loss of a close personal contact between students and instructor cannot, I think, be completely argued away.

On the other hand, we should also deplore the sort of self-consciousness which shrinks from television just because it is something new—or the sort of condescension which ridicules the method as being cold, unworkable, and excessively mechanical. My own experience convinced me that students can be reached by way of the screen, and that the camera can become quite as stimulating—indeed, quite as evocative—as a group of the most interested faces. Despite the skepticism of some of my colleagues, I do not plead guilty to having abetted an experiment which brought to the academy the sterile and de-emotionalized world of *1984*.

But perhaps what I am saying is that the differences between teaching by television and by the more conventional methods should be minimized rather than exaggerated. The camera, I take it, never transforms a fumbling lecturer into a brilliant one. Nor, conversely, does it seem likely to reduce to chaos what would otherwise be effective classroom techniques. The television apparatus is a medium, a link; and the more inventively and intelligently we utilize it, the better. But whether the demands it imposes are basically different from the demands of teaching in general seems rather doubtful. Again, I can only appeal to experience: and conclude that, after a day or two of adjustment, I found myself doing on television the things I would have done normally, and doing them in essentially the same manner.

ADA D. STEPHENS (University of Toledo): Perhaps the most significant areas of the conference, for me, were those devoted to discussions concerning research which has been done and which still needs to be done, and theories and principles of learning in relation to televised instruction. It has been fairly well established that when a course has been given by television and the same course has been taught by the same instructor in the traditional way, the results have been practically the same. This does not prove, however, whether the course has been taught better in both instances, because different kinds of preparation and presentation are necessary and possible for teaching via television.

As a person who has taught classes via television, particularly open circuit, I feel that I do prepare my work differently and more thoroughly than when I teach in the classroom.

This leads me to consider research in possible practices and procedures in both televised and classroom teaching. If teachers could consolidate some of their multiple-section classes and use the time gained for preparation and research, it is possible that they would better their instruction. This might mean increasing staff rather than decreasing it; it might be more costly, but it might also result in better instruction. Let's find out. Some possible areas for research which I have presented to our faculty are: (1) Will teaching by television mean teaching differently? (2) Are students given enough responsibility and/or time for study on their own, or do teachers continue to teach them as high school students? If so, can television improve the situation? (3) How valuable is discussion in class presentations, particularly in presentations of the lecture kind?

Television is with us and is going to be used increasingly as a teaching tool. The University of Toledo is currently using closed-circuit television for some classes. It is about to install an educational channel for area use. We must have some proper part in research since the opportunity is at our doorstep.

HARRY E. CRULL (Butler University): As I see the problem of television for instructional purposes in institutions of higher learning, I assume that what is meant is closed-circuit television within the institution rather than educational channel or commercial television utilized for instructural purposes.

It seems that one of the most significant problems is the training of instructors in the use of television. I have observed a number of instructors teaching by television, including a demonstration at a recent national meeting. The instructor who assumes that the classroom technique may be carried over to the television camera makes an error which can diminish the effectiveness. This seems to occur without the instructor having any notion of all that he is failing to get across.

Last summer at a national meeting I watched a closed-circuit presentation. It was very poorly done simply because the instructor taught exactly as he would in the classroom. He is an excellent teacher, but because of his failure to recognize the shortcomings of the television camera and failure to utilize its particular advantages, he was simply ineffective and, one might even say, disconcerting in his presentation. Seemingly, thorough training by a commercial television producer, if such is available, is the best answer to this problem.

I have taught credit courses on commercial television in the past, but have no experience with closed-circuit work. Our university presented over a period of several years a series of courses on a local station. The impact of these courses was not uniform nor was the polish or technique of the instructors. However, as a generalization, it seemed that those instructors who were most effective were the ones who recognized the strengths and weaknesses of television as well as the differences between presentation before the television camera and in the classroom.

While not everyone can hope to be a television star because he teaches a course on either a closed or an open circuit, nevertheless he can be trained to greater effectiveness if this training is properly handled by competent personnel. For example, in the closed-circuit demonstration mentioned above, the instructor paced constantly throughout the entire presentation until the audience was nearly dizzy from watching the oscillating background as the camera followed the instructor. His writing on the blackboard was far too small to be distinguished, and he had a number of mannerisms which distracted the viewers' attention. I have observed instructors using television and doing nothing which could not have been done on radio. To quote one critic, there is no great virtue in a lecture on the short story or the life of the bullfrog if for the period one stares at the professor's bald head. The use of visual aids is one of the advantages of television and a great deal of advanced preparation of charts and flash cards can increase the impact of the presentation enormously.

J. M. SACHS (Chicago City Junior College): I would like to discuss an aspect of open-circuit educational television which, it seems to me, provides us with an unusual opportunity to promote our institutions of higher learning and to serve our country well in the process. I was somewhat startled at the wide appeal of open-circuit college courses for credit. The Chicago experiment seems to indicate that educational TV brings the college to people who would not otherwise participate in collegiate education. Responses to questionnaires and unsolicited letters from registered and nonregistered viewers in the Chicago Junior College Program will bear this out. No doubt similar experiences have been recorded elsewhere.

We were thrilled to find that, in addition to the college-age and college-oriented students registered for courses, there was a large set of responses from people who could not attend traditional classes and people who had not been "college conscious" for a wide variety of reasons. Among these "side-effect" students were housewives whose responsibilities did not allow them to make frequent trips to a campus, working people who for reasons of schedule or home duties never thought of enrolling in traditional college courses, ambitious people who saw in this a previously unseen opportunity for advancement, older people who were reluctant to compete with youngsters in the classroom, people who through this medium had discovered in themselves a hitherto unexpressed cultural and intellectual interest, and, perhaps redundantly, a group of people who had simply not considered further formal education after high school. Furthermore, a large number of the people attracted to the Chicago Program have stated that they intend to go on to a degree. Thus, the stimulus provided by TV College in Chicago will bring to the campus many students who can profit from higher education.

This, at least to me, is an unexpected bonus from educational TV. But it also fits into a larger and more important niche. Our country needs more scientists, more mathematicians, more engineers, more technicians of every variety. Where are we to get them? I am well aware that college enrollments will rise sharply in the near future, and this will be a national blessing despite the strain it will impose on our institutions of higher learning. However, the best interests of the nation will be served only if in this expected flood of students we get a large percentage of the people who really belong in college.

By attracting more and more people who would not otherwise go to college, open-circuit educational television can help to provide the many technically trained experts needed so desperately in this atomic age world. Just incidentally we shall not only get more scientists and engineers, we shall get more poets, musicians, economists, novelists, classicists, and so on. It is a happy consequence of our democratic way that if we get enough talented people into higher learning, they will bring about a general broadening of cultural horizons as well as major deepening of manpower pools in critical areas.

The effects of open-circuit educational TV on the collegiate level is bound to be cumulative. The more people drawn into such a program, the more will be drawn into similar programs both on campus and on video in the future. The enthusiasm of one housewife expressed within her family circle may well change an anticollege orientation to a procollege orientation. Because it can successfully reach into the home, open-circuit television may very well be a key to maximum use of the talents and abilities of America.

JOHN R. MARTIN (Case Institute of Technology): The results of practically all studies of closed-circuit television as a medium of instruction have indicated that its use is entirely practical and that, in most cases, the learning process is as effective as that obtained by conventional teaching methods. It provides a new and powerful educational facility when applied to teaching situations where it is really needed.

There is, however, one disturbing problem which, if not actually stated, has been implied in a number of reports on studies made in the past. This is the opposition of both students and teachers to the use of closed-circuit television as a substitute for live class instruction. This is particularly noticeable in private institutions where problems of increased enrollments have not as yet become critical, and the student-instructor ratio is still low. Even in those cases where it is apparent that class size is an increasingly difficult problem, or where future problems are admitted, there is still apt to be a high degree of resentment, or at best a lack of acceptance, by either students or faculty.

Although there may be a number of valid reasons for these attitudes, in many cases it seems to be like a paraphrase of the nursery rhyme: no matter how well the material is presented, and no matter how well they may learn the material, they still do not like the medium of instruction. It is not surprising that these attitudes are even more prevalent among those who have had no experience with the medium than those who have actually participated in the program. Attitudes may vary from neutral, tinged with a high degree of skepticism, to downright horror, and as might be expected, the malcontents are much more verbal than those who are willing to accept the situation.

In some reports there is also the implication that closed-circuit television is an expensive and complicated method of instruction, involving a huge initial investment, high operating costs, and specialized staffs containing all the elements of commercial television programming. To the administrators of small institutions with limited budgets, this may be a factor sufficiently important to cause them to turn away from closed-circuit television as an answer to their enrollment problems. To underpaid faculties, it may seem that such expenditures would be better applied to higher salaries. Students, faced with increasing tuition costs, may view the program as a more costly way of obtaining second-rate instruction.

If costs are not a problem, the best equipment and facilities available should be used, particularly since inferior results sometimes obtained from less costly equipment may be a contributing factor to lack of acceptance. However, if instruction by closed-circuit television is fundamentally a sound educational method, it should not be considered as prohibitive for schools of limited financial resources. Everyone prefers a Cadillac to a jeep. But if the fundamental requirement is transportation, rather than elegance and comfort, the end result is the same regardless of the means by which it is accomplished.

If the problems presented above can be accepted as valid, the following approaches are suggested as possible solutions:

1. Greater emphasis should be placed on the objective of closed-circuit television as a method to *supplement* and not to *supplant* conventional teaching methods.

2. Closed-circuit television should be suggested *only* when there is a real reason for its use as a preferred alternative to other large-group instructional methods such as large lecture groups.

3. Studies in evaluation should be directed toward a comparison of subject matter most suitable for this medium of instruction rather than toward the accumulation of additional data on what seems to be a fairly well established fact, namely that it can be used effectively to teach large numbers of students.

4. Efforts should be made to find methods for improving acceptance by both students and instructional staffs, especially by providing more familiar and comfortable conditions under which the presentations are made. In particular, the wisdom of single central studios is debatable, quite aside from the factors of high initial cost and low use. However, when the conventional type of classroom is used as a program originating point, a number of opera-

tional problems are encountered which are not present in a studio operation. These problems, while not difficult of solution, should be clearly recognized if such a method of operation is to be successful.

5. In presenting the advantages of closed-circuit television as a teaching medium, less emphasis should be put on its demonstration values. While this may be quite important in some instructional areas, it should be recognized that there is much subject matter in which demonstrations play little part. It is difficult, for example, to imagine just what could be demonstrated in a course in advanced calculus.

6. At the same time, somewhat more emphasis should be placed on the value of closed-circuit television as a teaching aid even for small-group instruction. This can be realized with little expense and may have high educational value. It might well serve to reduce the prevalent attitude of distrust and dislike on the part of instructors and students alike.

7. Finally, it would seem more logical for educators in nontechnical fields to elicit the aid of their colleagues in technological fields for solving their operational problems, rather than depending on professional television engineers or equipment manufacturers. Our objective is education: theirs is entertainment. They may understand our problems no better than we know theirs. Members of the teaching staff on many campuses are interested and trained in both education and technological developments. This combination should be fully utilized to help solve the problems of educational closed-circuit television.

APPENDIX B

Selected Bibliography

The works listed here are primarily recent reports from colleges and universities and references judged useful for TV teachers:

BARROW, LIONEL C., and WESTLEY, BRUCE H. *Television Effects.* Research Bulletin No. 9. Madison, Wis.: University of Wisconsin, May 1958. 184 pp.

BECKER, SAMUEL L.; MURRAY, JAMES N., JR.; and BECHTOLDT, HAROLD P. *Teaching by the Discussion Method* [an experiment with television discussion, small and large group discussion, and the lecture method]. Iowa City, Iowa: State University of Iowa, 1958.

CARPENTER, C. R.; GREENHILL, L. P.; and Others. *An Investigation of Closed-Circuit Television for Teaching University Courses,* Report No. 2: The Academic Years 1955–1956 and 1956–1957. University Park, Pa.: Pennsylvania State University, Spring 1958. 110 pp.

CLEMENS, T. D. *TV and Teacher Education.* Duplicated. San Jose, Calif.: San Jose State College, 1956.

Credit Courses by Television. Washington: American Council on Education, 1955. 49 pp. $1.00.

DUNHAM, FRANKLIN; LOWDERMILK, RONALD R.; and BRODERICK, GERTRUDE G. *Television in Education,* Bulletin 1957, No. 21. Washington: Government Printing Office, 1957. 124 pp. $.50.

ERICKSON, CLIFFORD G., and CHAUSOW, HYMEN M. *The Chicago City Junior College Experiment in Offering College Courses for Credit via Open Circuit Television* [a report of the first year of a three-year project]. Chicago: Chicago City Junior College, March 1958. 54 pp.

An Evaluation of Closed-Circuit Television for Teaching Junior College Courses. Los Angeles: Division of Extension and Higher Education, Los Angeles City School Districts, 1957. 119 pp. Out of print. (Subsequent report in preparation.)

FILM EVALUATION BOARD OF DIVISION OF MATHEMATICS AND ADVISORY BOARD ON EDUCATION, NATIONAL ACADEMY OF SCIENCE—NATIONAL RESEARCH COUNCIL, *Films and Television in Mathematics Education.* Pub. No. 567. Washington: The Academy–Council, 1958. 20 pp. $1.00.

"Films and Television" (a series of 12 articles), *The American Mathematical Monthly,* LXV (June–July, 1958) 393–445. $1.00.

HAMILTON, T. H. *Closed-Circuit Television on the Michigan State University Campus.* Mimeographed. East Lansing, Mich.: Michigan State University, 1957.

HERMINGHAUS, E. G. *An Investigation of Television Teaching.* St. Louis, Mo.: St. Louis Public Schools, 1957.

HONIG, J. M.; SEIBERT, W. S.; and MOSES, D. F. *The Utilization of Audio-Visual Aids in the General Chemistry Laboratory Work at Purdue University.* Report No. 2. Lafayette, Ind.: Purdue University, May 1958. 73 pp.

KANNER, JOSEPH H. "Future Trends in Television Teaching and Research," *Audio-Visual Communication Review*, V (1957), 513–27.

KANNER, JOSEPH H.; MINDAK, WILLIAM A.; and KATZ, SANFORD. *The Application of Television and Kinescope Recordings to Reduce Instructor and Student Training Time and Training Costs.* A Report on Television in Army Training. Washington: Army Pictorial Service Division, 1958.

KANNER, JOSEPH H.; KATZ, S.; and GOLDSMITH, P. B. *Television in Army Training.* Long Island City, N.Y.: Army Pictorial Center, 1958.

KELLER, ROBERT J., and GOULD, ORRIN E. *Closed-Circuit Television in Teacher Education.* [The second report of investigations in progress at the University of Minnesota.] Minneapolis: College of Education, University of Minnesota, June 1957. 65 pp.

KENDIG, KATHRYN D., and MARTIN, GAITHER L. *The A B C's of TV* [a handbook on instructional and public service programming for educators and community leaders]. San Jose, Calif.: Spartan Bookstore. 238 pp. $3.85.

KLAPPER, HOPE LUNIN. *Closed-Circuit Television as a Medium of Instruction at New York University, 1956–1957: A Report on New York University's Second Year of Experimentation with Television in Classrooms.* New York: The University, 1958.

KUMATA, HIDEYA. *An Inventory of Instructional Television Research.* Ann Arbor, Mich.: Educational Television and Radio Center, 1956. 115 pp. Appendix 40 pp.

———. *Attitude Change and Learning as a Function of Prestige of Instructor and Mode of Presentation.* East Lansing, Mich.: Communications Research Center, Michigan State University, 1958.

KUMATA, HIDEYA, and DEUTSCHMANN, P. J. "The Mass Media—Journalism Broadcasting," *Review of Educational Research*, XXVIII (April 1958).

MACLEAN, MALCOLM S., JR., and ALLEN, WILLIAM H. *University Extension Through Television.* Madison, Wis.: Extension Division, University of Wisconsin, 1957. 31 pp.

MCKUNE, LAWRENCE E. *Telecourses for Credit: Vol. 4* [a compendium of institutions offering TV courses since 1951]. East Lansing, Mich.: Continuing Education Service, Michigan State University, September 1957. 78 pp. $2.00.

MACOMBER, F. G.; SIEGEL, LAWRENCE; HATHAWAY, S. C.; and DOME, J. E. *Experimental Study in Instructional Procedures.* Report No. 2. Oxford, Ohio: Miami University, 1957.

MARTIN, J. R. *Two-Way Closed-Circuit Educational Television.* Research Reports Nos. 948–1 and 2. Cleveland: Case Institute of Technology, 1957. 9 and 10 pp.

MAYES, M. A., and CHIPP, R. D. *Closed-Circuit Television System Planning.* New York: John F. Rider Publisher, Inc., 1957. 250 pp. $10.00.

MILLER, NEAL E., *et al.* "Graphic Communication and the Crisis in Education," *Audio-Visual Communication Review*, V (1957). 125 pp. Special issue, paper. $1.25.

NORTH CENTRAL ASSOCIATION OF COLLEGES AND SECONDARY SCHOOLS, SUBCOMMITTEE ON TELEVISION OF THE COMMISSION OF RESEARCH AND SERVICE, "Appraisal of the Current Status of Television as a Medium of Instruction," *North Central Association Quarterly*, XXXII (April 1958), 353–72.

POLLOCK, THOMAS C., *et al. Closed-Circuit Television as a Medium of Instruction, 1955–1956.* New York, New York University, October 1956. 56 pp.

POOLE, LYNN. *Science via Television.* Baltimore: Johns Hopkins Press, 1950. 197 pp.

SAWYER, J. W., and WOODLIFF, C. M. *A Survey of Policies and Procedures for Selection, Administration, Production, and Evaluation of Formal Adult Instruction for College Credit by Television.* Syracuse, N.Y.: Radio-Television Dept., Syracuse University, 1957.

SEIBERT, W. F. *A Brief Report and Evaluation of Closed-Circuit Television Instruction in the First Semester Calculus Course.* Mimeographed. Lafayette, Ind.: Audio-Visual Center, Purdue University, 1957.

SIEPMANN, CHARLES A. *TV and Our School Crisis.* New York: Dodd, Mead & Co., 1958. 187 pp. $3.50.

STODDARD, ALEXANDER J. *Schools for Tomorrow: An Educator's Blueprint.* New York: Fund for the Advancement of Education, 1957. 62 pp.

Teaching by Closed-Circuit Television. Washington: The American Council on Education, 1956. 66 pp. $1.00.

Television in Instruction: An Appraisal. [Report of a seminar of the Department of Audio-Visual Education, National Education Association, September 1957.] Washington: The Department, 1957. 24 pp. $1.00.

WASHINGTON COUNTY BOARD OF EDUCATION. *Closed-Circuit Television Project Notes.* Hagerstown, Md.: Washington County Board of Education, 1957.

WATTS, PHYLLIS W., *et al. Preliminary Report of the Committee Evaluating Education 107 TV.* Duplicated. Fresno, Calif.: Fresno State College, 1957.

WEISS, J. K. "Opportunities ETV Offers," *NAEB Journal,* XVII (1958), 3–12, 23–25.

ZORBAUGH, HARVEY (ed.). "Television and College Teaching," special issue of *Journal of Educational Sociology,* May 1958. 48 pp. Includes preliminary report on televised instruction at New York University in 1956–57.

APPENDIX C

Program of the Conference

Presiding Officer: JOHN C. ADAMS, President, Hofstra College; Chairman, Committee on Television, American Council on Education

SUNDAY, OCTOBER 20
Nittany Lion Inn

4:00–6:00 P.M.   Registration

8:30 P.M.   Buffet Supper

MONDAY, OCTOBER 21
Hetzel Union Building

9:00–11:45 A.M.

Introductory Remarks, JOHN C. ADAMS

Address of Welcome, LAWRENCE E. DENNIS, Vice-President for Academic Affairs, Pennsylvania State University

Greetings, ARTHUR S. ADAMS, President, American Council on Education

A Perspective on Televised Instruction, C. R. CARPENTER, Director, Division of Academic Research and Services, Pennsylvania State University

Panel Discussion on A Perspective on Televised Instruction
JOHN W. TAYLOR, Executive Director, Chicago Educational Television Association
F. GLENN MACOMBER, Director, Experimental Studies of Instructional Procedures, Miami University
HARVEY ZORBAUGH, Chairman, Communications Arts Group, New York University

1:30–4:00 P.M.

Theories and Principles of Learning in Relation to Televised Instruction
NEAL E. MILLER, Professor of Psychology, Yale University
JOSEPH H. GROSSLIGHT, Professor of Psychology, Pennsylvania State University

Concepts of Televised Instruction, presented by selected conference participants

227

6:30 P.M.   Informal Dinner, with members of the faculty of Pennsylvania State University serving as hosts

8:30 P.M.   Examples of Teaching by Television (Sparks Building)

Critique, RICHARD GOGGIN, Chairman, Department of Television, Motion Pictures and Radio, New York University

TUESDAY, OCTOBER 22
Hetzel Union Building

9:00–12:30 P.M.

The Need for Evidence, ERIC A. WALKER, President, Pennsylvania State University

Review of Relevant Research Results on Instruction by Television
   LESLIE P. GREENHILL, Assistant Director, Division of Academic Research and Services, Pennsylvania State University
   HIDEYA KUMATA, Associate Professor, Communications Research Center, Michigan State University

Effects of College Cultural Patterns on Students' Learning from Televised Instruction: Panel Discussion
   JOHN E. IVEY, JR., Executive Vice-President, New York University
   ROBERT R. BLAKE, Professor of Psychology, University of Texas
   ARTHUR HENRY MOEHLMAN, Professor of Education, University of Texas

1:30–4:00 P.M.

Practical Problems on the Improvement of Televised Instruction: Panel Discussion
   W. S. RAY, Associate Professor of Psychology, Pennsylvania State University
   HENRY S. DYER, Vice-President, Research Division, Educational Testing Service
   HERMANN H. REMMERS, Director, Educational Reference Bureau, Purdue University
   HARRY K. NEWBURN, President, Educational Television and Radio Center

Concepts of Televised Instruction, presented by selected conference participants

6:30 P.M.   Dinner Meeting (Nittany Lion Inn)

Presiding Officer: ARTHUR S. ADAMS, President, American Council on Education

Reservation of TV Channels for Education, RALPH STEETLE, Executive Director, Joint Council on Educational Television

Cooperation of Educational Broadcasters, BURTON PAULU, President, National Association of Educational Broadcasters

Educational Philosophy and Television, CLARENCE H. FAUST, Vice-President, The Ford Foundation, and President, Fund for the Advancement of Education

9:30 P.M. Demonstrations of Teaching by Television (Sparks Building)

Discussion, leader: FRED MCKINNEY, Professor of Psychology, University of Missouri

WEDNESDAY, OCTOBER 23
Nittany Lion Inn

9:00–10:00 A.M.

Summary of the Conference, JOHN E. IVEY, JR.

Review from the Fifth Milestone—The 1952 TV Institute at Penn State, with a Glimpse into the Future, ARTHUR S. ADAMS

APPENDIX D

Conference Roster

ARTHUR S. ADAMS, President, American Council on Education, 1785 Massachusetts Ave., N.W., Washington 6, D.C.

JOHN C. ADAMS, President, Hofstra College, Hempstead, N.Y.

EDWIN P. ADKINS, Director of Education, State University of New York, College for Teachers at Albany, Albany 3, N.Y.

JOSEPH ALLEN, Administrator, National Scholarship Program, Alfred P. Sloan Foundation, Inc., 630 Fifth Ave., New York 20, N.Y.

J. W. ASHTON, Vice-President, Indiana University, Bloomington, Ind.

JOHN BAXTER, Professor of Chemistry, University of Florida, Gainesville, Fla.

DAVID W. BERGSTROM, Assistant Professor of Zoology, Miami University, Oxford, Ohio

A. B. BISCOE, Dean of Faculties, University of Georgia, Athens, Ga. (Representing Southern Regional Education Board)

ROBERT R. BLAKE, Professor of Psychology, University of Texas, Austin, Tex.

FREDERICK J. BOGARDUS, Associate Professor of Mechanical Engineering, Purdue University, Lafayette, Ind.

DAVID S. BRODY, Professor of Psychology, Oregon College of Education, Monmouth, Ore.

ROBERT D. BROWN, Dean, School of Chemistry, University of Alabama, University, Ala.

C. R. CARPENTER, Director, Division of Academic Research and Services, Pennsylvania State University, University Park, Pa.

HARRY E. CRULL, Head, Department of Mathematics and Astronomy, Butler University, Indianapolis 7, Ind.

VERNON DAVIES, Professor of Sociology, State College of Washington, Pullman, Wash.

HORANCE G. DAVIS, JR., Assistant Professor, School of Journalism and Communications, University of Florida, Gainesville, Fla.

LAWRENCE E. DENNIS, Vice-President for Academic Affairs, Pennsylvania State University, University Park, Pa.

PAUL T. DIXON, Coordinator of Secondary Education and Director of the Summer Sessions, Kansas State Teachers College, Pittsburg, Kan.

HAROLD B. DUNKEL, Professor of Education, University of Chicago, Chicago 37, Ill. (Representing American Association of University Professors)

HENRY S. DYER, Vice-President, Research Division, Educational Testing Service, 20 Nassau St., Princeton, N.J.

WILLIAM E. ENGBRETSON, Associate Secretary, American Association of Colleges for Teacher Education, 11 Elm St., Oneonta, N.Y.

CLIFFORD G. ERICKSON, Assistant Dean in Charge of Television Education, Chicago City Junior College, 34 North Austin Ave., Chicago 34, Ill.

RICHARD I. EVANS, Associate Professor of Psychology, University of Houston, Houston 4, Tex.

CLARENCE H. FAUST, Vice-President, Ford Foundation, and President, Fund for the Advancement of Education, 477 Madison Ave., New York 22, N.Y.

REED FERGUSON, Director, Conference Center, Pennsylvania State University, University Park, Pa.

MARTIN FLECK, Associate Professor of Biology, University of New Mexico, Albuquerque, N.M.

JOSEF W. FOX, Associate Professor of English, Iowa State Teachers College, Cedar Falls, Iowa

SISTER MARY GABRIEL, S.S.J., Saint Bernard School, 401 Washington Rd., Pittsburgh 16, Pa. (Representing National Catholic Educational Association)

RICHARD J. GOGGIN, Chairman, Department of Television, Motion Pictures and Radio, New York University, New York 3, N.Y.

LESLIE P. GREENHILL, Associate Director, Division of Academic Research and Services, Pennsylvania State University, University Park, Pa.

EUGENE F. GREWE, Assistant Professor of English and Chairman of Freshman English Department, University of Detroit, Detroit 21, Mich.

CLARK GRIFFITH, Assistant Professor of English, State University of Iowa, Iowa City, Iowa

JOSEPH H. GROSSLIGHT, Professor of Psychology, Pennsylvania State University, University Park, Pa.

ERNA GUNTHER, Professor of Anthropology and Director of the Washington State Museum, University of Washington, Seattle 5, Wash.

MICHAEL F. HANNON, Coordinator of Educational Telecourses, New Haven State Teachers College, New Haven 15, Conn.

DALE B. HARRIS, Director, Institute of Child Welfare, University of Minnesota, Minneapolis 14, Minn.

GEORGE HARRIS, Chairman, Department of Music, Memphis State University, Memphis, Tenn.

ARMAND L. HUNTER, Director, Television Development, Michigan State University, East Lansing, Mich.

SHEPARD A. INSEL, Assistant Professor of Psychology, and Coordinator, Counseling Center, San Francisco State College, San Francisco 27, Calif.

JOHN V. IRWIN, Director of the Speech and Hearing Clinic, University of Wisconsin, Madison, Wis.

JOHN E. IVEY, JR., Executive Vice-President, New York University, New York 3, N.Y.

FREDERICK H. JACKSON, Executive Associate, Carnegie Corporation of New York, 589 Fifth Ave., New York 17, N.Y.

WILLARD JOHNSON, Vice-President, Educational Affairs, U.S. National Student Association, 1234 Gimbel Bldg., Philadelphia 7, Pa.

W. BERNARD KING, Professor of Chemistry, Iowa State College, Ames, Iowa

HOPE LUNIN KLAPPER, Assistant Professor of Education, Department of Educational Sociology and Anthropology, New York University, New York 3, N.Y.

HIDEYA KUMATA, Associate Professor, Communications Research Center, Michigan State University, East Lansing, Mich.

BARCLAY S. LEATHAM, Chairman, Department of Dramatic Arts, Western Reserve University, Cleveland 6, Ohio

RALPH LEYDEN, Assistant to the Dean as Coordinator, Stephens College, Columbia, Mo.

F. GLENN MACOMBER, Director, Experimental Study in Instructional Procedures, Miami University, Oxford, Ohio

JOHN R. MARTIN, Associate Professor of Electrical Engineering, Case Institute of Technology, Cleveland 6, Ohio

CHARLES N. MCCARTY, Associate Professor of Chemistry in charge of General Chemistry, Michigan State University, East Lansing, Mich.

KEITH MCKEAN, Professor, School of General Studies, North Carolina State College, Raleigh, N.C.

FRED MCKINNEY, Professor of Psychology, University of Missouri, Columbia, Mo.

W. C. MCNELLY, Chairman, Department of Physiology, Miami University, Oxford, Ohio

ROSS R. MIDDLEMISS, Professor of Mathematics, Washington University, St. Louis 5, Mo.

NEAL E. MILLER, Professor of Psychology, Yale University, 333 Cedar St., New Haven, Conn.

ARTHUR HENRY MOEHLMAN, Professor of Education, University of Texas, Austin 12, Tex.

DAVID G. MONROE, Professor of Political Science, University of North Carolina, Chapel Hill, N.C.

L. O. MORGAN, Associate Professor of Chemistry, University of Texas, Austin 12, Tex.

REV. HERMAN J. MULLER, S.J., Assistant Professor of History, University of Detroit, Detroit 21, Mich.

HARRY K. NEWBURN, President, Educational Television and Radio Center, 2320 Washtenaw Ave., Ann Arbor, Mich.

JAMES C. OLSON, Chairman, Department of History, University of Nebraska, Lincoln, Neb.

BURTON PAULU, Director, Department of Radio and TV Broadcasting, University of Minnesota, Minneapolis, Minn. (Representing National Association of Educational Broadcasters)

WALTER PETERSON, Program Director for Education in the Sciences, National Science Foundation, Washington 25, D.C.

W. S. RAY, Associate Professor of Psychology, Pennsylvania State University, University Park, Pa.

ANNA REARDON, Head, Department of Physics, Woman's College of the University of North Carolina, Greensboro, N.C.

HERMANN H. REMMERS, Director, Division of Educational Reference, Purdue University, Lafayette, Ind.

SISTER M. RICARDA, Principal of Saint Bernard School, 401 Washington Rd., Pittsburgh 16, Pa.

RENE ROCHON, D.D.S., Dean, School of Dentistry, University of Detroit, Detroit 28, Mich. (Representing American Association of Dental Schools)

H. BURR RONEY, Professor of Biology, University of Houston, Cullen Blvd., Houston, Tex.

J. M. SACHS, Assistant Dean in Charge of Southeast Branch, Chicago City Junior College, Chicago 17, Ill.

KURT C. SCHREIBER, Head, Department of Chemistry, Duquesne University, Pittsburgh 19, Pa.

WARREN F. SEIBERT, TV Program Research Consultant, Purdue University, Lafayette, Ind.

JAMES R. SHIPLEY, Head, Department of Art, University of Illinois, Urbana, Ill.

JAMES F. SHORT, JR., Assistant Professor of Sociology, State College of Washington, Pullman, Wash.

HAROLD P. SKAMSER, Director of the JETS Program, Michigan State University, East Lansing, Mich. (In 1958 appointed Dean of Engineering, California State Polytechnic College, San Luis Obispo, Calif.)

MRS. DOROTHY R. SMITH, Secretary, Committee on Television, American Council on Education, 1785 Massachusetts Ave., N.W., Washington 6, D.C.

G. KERRY SMITH, Executive Secretary, Association for Higher Education, National Education Association, 1201 Sixteenth St., N.W., Washington 6, D.C.

MRS. ANN C. SPINNEY, Executive Associate, The Fund for Adult Education, 320 Westchester Ave., White Plains, N.Y.

GLENN D. STARLIN, Associate Professor of Speech, Director, Inter-Institutional TV Teaching Project, University of Oregon, Eugene, Ore.

RALPH STEETLE, Executive Director, Joint Council on Educational Television, 1785 Massachusetts Ave., N.W., Washington 6, D.C.

ADA D. STEPHENS, Associate Professor of Elementary Education, University of Toledo, Toledo 6, Ohio

DAVID C. STEWART, Assistant Director, Joint Council on Educational Television, 1785 Massachusetts Ave., N.W., Washington 6, D.C.

OLIVER M. STONE, Head of Engineering Drawing Department, Case Institute of Technology, Cleveland 6, Ohio

JOHN W. TAYLOR, Executive Director, Chicago Educational Television Association, 1761 East Museum Drive, Chicago 37, Ill.

FRANK S. TRUEBLOOD, Assistant Dean, Los Angeles City College, Los Angeles 29, Calif.

EUGENE UDELL, Director, Audio-Visual Center, Temple University, Philadelphia, Pa. (Representing Association of American Colleges)

ERIC A. WALKER, President, Pennsylvania State University, University Park, Pa.

RICHARD A. WATERMAN, Associate Professor of Sociology and Anthropology, Wayne State University, Detroit 1, Mich.

JOHN K. WEISS, Assistant Vice-President and Treasurer, Fund for the Advancement of Education, 477 Madison Ave., New York 22, N.Y.

HAROLD E. WHITEHALL, Chairman, Linguistics Department, Indiana University, Bloomington, Ind.

HARRIS W. WILSON, Associate Professor of English, University of Illinois, Urbana, Ill.

HARVEY ZORBAUGH, Chairman, Communication Arts Group, New York University, New York 3, N.Y.

PENNSYLVANIA STATE UNIVERSITY HOSTS

CLIFFORD R. ADAMS, Professor of Psychology

MARY BROWN ALLGOOD, Associate Professor of Home Equipment and Commercial Consumer Services

B. G. ANDERSON, Professor of Zoology

C. K. ARNOLD, Staff Assistant to the President

R. G. D. AYOUB, Associate Professor of Mathematics

SIMON BELASCO, Associate Professor of Romance Languages

LOUIS H. BELL, Director of Public Information

JESSIE BERNARD, Professor of Sociology

R. G. BERNREUTER, Assistant to the President for Student Affairs

P. W. BIXBY, Professor of English Composition

I. C. BOERLIN, Supervisor of Audio-Visual Aids

J. S. BOWMAN, Professor of English Composition

R. W. BREWSTER, Professor of Political Science

F. G. BRICKWEDDE, Dean, College of Chemistry and Physics

C. D. BRIGHAM, Assistant Professor of Air Science

HUGH S. BROWN, Professor of Education

A. F. BUFFINGTON, Professor of German

J. H. BURDEN, Instructor of Music

R. C. CARPENTER, Director, Division of Academic Affairs and Research

T. H. CHENG, Professor of Zoology

ALBERT CHRIST-JANER, Director of the School of Arts

W. F. CHRISTOFFERS, Research Fellow

R. M. COLWELL, Lecturer in Accounting

H. B. CURRY, Professor of Mathematics

H. A. CUTLER, Coordinator of General Education

H. M. DABISON, Professor of Education

R. H. DAVAGE, Assistant Professor of Psychology

LAWRENCE E. DENNIS, Vice-Presirent for Academic Affairs

McKAY DONKIN, Vice-President for Finance, and Treasurer

J. P. DRISCOLL, Assistant Professor of Education

BEN EUWEMA, Dean, College of the Liberal Arts

M. A. FARRELL, Vice-President for Research

HUMMEL FISHBURN, Professor of Music and Music Education

W. H. FOLWELL, III, Assistant Professor of Extension Information

W. H. GRAY, Professor of Latin American History

LESLIE P. GREENHILL, Associate Director, Division of Academic Research and Services

SANDRA GREENSPUN, TV Production Assistant

J. H. GROSSLIGHT, Professor of Psychology

C. G. HAAS, JR., Assistant Professor of Chemistry

BRICE HARRIS, Professor of English Literature

FRANK HARTMAN, Research Associate

GRACE M. HENDERSON, Dean, College of Home Economics

H. S. HOFFMAN, Assistant Professor of Psychology

C. B. HOLT, JR., Associate Professor of Electrical Engineering

C. L. HOSLER, Associate Professor of Meteorology

G. R. HUDSON, Assistant Professor of Education

J. D. HUNDLEBY, Research Assistant

LYMAN HUNT, Associate Professor of Education

A. W. HUTCHISON, Professor of Chemistry

LT. S. E. KANE, JR., Assistant Professor of Air Science

W. E. KENWORTHY, Executive Assistant to the President

LUTHER F. KEPLER, JR., Coordinator of TV Operations

COL. A. W. KOGSTAD, Professor of Military Science and Tactics

H. L. KRALL, Professor of Mathematics

F. B. KRAUSS, Professor of Latin

O. E. LANCASTER, Professor of Engineering Education

OSSIAN MACKENZIE, Dean, College of Business Administration

R. C. Maloney, Associate Dean, College of the Liberal Arts

K. V. MANNING, Associate Professor of Physics

BERTHA W. MATHER, Instructor of Mathematics

W. C. MATHER, Professor of Sociology

M. B. MATSON, Assistant Professor of Sociology

F. R. MATSON, Professor of Archaeology

M. N. McGEARY, Professor of Political Science

D. H. McKinley, Associate Dean of the College of Business

W. W. MILLER, Associate Professor of Chemistry

J. A. MURNIN, Research Assistant

G. R. MURRAY, Assistant Professor of Chemistry

G. K. NELSON, Professor of Accounting

H. E. NELSON, Associate Professor of Speech

HANS NEUBERGER, Professor of Meteorology

C. I. NOLL, Associate Dean, College of Chemistry and Physics

E. K. OXHANDLER, Assistant Professor of Audio-Visual Education

LAWRENCE J. PEREZ, Assistant Dean, College of Engineering and Architecture

W. F. PROKASY, JR., Assistant Professor of Psychology

H. G. PYLE, in charge, Division of Informal Instruction

JOHN R. RACKLEY, Dean, College of Education

W. S. RAY, Associate Professor of Psychology

A. H. REEDE, Professor of Economics

SARA A. RHUE, Associate Professor of Elementary Education

A. C. RICHER, Professor of Soil Technology

A. L. RODGERS, Associate Professor of Geography

C. J. ROWLAND, Professor of Accounting

CHRISTINE F. SALMON, Associate Professor of Housing

J. A. SAUER, Professor of Physics

H. K. SCHILLING, Dean, Graduate School

A. J. SHALER, Professor of Metallurgy

P. A. SHELLEY, Professor of German and Comparative Literature

H. D. SHERK, Coordinator of TV Presentations

A. C. SUTHERLAND, Professor of English

C. B. TATE, Associate Professor, Agriculture Extension

B. M. TORKELSON, Assistant Professor of Education

A. W. VANDERMEER, Assistant to the Dean, College of Education

E. C. VEREB, Chief TV Engineer

J. C. WAGNER, Assistant Professor of Metallurgy

ERIC A. WALKER, President of the University

W. H. WALTERS, Associate Professor of Theater Arts

E. C. WAREHAM, JR., Instructor of Music

THOMAS WARTIK, Associate Professor of Chemistry

R. H. WATERS, Professor of Transportation

WAYNE WEBB, Professor of Physics

R. L. WEBER, Associate Professor of Physics

A. M. WELLINGTON, Professor of Counselor Education

F. L. WHALEY, Associate Professor of Psychology

M. W. WHITE, Professor of Physics

C. S. WYAND, Vice-President for Development

AMERICAN COUNCIL ON EDUCATION

Arthur S. Adams, *President*

The American Council on Education is a *council* of national educational associations; organizations having related interests; approved universities, colleges, teachers colleges, junior colleges, technological schools, and selected private secondary schools; state departments of education; city school systems and private school systems; selected educational departments of business and industrial companies; voluntary associations of higher education in the states; and large public libraries. It is a center of cooperation and coordination whose influence has been apparent in the shaping of American educational policies and formation of educational practices during the past forty years.